STRICTLY ME

Strictly Me

My Life Under the Spotlight

Mark Ramprakash

With Mark Baldwin

MAINSTREAM
PUBLISHING

EDINBURGH AND LONDON

First published in Great Britain in 2009 by
MAINSTREAM PUBLISHING COMPANY
(EDINBURGH) LTD
7 Albany Street
Edinburgh EH1 3UG

ISBN 9781845965129

A catalogue record for this book is available
from the British Library

Typeset in Caslon and Century Gothic

Printed in Great Britain by
CPI Mackays of Chatham Ltd, Chatham, ME5 8TD

To Mum, Dad and my sister Zara, and to my wife Van
and our daughters Cara and Anya, for their constant love and support
throughout this journey that is ongoing

CONTENTS

FOREWORD BY DARREN GOUGH

As a cricketer, Mark Ramprakash is among the top three English players whom I came up against regularly in my own career. In recent years you could add Kevin Pietersen to that shortlist, as the best England batsman of the current era, but for most of my time it was Graeme Hick, Alec Stewart and Ramps.

That is how highly I rate him. And although he underachieved in the early part of his own England career, I think Ramps is very unfortunate not to have played more than his 52 Tests; certainly, his best years were his mid-30s – after his last Test cap was won – and during that time he should definitely have been selected again for England.

To me, it is inconceivable, for example, that he did not win selection for both of England's last two Ashes tours of Australia. Ramps averaged more than 40 against the great Australia sides of the 1990s and 2001, but he was ignored in 2002–03 (he should have been called up when Graham Thorpe withdrew, let alone in the initial squad) and also for the 2006–07 tour.

With Michael Vaughan out of that latter series through injury, Ramps would have been the perfect experienced batsman to have called upon in his place. As it was, we got our selection very wrong for most of the trip and ended up losing 5–0.

I consider it a very great privilege that I was playing for Yorkshire against Surrey in the match in which, in 2008, he completed his hundredth first-class hundred. In fact, after he had cut away a ball from David Wainwright, our left-arm spinner, for the boundary that took him to that great landmark, I was the first person to shake his hand. I was so pleased for him.

We had never looked like getting him out in that second innings, and before the match I had reminded him that he got his maiden first-class century against Yorkshire at Headingley and so it was a foregone conclusion that he would get his hundredth there as well! I think that helped to relax him, actually.

Ramps and I have played against each other for all of my own first-class career (he started before me, and is still going!) and for quite a lot of that time with one another for England. We have toured often together and, in fact, first came across each other when we were on England Under-19 duty.

Today, of course, we are both better known for our exploits on *Strictly Come Dancing*. It's amazing, and really quite comical. Between us, we have played in more than 100 Tests for England, I have taken getting on for 500 international wickets and Ramps has scored more than a hundred hundreds – but both of us are more widely known for dancing than we are for cricket!

Then again, when you look at the viewing figures for *Strictly* – 12 million, or something – and then how many people watch England play cricket on Sky, which is an awful lot less, I suppose it is not that remarkable.

Ramps rang me for advice as to whether he should accept the invitation to go on *Strictly* in 2006 and I told him that if I could win it, then he would have no problems. He was always more into music than I was – he would always have music to listen to before going in to bat – and he was definitely more of a natural dancer! On tour, whenever we found ourselves in a club, it would always be Ramps rather than me who would be keen on getting onto the dance floor.

I think, when he first began on *Strictly*, that he was quite nervous about following another cricketer who had won it, but as soon as I saw him that first week I knew he had the ability to make it. It was fantastic for Ramps – and for English cricket, to be honest – when he did follow me to the *Strictly Come Dancing* title.

So, who is the better dancer? I couldn't possibly say. What I will say is, I beat him on that *Strictly Christmas Special*, didn't I? Actually, in all seriousness, I would suggest that I'm better at ballroom and he's better at Latin!

When we meet up now, of course we have a lot of banter with each other about our dancing. And during both the 2007 and 2008 cricket seasons, I think our dancing achievements actually spiced things up even more when we came up against each other on the field. We found we were even more competitive with each other and, over the years, I have really enjoyed our on-field battles.

Ramps is a great guy, and a great character. So many people don't really know him because he is a quiet person who keeps himself to himself. People think he's aloof but when you get to know him, as I have, he will open up a little bit more, and he is a loyal, dependable friend to have.

I am very pleased to be able to call Ramps a friend, as well as a fellow England cricketer and fellow dancer! I hope this book reveals more of his personality to the wider public and also serves as a true monument to the great achievements of one of the most talented players English cricket has ever seen.

* Darren Gough played 58 Tests for England, taking 229 wickets at 28.39. He also won 158 ODI caps, taking another 234 wickets at 26.29.

FOREWORD BY KAREN HARDY

Meeting Mark Ramprakash . . . well, where do I start? I remember opening the door for our first meeting and being bowled over (pardon the pun) by this shy but handsome man standing in front of me. 'Result,' I thought, until I found out that he was a cricketer. How could a cricketer win for a second year? He was also possibly one of the least known celebrities on the show, but worse than that . . . he didn't speak!

So, why had this man entered one of the biggest and most glamorous shows on television? A show that was about being a personality and a performer – neither of which I initially thought Mark was. I don't think Mark knew either, but he embarked on a three-month journey which neither of us ever thought would end with us holding the trophy as champions of *Strictly Come Dancing* 2006.

It only took a very short time for the ice to be broken between us. When, on our initial meet, I asked what his surname was, he said, 'It's long!' so I naturally put Mark Long into my mobile phone, only to be told an uncomfortable second later that he meant it was a long surname, as in Ramprakash! A story that will stay with me forever and, yes, Mark, I was desperately embarrassed!

The journey that Mark and I took, I think, was a shock to everyone, especially to those of you who really know him. From walking out and exposing his body in those sequinned tops to mastering the skill of shaking his hips around, I don't think anyone would have believed Mark Ramprakash would open up as much as he did over the weeks.

Each time Mark came into the studio I could see his nerves, dreading what I had planned for him that day. And as a coach, until I could work out what was going on in his head, my job proved to be more of a challenge than I had anticipated. I started to push buttons mentally and physically with Mark to see just how far I could go.

He took every punch I gave him, but halfway into the show I had overlooked just how hard this really was for Mark to deal with. It was at this point in the competition that I came face to face with 'the Bloodaxe', a nickname everyone had told me about, but an aspect of Mark I never in a million years thought I would meet. I can't say it was one of the highlights of the show, but it took seeing this side of him for our relationship to change from being a student and teacher to an unstoppable team.

I found out that this man was made of so much more than he was letting on to anyone. He dealt with awkward moments that could have caused an absolute meltdown, when I apparently 'got into his personal space' with that whole body touching thing, and when our microphones got tangled up in the salsa. Did anyone expect a certain shy person who, until then, had probably said a maximum of ten words on TV to turn around and shout out: 'Please can we have another go?'? Well, I certainly didn't, and I am just so happy he did, as he danced out of his skin. I will never forget him singing in my ear halfway through because he was enjoying it so much.

Memories of the semi-final and dancing the Argentine Tango will never leave me, as it was the night we got the three tens! Mark wowed the audience and got us into that final. It was a magical moment when the dance finished and the audience just exploded. I thought the cameras had left us when I mimed, 'Oh yes,' to Mark at the end of the dance, but I just needed him to know how well he had done.

Finale night and the showcase! How he lifted me, I'll never know, I think it was just pure adrenalin and a stubborn determination that, no matter what, I was going up! Those lifts have to work and he pulled every one off – even if it was 'dead weight' that you had to lift, Mark!

Over the weeks Mark showed me what being a true competitor was all about; whether it's walking out onto a cricket pitch, hoping to score that century, or dancing an Argentine Tango and scoring tens, he proved it's all down to respecting your team players, and a lot of hard work, heart and determination. That is what I was to learn Mark Ramprakash was all about and so much more.

I have so much to thank Mark for, more than he will ever realise. For believing in me as his coach, for training for so many long hours, for dealing with all his mental demons, for always giving me more than his best, but most of all for allowing me to re-live my dreams as a dancer and giving me the time of my life. Mark, you may have been Bruce's favourite, but you were also mine, and I thank you.

The greatest thing of all was realising a new friendship had grown overnight, not only between Mark and me, but also between my husband and son and his wonderful family and friends, whom we are so happy to have had the chance to meet.

Best wishes for this book, which tells the fascinating story of your cricket life as well as your *Strictly Come Dancing* triumph. I am honoured to have been asked to write this foreword.

Your coach, partner and friend,

Karen Hardy

World Masters, International, United Kingdom and British National Champion of Latin American Dance

INTRODUCTION

Since winning *Strictly Come Dancing* I have often been asked whether I would swap the thrill of that for another Test match century, or one more chance to play for England.

No, I wouldn't. What I experienced on *Strictly* was magical, and irreplaceable. I felt a huge sense of achievement, which was all the more amazing for being so totally unexpected.

To have been given the opportunity to do something like that, to meet and perform with a wonderful dancer and person like Karen Hardy, and to form a fantastic friendship with someone I had not even heard of before I went on the show is truly an experience I would not have missed for the world.

In a big way, too, winning that title and proving that I could perform under massive pressure in a field so different from international cricket has made up for a lot of the disappointments and deep frustrations of my cricket career.

Catharsis might be a bit strong and overdramatic, but not by too much. To walk out from behind that curtain and perform an intricate dance routine in front of an audience and also another 12 million or so people on live, prime-time television is not easy!

Moreover, having had to put up with a lot of criticism during my cricket career for a perceived failing of temperament, or of bottle, on the big stage, I do feel that the way I competed on *Strictly Come Dancing* was a big statement about my character, my competitive nature, my concentration and my desire to do well.

17

From signing up for the show to holding the trophy aloft with Karen, I went on a remarkable journey. It changed my life, in many ways, and it also fulfilled me in a manner that my career as a professional cricketer has not done – and could never do. Almost three years on from becoming *Strictly* champion, it also continues to do so.

Since then I have also realised a massive cricketing ambition by becoming only the 25th batsman in the game's history to score a hundred first-class hundreds. My aim is to play on for two more seasons at least with Surrey, too, so hopefully there will be a few more centuries to come before I retire.

A lot of my life has been played out in public view, whether on *Strictly* or on the cricket grounds of the world. Lots of people will also imagine they know at least a bit about what sort of person I am, again either from watching me on television or from watching me play cricket. One of the reasons for writing this book was to set out my account of all that has happened to me, on the cricket field and on the dance floor, because in many respects the popular image portrayed of me has been too simplistic, too ill-informed, and in some cases misrepresentative and inaccurate.

My cricket career is soon to go into a fourth decade, because I made my first-class debut as long ago as 1987, when I was still a 17-year-old schoolboy. I have played in 52 Tests for England, scoring hundreds against the West Indies in Barbados in 1998 and against Australia at the Oval in 2001.

It is a source of regret that the England selectors have chosen not to call on me since 3 April 2002, the day when we were beaten by New Zealand in Auckland at the end of a Test series that was drawn 1–1.

There must have been a chance of me being selected for the 2002–03 Ashes tour, especially when Graham Thorpe withdrew for personal reasons, and also the 2006–07 Ashes tour when Michael Vaughan was unfit, while there was a considerable campaign in the media for my name to be included in the England squad that went to Sri Lanka for three Tests at the end of 2007.

That summer I had scored more than 2,000 first-class runs and averaged more than 100 per innings for the second successive season, which no one else has ever done. In 2006, I had set world records by reaching the 2,000-run landmark in only twenty innings and by passing 150 in five successive innings.

But, sadly, it seemed that even this sort of sustained run-scoring for Surrey was not enough to persuade the selectors to resurrect my England career. I had struggled at Test level for a variety of reasons, which I hope this book will address, but it would have been nice to have had the chance to show what I could have done at the top level in my more mature years, given that I was still 32 when I made my final Test appearance.

Scoring a hundred hundreds has fulfilled me as a cricketer to a large extent, and despite being ignored by England in recent times I do not find myself bitter and twisted about the fact that my Test average of 27.32 classifies me as an underachiever, especially when put next to my overall first-class average of more than 50.

I am very proud of what I have achieved on the cricket field. It is a game that has consumed me, and which continues to be a passion, even though I have just gone past my 40th birthday. I am fascinated by the demands of cricket and by the technique of batting, and I have in recent years become a Level Four coach. Perhaps coaching is a direction I will go in when my playing days finally come to an end.

Practice has never been a chore for me, ever since I was a boy. My father has always said that if you enjoy something it doesn't seem like practice. Both my dad, Deonarine, and my mum, Jennifer, were sitting in the stands at Headingley on 2 August 2008 when I completed my hundredth first-class hundred.

That achievement, perhaps more than anything else I have done, was a culmination of half a lifetime's dedication to my sport – and to batting – and it was an achievement to be shared in particular with my wife, Vandana, my two daughters, Cara and Anya, my parents and my sister, Zara. They are the ones who have been with me all the way, and the real pleasure for me of reaching my hundredth hundred was that it was for them.

Van and I met in 1990, the year before I first played for England, and we were married in 1993. She has put up with a hell of a lot, like so many cricket wives because cricketers are away from home so much in their careers, but she has been incredibly supportive to me.

Of course, when I played for England, I was away on tour for two or three months sometimes during the winter, but summer also means a huge amount of time away from home, as you travel around the country to play for your county team, or for England.

Van has always been so understanding of the realities of playing professional cricket for a living, of the fact that I will often be dog-tired when I get in from a long day batting or in the field, and she has gone out of her way to make sure things at home are easier for me. As players in the public eye, we get all the praise when we are successful, but believe me when I say that Van deserves an awful lot of those plaudits too.

All these years I have been able to follow my dreams and my ambitions, and she has been there with me. Little things mean so much: like when both our daughters were small babies, I never once needed to get up in the middle of the night to feed them or comfort them. Of course, I helped out at other times, but Van believed it was important for me not to have my sleep disturbed, as I needed my energy for my job of playing sport or training for it.

No words can express just what a huge part she has played in my life, and when that hundredth run of my hundredth hundred was scored against Yorkshire at Headingley, it was her achievement as much as mine.

To have my parents present to witness that landmark was also special. In recent years, and since my dad retired, they have made a few little trips around the country to combine a mini-holiday with the chance to see me play for Surrey. They had also come up to Leeds to see if I could complete my hundredth hundred on the same ground on which I had made my first, for Middlesex on 20 July 1989.

They stayed at a bed and breakfast very close to the Headingley ground and, in Surrey's first innings, I was out for just 6 when I was bowled by a superb delivery from Deon Kruis. That evening I went out to dinner with my parents in Leeds, to an Italian restaurant, and we were talking about my desire to get that hundredth hundred.

I said that I had come to Headingley with a good feeling about the game, especially as it is a ground that holds some great personal memories for me and is a place where I have made a lot of big scores. Then my mum said that I should remember that there was always the second innings!

She was proved right, of course, and I couldn't have asked for anything more than the fact that they were there, just after tea on that last afternoon of the game, when I reached the hundred. As I celebrated on the field, I was also able to see them in the stand and was able to acknowledge them from the middle.

My parents knew everything that had gone into my career; they had lived my career with me, in that sense. During the 2008 season they had been aware of the media attention surrounding my progress towards that hundredth hundred, and they knew about the additional responsibilities I had been dealing with, in terms of both my testimonial year at Surrey and in taking on the captaincy on the field in Mark Butcher's injury absence.

More than all of that, though, they had endured as parents all the tough times that I had been through – especially with England. As well as watching me succeed, they had also sat in grounds and seen me fail on the Test stage, which would have been hard for any parent. They deserved that day at Headingley.

Afterwards, when all the media interviews were over, and after Yorkshire had very kindly marked the occasion by making a presentation to me, I went over to spend some time with my mum and dad in their B&B just outside the ground. We just sat in their little hotel room, had a cup of tea and savoured the moment. We didn't need to say too much. It was early evening by this time and I remember that rain was falling outside. We reflected on my career and recalled how it had been at Headingley, too, that I made my England Test debut 17 years earlier.

Surrey had a Pro40 League match at Chesterfield the following day, however, so I soon had to get in my car and drive off to rejoin my teammates at our hotel for that night. It was special, though, to spend that quiet time with my parents before driving off to prepare for another match, and another day.

I know that there are others who took a quiet satisfaction in my achievement, from my coaches when I was a boy to the other big influences on me as a cricketer and a person such as Mike Gatting, Don Bennett and Alec Stewart, who always seemed to do things right. Apart from my father, though, the biggest influence on the way I have played the game was probably Desmond Haynes, the great former Barbados and West Indies opener, who was a teammate at Middlesex for a number of years early in my career.

The necklace he wore had the inscription 'live, love, laugh' and his enthusiasm for cricket was so great. He was also incredibly approachable and was always willing to talk cricket. He might have played for the world champions, as the West Indies then undoubtedly were, but he had no ego: he didn't just go in for big shots when he batted, he wanted all the short singles, too.

I remember when we were batting together against the New Zealand touring team in 1990 and I was about to face my first ball from Richard Hadlee. 'Dessie' came down the wicket and told me that this first ball would be straight and fast and that I should make sure I didn't get my leg in the way, as Hadlee would be looking for an lbw. He was absolutely right, and I just managed to jam the bat down on it.

I learned an awful lot from Haynes in terms of my approach to batting and, as I will outline later, technically. But he also taught me a great deal about cricket generally and about having belief in your method. Being in that Middlesex dressing-room as a young professional, with Haynes and Gatting and John Emburey around, made me realise very clearly how important it was to have a number of good senior players in the mix. I was very lucky to be at Middlesex at that time.

Working hard and practising with a focus on what is important for the match you are preparing for is something else I learned very early from senior batsmen like Haynes and Gatting. And that's how it was with the dancing, too, and I think that's another reason why I managed to do so well. Preparation was also something Karen was very hot on, so we both wanted to practise as much as possible as a matter of course, and we ended up doing more hours of work every week than any of the other couples on the show that year.

The first performance on *Strictly* was a serious moment for me. I was an absolute beginner, and although our practice had gone well it was something else to go out and actually perform.

I have never been more nervous in my life, and it was an incredible feeling. I had really suffered from nerves at certain stages of my Test career, to the extent that it had inhibited my performances on occasions. So, although I had faced that sort of feeling before, this was something entirely new.

Of course in cricket, as a professional player, you are expected to go out there and perform because it is your job and you are supposed to be good at it, whereas at the start of *Strictly Come Dancing* it was more a case of me not wanting to do anything other than not make an utter fool of myself and fall flat on my face.

For that first dance I was massively out of my comfort zone and although all the other amateur competitors were also feeling similar emotions it did not help much: they couldn't come out there and share your discomfort or fear. You were on your own.

I suppose, in that respect, it was like cricket. When you are batting, you only have one of your teammates at the other end of the pitch and all the rest of the team are sitting back in the dressing-room. They can all encourage you, both before a game and during it, but when the bowler starts to run in you are completely on your own as a batsman.

On *Strictly*, I had Karen as my partner and that was a very big help. She could help me with the timing of the dance and even pull me into a certain position at times or stop me doing something wrong. But, still, there is a large element of being on your own, especially as the male dancer has to lead the dance and it is for the female to follow.

When you are behind that curtain and the announcer says your name, the nerves are simply incredible. However, once the music started, I found that things changed very quickly. And, in my opinion, because this was certainly the case with me, the first five seconds of every dance are vital.

In those first five seconds I could tell if things were going to go well or not because of the way my body responded to the piece of music accompanying the dance. And if I really felt the music and enjoyed the music, I found that I danced so much better.

Some dances suit certain people more than others, of course, but when you get those first few movements right your feelings are so strong that all the nervous energy in you can then work for you; alternatively, if you don't feel right, you cannot shake off those nerves or make them work for you. It just becomes hard to get into the dance.

With cricket, there are definitely times that you feel good before an innings and you go out there and, yes, you are off and running straightaway. But that is in the minority of cases. Indeed, I would say that at least eight times out of ten you go out to bat and you don't feel good about everything.

But experience has taught me, over time, to deal with the fact that you don't feel entirely comfortable. You need your technique to help you, certainly, and you also need a mental resolve to stick it out, to survive. Because you know that the longer you survive, the longer you stay out there at the crease, the easier batting will become and the better you will feel.

The huge and obvious difference between batting and dancing is that, in dancing, you have just ninety seconds to perform and therefore if you don't get it right in those first five seconds you are struggling.

There were, however, many similarities between the two in terms of the physical and mental requirements. Yet it is only since *Strictly* that I have really recognised fully the link. In many ways, though, I would say that, subconsciously, cricket prepared me to do well on that show.

Apart from fitness, footwork and a desire to practise and prepare, I would say that the major thing that being a professional cricketer brought to my dancing was mental skills.

Throughout the Saturday rehearsals on the set, for instance, I would spend some quiet time in my dressing-room visualising what I was about to do. I would think about going out there and how I was going to do the dance. I would also pick two or three key things out of the routine to help me to remember what was most important in that particular dance. It would help things flow.

In batting, I have found it is essential for me to have two or three key words in my head when I am out there at the crease. They are private to me, but they are words that switch me on to batting.

During my early cricket life I suffered a lot of heartache in my effort to reach the top of my chosen profession. It took me seven years, from my Test debut in 1991, to score my first hundred for England and there were a lot of ups and downs in that time. I had to deal with that constant question: did I have what it took to be successful at Test match level?

Scoring a Test hundred is, for a batsman, perhaps the ultimate thrill in cricket from a personal achievement point of view, and for me that thrill was heightened even more because of the long wait I had to endure before experiencing it.

I also scored a century in an Ashes Test, against an Australian bowling attack which was perhaps the greatest in the history of the game; certainly two of the bowlers, Glenn McGrath and Shane Warne, will go down as two of the greatest there have been.

That was also a massive thrill, but I would equate it with achieving what I did on *Strictly Come Dancing*. That is a measure of the fun I had doing the show. And although my life has been in cricket I value hugely the positive feelings that I still get – three years on – from achieving something so worthwhile in another part of my life.

The fact that it was such a high-profile show is also very relevant to what I feel about my achievement with Karen. The knowledge that all those many millions of viewers were watching every show – and especially when we got to the final itself – meant that there was an incredible nervous tension. It was live; it was now or never. And because I found myself able to go out there and perform, time after time, and to be able to express myself and enjoy the experience, I now have a ready answer to those people who say that in Test cricket I didn't perform because I was not mentally tough enough.

Believe me, to go out there in Lycra, sequins and Cuban heels and perform over a 14-week stretch, and perform to a level where you end up winning . . . well, that takes a bit of doing, and it means a hell of a lot to me that I was able to do it.

There were some tough weeks learning particular dances, and then rehearsing them again and again in an effort to get them right, but I found I enjoyed the whole process of it. As a competition, though, it is not something that you can go out and say you are going to win because you cannot predict the public vote element of it. I am very competitive, of course, but my whole approach was simply to do my best and to enjoy it, and then see if the outcome was a good one!

Over and above everything else, though, it was Karen who made the experience for me. She is such a great coach, as well as being a multiple world champion in her own right, and she got me to relax and to enjoy the whole experience.

This was crucial because she read my personality very well. Naturally, I am a bit quiet and reserved, but she understood that and gradually dealt with it. It was very important for me to have fun, going to training every day, and I know there were times when she was praising me to encourage me; I knew I wasn't doing it particularly well, but Karen spotted the right time to offer that encouragement and it helped me so much.

So what kind of person am I? Cricket followers will have made their impressions over the years, while viewers of *Strictly Come Dancing* have had a different insight into my character, I'm sure. My Level Four coaching course covered this kind of question, actually, and I found it very interesting to look at oneself in this way.

I know that I am and always have been quite reserved, especially with people I don't know. This can be perceived as me being quiet, or even moody and aloof. Initially, I don't open up too much, but once I know someone and they become a friend, then I open up a lot. I think when people get to know you, you come across very differently.

Early on in my cricket career, I got tagged as bad-tempered, or temperamental and moody, and I think unfairly so. If you had asked me at the time, I would have agreed that cricket was a serious business to me and that I made no apology for wanting to do well.

I was very ambitious, and when things didn't go as well as I wanted them to it did affect me.

Looking back at those early times, in particular, I wish I could have handled a few incidents much better. I was naive. All I needed was some help to deal with how to handle disappointment, but when I was younger I didn't realise that all I needed was to be told to keep working hard and that things would turn out the right way.

I always tried my very hardest in the field, and I desperately wanted the team I was playing for – whether that was Middlesex, England A or England – to win. I was totally committed to the team, sometimes too much so.

But in any given situation, whether I had done well or badly, I would always look very closely at myself and analyse what I could have done better. I would ask myself where I could have improved my own performance. On *Strictly*, if I couldn't do a rumba properly, then it would not be for want of trying or of preparation or training. And it has been the same with my cricket. I could always go to sleep at night knowing that I could not have done more to be successful.

I have always been a student of the game, I have tried to learn and to listen to people, and I have tried to learn from my mistakes. I have looked at all areas of my cricket career: lifestyle, technical, tactical, mental. I have tried to be as good as I could be.

And that, definitely, is me.

If I had to describe myself further, however, I would say I am a hard-working and conscientious person. If I am given a task, I try to do it on time and as well as I can. Loyalty is also important to me, and if you are a friend of mine then I will back you through thick and thin.

I also think it is important to present yourself well in official situations. For instance, if I am attending a function on behalf of Surrey or my bat manufacturers Gray-Nicolls, then I will take time over my appearance and dress appropriately. I would also say I have always been like that – polite, helpful and dependable – even when I was younger and the fires of ambition burned most strongly.

It is cricket and a deep passion for the game that has really dominated my life and defined who I am. Sometimes, indeed, cricket has seemed more important to me than life and death.

These days, however, I have much more of a balance in what I do – even though I am still playing professional cricket – and my two daughters Cara and Anya are a huge part of my life. They are twelve and seven respectively, and it is so important for me to spend time with them, and to use all my own experiences of life to guide them as they grow up.

In the past seven years or so, I have been more at ease with my life, and my cricket. I am actually a big believer in fate, in cricket and in life, especially as there are so many things you can't control. In cricket, you might get a bad decision, or be run out by a bowler's deflection or certain things might just go your way. I remember one innings earlier this year when I got a hundred against Middlesex at Lord's but, on 1, I edged a ball that could have been caught low down by the fielder at first slip. It wasn't on that occasion, and that's why I believe that, ultimately, fate will decide whether you do well or not.

What I learned, in the late 1990s and largely with the help of Steve Bull, the England psychologist, is that all you can do is concentrate very hard on your preparation, and train and eat properly, and then, when you bat, watch the ball as closely as you can.

A lot of my tough times in the game – which affected my belief and my confidence – are now in the past, and completing my hundredth hundred really was a fulfilling experience. Yet even when I was in the process of getting that hundredth hundred, in 2008, some of the media were trotting out the same old story about me failing to nail it down under the pressure. It was so frustrating, and so wrong.

In my career I've averaged one century in just about every seven first-class innings and between my 99th hundred and my hundredth were ten innings. Not very out of the ordinary, then, especially when you consider that as great a batsman as Wally Hammond – indeed, probably England's greatest-ever batsman – took 24 attempts to get to the milestone (he ended up with 167), but if you read the press you might have thought so.

The perception, because of the way my 'wait' was being reported – and being linked to my supposed temperamental failings – was that I was taking an abnormally long time to get it. In fact, there was also almost a month during the time between my 99th hundred in early May and my hundredth in early August – virtually the whole of June – when Surrey didn't even play a first-class game, mainly due to the Twenty20 Cup group stage. Also, on the morning of 16 July, I woke up feeling so bad with a severe bout of food poisoning that I had to miss the four-day Championship game against Durham, at Guildford, that started that day. That, in effect, took another week out of my season and it was in the very next match, at Yorkshire, that I got the hundred.

My view, when you look at all I have achieved, and all the runs I have scored, is that I have squarely answered those who have said – and might continue to say – that I am not mentally tough. I believe I have answered that question emphatically.

Mark Ramprakash
September 2009

CHAPTER 1

SHALL WE DANCE?

'I love Mark! I enjoy watching him, and for a beginner and a non-dancer like him to master what he has mastered, and do it so well, is amazing. I love seeing that natural ability in anyone – and it is really, really exciting when they have not come from a background of dance'
– Arlene Phillips, *Strictly Come Dancing* judge

Since my appearance on *Strictly Come Dancing* there are three questions that I get asked more than any others. The first is how did I get to do the show, the second – from the ladies – is what is Karen Hardy actually like, and the third – from the blokes – is 'Did you?'

That's males for you, I suppose. All I can do whenever it is trotted out is smile and shake my head and generally give a bit of banter back, as if it is the very first time that I've heard that line.

Karen, her husband Conrad and their family are people that I'm just so thrilled to have had the chance to get to know and, looking back now, it is amazing to think that in July 2006 – when I was first approached about being involved in *Strictly* – I didn't even know who Karen Hardy was.

Indeed I had only watched a single show of the previous series, to see how Darren Gough got on in his very first appearance in the 2005 edition of *Strictly* – in which he ended up winning the title, of course. I did hear about that, naturally, but I'd only ever watched the one whole programme and I'd ended up virtually cringing behind the sofa as Goughy strutted around wearing a waistcoat with nothing on underneath. Sorry, Goughy.

I was in my local north London park with my two girls when I got that fateful first call, from an agent whom I'd known for a few years. He asked me what I thought about being on *Strictly Come Dancing* and I must admit my initial reaction was 'Sorry, mate, no chance . . .'

At that stage, in my defence, I really didn't know much about the programme – apart from it being the thing that Goughy had won, and kept on letting people know he had won – and I certainly didn't know that it was such a high-profile, highly popular programme. And when I got home and mentioned the call to my wife and my daughters, the two girls' initial reaction was to fall about laughing.

I also knew all about Darren Gough, and his extrovert personality. He comes alive in the spotlight, on the cricket field and off it, and he loves attention. He is a very different character to me. I am certainly no extrovert.

But then Van said to me: why not? By this stage of my cricket career, too, I had begun to get interested in the process of doing my coaching badges, and being encouraged to think outside the box and learning new ideas was all part of that. I knew, too, that one of my weaknesses was a tendency not to want to do anything different. So, the more I thought about it, and the more Van and I talked about it, the more I felt it might be a good thing to try. After 20 years in cricket, indeed, why not?

There was also for me, however, more than a touch of not really knowing what I was letting myself in for; at first, after confirming that I was interested, all I had to do was go along to what in effect was a BBC interview. Two delightful ladies called Charlotte Oates and Sam Donnelly have the task of chatting to potential contestants and, I suppose, sussing you out.

After meeting them, and chatting about various aspects of my cricket career and what the programme would entail, they said they would let me know. There was no indication at all about whether I was thought suitable or not.

Also, as the 2006 cricket season was still going on, I was very much in the thick of what was a marvellous summer, both for me and for Surrey, and so I didn't actually think too much about whether I would make the final selection. It was also a good few weeks before I got the call confirming that I had, indeed, made the cut.

One thing I did do, though, during those weeks was call Darren Gough. I had intended to ask him a few questions about the show, simply to get my mind around what I might end up doing, but all I ended up doing was listening to Darren for half an hour or so as he went on and on about why I just had to do it, and how stupid I would be if I even thought about not doing it.

Goughy stressed just what a great time he had had throughout the whole show, and he explained, too, how much he had got into it – the whole process of learning to dance from scratch – and said that I would kick myself if I didn't take the opportunity to have a go myself.

To be fair to him, he was so incredibly enthusiastic – even for him, which is saying something – that he did help to push me towards believing that it would be fun and a great chance to do something very different from cricket. The call had come out of the blue, but I felt that was even more of a reason to grab it. I've still no idea who it was that put my name forward in the first place – other than that the BBC do tend to look quite closely at sportspeople generally when they are surveying potential candidates.

My first glimpse of the glamour of *Strictly*, and the new world that I was about to experience, came when I had to go to a BBC studio to start the filming for the opening credits. Karen was not around at this stage, as she was still in Japan doing some coaching and teaching, and I remember I took along my eldest daughter Cara for some moral support. Cara, who was nine at the time, absolutely loves dance and has done tap, ballet and modern.

I didn't know how to stand or what to do, but it was at that first filming session that I met an extremely confident young man from New Zealand called Brendan. He seemed to know how to do everything, and so he showed me a couple of moves and also how to stand. It was kind of him.

A lot of people seem to want to know what Brendan Cole is like too, and whether he is as much of a prat as he seems on the show. I always just give them a look, and they say, 'Oh, right, he is.' I don't have to say anything else!

As the show progressed, though, Brendan was the one person whom I didn't seem to hit it off with. I suppose we just didn't have a lot to say to one another, which is surprising in a way because, as a New Zealander, he is one of the few professional dancers who have even heard of cricket, let alone know what I do for a living.

It was even more disappointing, though, that he didn't seem to give Karen and me more support and backing as the show went along because he is very friendly with Karen's husband, who is also from New Zealand. He kept being more supportive of others in the competition, and some of the comments he made about us were perhaps a bit surprising. I didn't have a problem if he preferred to support other couples, of course, but there did seem to be a little bit of tension there when it came to us.

The first time I met Karen was obviously a big moment – for both of us, I would guess! I was taken to a dance studio in Hackney (which we were to use a lot for our training), but it was all a bit top-secret at the time, and of course there were cameras there to record our meeting and the subsequent first session together.

I was pretty nervous about meeting her, but from the moment she walked through the door she made me feel very much at ease. She was very relaxed and very friendly, and a gorgeous lady. What she also did at that first practice session, which I appreciated, was to sit me down and talk about the fact that, as dance partners, we would have to be very close to each other – and to be in each other's personal space in a way that is not natural at all for people who have never met before.

Karen said that I was not to worry about it, and that it was something that we would quickly get used to. It is obviously an important aspect of dancing – you simply have to get physically very close to someone in order to dance properly and well – but it was good that she flagged this up very early and therefore dealt with this awkward aspect of our partnership right at the outset.

She also didn't know anything about cricket, or who I was, which I loved, and you will already have read in Karen's foreword about what happened at the end of our first session, when she asked me for my full name in order to put my number into her mobile phone. But that was funny, and it further broke the ice, and I left for home that day feeling that I had been very lucky indeed to be partnered with such a nice person.

One thing, too, that immediately became clear at our first meeting was that Karen likes to talk . . . a lot. But that was good, because I don't! Right from the start, our two personalities seemed to complement each other, and I did feel very much at ease despite that first dancing session being anything but comfortable for me. It was so different. And I felt a bit weird, to be honest. It's just that it feels that you are mincing around the floor, which is hard to do in a serious way, and for me that was something else to overcome all the way through the show.

What became abundantly clear very quickly, meanwhile, was the fact that Karen is very popular with everyone connected to the show. She's very good with people, and very bubbly, but whoever it was – camera crew, make-up, wardrobe – you got to see that they lit up when Karen was around.

And it was her special personality that helped me to come out of myself as the show went on; it is highly unlikely that I could have built the same rapport with any of the other dancers. For that, of course, I must say a huge thanks to the ladies in casting. They make the decisions, based on their interviews with the amateurs, about who gets paired with whom and, as far as I am concerned, they did their job brilliantly.

At our first practice, after a bit of an initial chat, we began with a cha-cha to the J-Lo song 'Let's Get Loud'. It was pretty cringe-making for me, as it was the first experience of seeing myself in the full-length mirrors that are on the wall of the studio. You soon get used to it, of course, but initially you are so self-conscious. I did pick up the steps reasonably quickly, though, and it was encouraging that Karen seemed very happy with what we had done as a start.

It was obvious, right from the first minutes of our partnership, that Karen was also a quite outstanding teacher. I knew by then that she had been the last British female dancer to be a world champion at Latin dance, and so that meant an immediate respect for her own individual ability. In my eyes, that put her up on a level with some of the very best cricketers I had ever played with or against. But it was her patience, and her coaching skills, which struck the most powerful chord with me.

She had been retired from competitive dancing for five years, but it is not for nothing that she is rated as a top coach. She managed me very cleverly and very well for the whole 14 weeks of *Strictly*, whether that was by encouraging me and boosting me up or by judging perfectly when she could take the mickey, or needle me, in the knowledge that it was exactly the right way at that time to push me on again and drive me to improve my performance.

The first time I met my fellow competitors was on the first performance day. That, too, was quite an occasion because some of them – Emma Bunton, Peter Schmeichel, Matt Dawson – were people who had achieved massive things in their respective fields. I hadn't met any of them before, either, and so in some ways that was quite daunting.

What I also remember about that day was that I felt a right idiot because I turned up a bit late and was the last there – and I was still dressed in my scruffy old Surrey training top and tracksuit trousers. All the other celebrities were in casual clothes, or rather designer tops and jeans or smart casual. Karen had suggested that we do some training earlier in the day and I had just not bothered to change. One of the girls said, 'Oh, so you must be the cricketer,' and I wanted to curl up!

For the first three or four days of our training, everything seemed to be going smoothly and, by and large, it was all very nice and well-mannered and polite between us. But Karen wants to have fun when she is working, too, and she was keeping up a constant stream of banter with me.

I remember, after the fourth day, thinking to myself that night that it was time that I had a bit of a go back. I decided that I shouldn't just be on the receiving end of the banter. And so, the next day, I came back at her on a couple of early occasions and she loved it. Indeed later she told me she was delighted to see that change in my personality – or, rather, the real me coming out. She said that it was the moment she felt we began to establish a chemistry and a rapport.

It was when we really began to get a lot of fun out of the dancing that Karen believed that we might be proper contenders.

When I look back at those three months or so of intense training myself, I also recognise just what a privileged position I was in. There I was, a complete and utter beginner, being coached and taught to dance by a world champion. Try to imagine a cricketing equivalent: it's like a world star putting in five or six hours a day of coaching, for fourteen weeks, with someone who had never picked up a cricket bat or bowled a ball. She must have had the patience of a saint.

Some of the show's early publicity shots were also filmed at the Oval, which was rather embarrassing for me, as all the Surrey offices look out over the pitch – and that's where the promotional video was going to be filmed! Needless to say, a lot of the staff also 'just happened' to be wandering around the ground as I was walking out in all my dancing gear.

Getting ready for the shot was also quite amusing. It took me five minutes in the make-up room, but of course Karen and the other girls were in there for hours, getting their hair just right and all the rest. This was a routine that I was to become all too familiar with over the weeks ahead!

But it was also funny to see her, just for that day, come into my environment. I knew my way around the Oval, and I knew everyone there, whereas she had never been there before. Karen was struggling a little bit at the time with a shoulder niggle, so I took her to see the Surrey physio, Dale Naylor, and he was able to help her with the problem. This was about a week into the show, so it was nice for me to be able to introduce her to a bit of my world.

For the professional dancers, the weekly schedule of *Strictly Come Dancing* is full-on and very stressful. Not only do they have to try to teach people like me, they also have to arrange the choreography, decide on the outfits, choose the music and tailor the daily training routines so that – hopefully – a peak is reached with the live performance on the Saturday night.

A feature of every *Strictly* show has been the public acclaim for the standards reached by the leading celebrities, but to my mind it is the professionals who deserve all the credit. We all get very pampered, and so much pressure is heaped upon them. The whole look, and feel, of what is performed on the show is down to them.

Karen, of course, was totally on top of all of that, as well as being incredibly relaxed and fun and great to be with. Knowing when to boost up their partners, and when to push them on in a bid to make an improvement to the amateur's performance every week, is not an easy thing to do for the professionals. I take my hat off to all of them.

After about six weeks of the show, my former Middlesex cricket teammate Simon Hughes, who is now a leading sports journalist and broadcaster, came along to a practice to watch some of the session that Karen and I were putting in and to interview me for a column he was writing for the *Daily Telegraph*. During our chat Simon made an interesting observation.

He said that he felt I could become very good at dancing because, in my early cricket career in particular, I had been an excellent impressionist when it came to mimicking bowlers' actions. Early in my teens, I had even modelled my own batting style – right down to my stance at the crease – on my hero, Viv Richards.

It was a bit of a party piece of mine when I was a young player. I had grown up watching all the famous Test bowlers on the television and, like a lot of cricket-mad youngsters, I had gone out into the garden or into the park and then tried to impersonate them when I bowled myself. People such as Bob Willis and Michael Holding were on my 'list' of those I could mimic and it even got to the stage, as a young Middlesex player, when I would get asked to do a bit of a routine right at the end of County Championship matches that were going to be draws.

For fun, Mike Gatting (the captain) used to throw the ball to me and the rest of the lads used to find it funny. There was one game in particular I remember, against Yorkshire at Headingley, when I tried to enliven the last few minutes of the contest by bowling an over of six different impressions.

Anyway, Simon felt that my ability to copy those bowlers' actions was playing its part in my ability to pick up the steps and the actions required by a particular dance. He felt that when Karen demonstrated a step or a move to me, I found it easier than most to copy and, in effect, mimic.

I have played a lot of football, both as a youngster and in my adult life, and this was something I definitely think added to my ability to have quick feet on the dance floor, and being a batsman, too, must have helped, in that batting is all about footwork. You need to be quick and assured in your footwork, against all types of bowlers. Then again, that couldn't have been much of a factor in the *Strictly* success of Darren Gough: he's a fast bowler, and a completely different shape and physique to me!

People do often say to me that I must have had some dancing experience before going on the show, but I can categorically say that I had never done anything that could be described as proper dancing. The only dancing I had done was in the nightclubs when I was younger and that was strictly informal. Yes, I loved dance music, and I would dance around happily in a group. But I would never be the first one up!

Soon, Karen and I settled into the routines of our training weeks and, very soon, I really began to enjoy the experience and to look forward to the different challenges that each week would bring. Fitness was not so much of a problem for me as it was for some of the other contestants, although it was physically very demanding and I did get very tired at times, but both Karen and I thought nothing of doing more and more training and upping the intensity. As we got into it, our competitive natures took over. But we were also enjoying ourselves, and that was the most important thing of all.

Our training week would go like this: on Monday and Tuesday we would plot through the steps of the routine. It's not rocket science: it is just a question of repeat, repeat, repeat. That is how you learn it. Then, later on a Tuesday and on a Wednesday we would put the routine to music, getting the steps in time to the beat of the piece of music chosen to accompany the dance. Part of Wednesday and all of Thursday would be spent polishing the routine, whether it was about the correct use of arms or posture or whatever, and on Friday we would have three run-throughs of the routine at the BBC studio in the afternoon.

During the third week, however, I experienced my first real panic. It was incredibly stressful, but it also taught us a lesson.

We were doing a tango, and for four days – as just described – we practised and polished our routine and felt we were in good shape. We had been in the same studio for all four days and so we had started (and, therefore, finished) the routine in exactly the same area of the room because Karen put the music tape in the machine before each practice. We started, of course, from a place near to that tape machine.

Then, on the Friday, we went to the BBC studio and when the music started I found that, after about three steps, I had completely lost it. I couldn't remember anything about how the routine went after that. My mind was a total blank and the harder I tried to remember it, the worse it got. It was ridiculous.

It soon became obvious what was producing this memory wipeout and the sheer terror and panic that was coming with it. In the dance studio there were the floor-to-ceiling mirrors on the wall and seeing myself in the mirror had become an aid to remembering the steps in the dance. It was subconscious more than anything, but doing the practice routine in exactly the same part of the same studio had meant that I was picking up little cues from my surroundings. Now, without them and in a very different room, I was lost.

Horrendous is not a strong enough word for that experience. It was frightening, really, because it was Friday afternoon and it was still quite early on in the show. The prospect of having to dance live 24 hours later was truly terrifying. Nerves were pretty frazzled on Saturday evenings at the best of times, let alone when you have seemingly forgotten everything about your routine!

Karen tried to calm me down, but what made it worse was that other competitors were around, too, waiting for their own dance-throughs. And, with every failed attempt that we had, more of them were beginning to watch what was happening with us.

Everyone is only supposed to have three run-throughs, so as to be fair to each couple in terms of having an equal amount of time on the floor, but we must have attempted to get through the routine about five times and, on the last one, Karen literally dragged me around to get it done. Hopeless.

Later that night, at around 11 p.m., I found myself in my kitchen at home going through the routine over and over again. I had my eyes closed, and I was trying to visualise Karen being there and what I had to do. I'm afraid it was sheer panic taking over. I didn't get too much sleep that night either; I just kept going through it in my head.

As it happened, all that visualising must have worked because the live performance went as well as we could have expected. Well, better, actually! We were a bit lucky to get through that week, but it often happened in the live dance that your performance was worse than in practice, or sometimes above your expectations. That's the beauty of a live show, I suppose: it's all on the night, and that creates such a lot of excitement and unpredictability. For the contestants, it can be both a blessing and a curse.

In every subsequent week, however, Karen and I made sure that we never repeated the error of that tango week. We made sure we practised each dance in different areas of a studio, or in different locations, and thankfully I never experienced my mind going blank again.

Those early weeks of the competition were truly eye-opening for me – and not just because I had been thrust into this alien, show-business world and was doing something that I never thought I would ever do. It hadn't dawned on me that *Strictly Come Dancing* was such a popular show!

As I've said, I went into it with no real knowledge of the level of its profile, but I remember after the first Saturday night show we were told that all the male celebrities would be required to come in to the BBC studio again the following day – Sunday was normally a day off – in order to learn a group dance which we were to perform as an extra element to the following week's programme.

It was on that morning, as we all gathered, that someone from the BBC casually told us that they had just got the official figures in and that more than nine million people had tuned in the previous evening. That is when it hit me that I was involved in something a little bit out of the ordinary.

As the weeks went by, and the contestants got whittled down to the main contenders, it became obvious that Matt Dawson would be one of those capable of going all the way. He had also improved hugely since the start of the show, and therefore he had real momentum on his side, and that recognition from the public and judges alike that – as Goughy had done the year before – he was making that transition from total amateur to something beginning to approach professional standard.

Why have sportspeople – and others include Colin Jackson, Denise Lewis and Austin Healey – been significantly successful on *Strictly*? I suppose the fact that we have to be competitive every day of our working lives is a big factor, as is also a natural fitness and flexibility in most cases.

We are used to performing in the moment, too. In our jobs, it's all about the live performance. Moreover, generally speaking, sportsmen and women have a perfectionist streak in them and the vast majority of us are also big on preparation and making sure we can perform to the best of our ability. We don't like being ill-prepared because we know it will impact on performance.

In cricket, my mantra is being able to walk out on to the ground to bat – or to field, for that matter – knowing that I have prepared as well as I can for that particular innings or match. That also means, whatever happens, I will have no regrets. There would be nothing worse, for me, and I suspect for virtually all professional sportspeople, than failing to perform after failing to prepare. I couldn't live with that.

Translated to *Strictly*, the sporting contestants would look upon the live Saturday evening dance, or dances, as the focus and the point of all the practice and, if you felt that you couldn't have done any more, you could take the consequences with equanimity.

I also feel that every sportsperson who has appeared on *Strictly* has a bit of an advantage over actors, or newsreaders, or other less physical professions, in that we are predominantly much fitter – and in some cases much younger. For some, two hours a day of practice is more than enough and they might even struggle to keep up that sort of schedule over a period of time. For us, though, more practice hours are not a problem. In my own case, I never felt physically tired to an extent that I could not have gone on.

The mental side of doing the show is another area in which I felt prepared, as a sportsman. Mentally, performing live is very stressful and tough, but I was able to draw on a lot of the things that I had worked on with Steve Bull, the England cricket team psychologist who had helped me during the second and most successful part of my international career.

I found the visualisation exercises I had learned from Steve were very valuable, plus the ability mentally to embrace the challenge and to enjoy the challenge.

Performing in front of a live audience on the Saturday shows could also be extremely off-putting for the amateurs. You often have a number of friends and family in the audience and it only takes catching the eye of someone you know for a split-second to throw you off your routine.

Again, you learn very quickly that the professional dancers are superb at looking as if they are interacting with the live audience when, in fact, they don't focus at all on anyone. Mental preparation, and visualisation, was important to me in this area too, although actors and singers have the biggest advantage here in that this ability to look out at the audience but not actually see any of them is a technique they must employ in their own professions.

Often the amateurs get pulled up by the judges for looking like they are not enjoying the dance and not communicating with the audience; it is just that they are concentrating so hard on the steps and not looking at anyone in the audience for fear of losing their way. They are genuinely worried, and nervous, so it's hardly surprising that they look it!

But while the professional dancers literally act out the dance, as their way of expressing themselves to the audience, I found that it was the music which made the real difference for me. If I liked a particular piece of music, it became that much easier to express myself through the dance. If I didn't like the music that much, it was much harder. I reckon it would be straightforward to look back at the tapes and guess which music I liked the best, simply from my body language.

For instance, I am a big James Bond fan and I loved dancing to the *GoldenEye* theme. We also did a group dance to 'Diamonds Are Forever', which was brilliant fun. Then there was 'Hot, Hot, Hot' – the song I did my salsa to. I had heard that song since I was a kid and always liked it. Dancing to it, therefore, was at once an enjoyable sensation.

As in cricket, with regard particularly to batting, it was extremely helpful to have a few key words in my head when I went out to dance. Again, this is central to a strong mental approach in that it helps to keep you focused on the job in hand. On *Strictly*, it was interesting to me that Karen also dropped some of these key words into our practices. Clearly, it was an aid she herself used in her professional dancing career and words like 'smile', 'keep your frame' and 'head up' were etched in my mind when we took to the floor.

Despite all the hard work in practice, however, and all the things I could bring myself to the task – like my fitness and the ability to mimic, and good footwork and mental preparation – I still depended hugely week to week on Karen.

An example of just how good the professionals are came in our semi-final, when we were performing the quickstep. As its name suggests, this dance is quick and energetic, and the adrenalin was flowing so much for me that I was going too quickly. Our dance routine, though, had a pause in the middle and as I was stepping so fast I got to this point too early. Karen, though, simply made up something on the spot so that she could catch me up; 99.9 per cent of the people there (i.e. everyone except Karen and me) would not have known that this was not part of our rehearsed routine. The judges certainly did not pick up on it.

Also, during the final itself and in our crucial show dance, we were coming to a step called the New Yorker and I was about to go into it way too early. Karen came towards me and pointed a finger and her eyes told me to wait . . . and, again, her action just seemed natural and part of what we were doing. She was exceptional at keeping me in check!

Karen found it very amusing that I did not have a clue about how to count music. When she initially asked me, I would go 'one, two, three, four' to the beat and she would fall about. And, even after 14 weeks, I never really managed to pick up a basic method of counting the music, but as Karen had everything totally under control I didn't need to, in reality.

Again, in the final, during our routine to 'Shout' by Lulu, I was going far too fast. When we soon got to the bit where we had to hold hands, she gripped me a bit tighter and gave me that warning look. We then waited a split second, so as not to go ahead of the music, and then carried on. I'm sure none of the judges would have spotted that, either.

I only live about half an hour from the BBC, so on the live performance days – Saturdays – I didn't need to get up too early. I would be in the studios by about 9.30 a.m. Of course, all the ladies had been there for quite a while by then, getting ready for the day.

Everyone would be on set by about 10.30 a.m. and then we would do rehearsals. This would also involve walk-throughs of where we all had to be and what we had to do during the opening bit of the show, when Bruce Forsyth and Tess Daly would introduce each couple and we would walk down the steps onto the floor.

Then it would be time for lunch, and during my 14 weeks on the show I had the same thing each Saturday for my lunch meal – jacket potato with tuna. I am such a creature of habit, anyway, but this became something of a routine for me. Why change when things are going well? But most of all, during lunch, I tried to sit and watch *Football Focus*, which was being recorded in the same building, of course.

In early afternoon, we all had to do what is called Band Call.

During the week you are practising to your selected piece of music on CD, so it is important that the live band play that piece at the same pace and as near as possible in sound to the CD version of it. Karen was meticulous in getting this right, even though a live band will always play a piece slightly differently in some parts. That is unavoidable, but the pace was the key thing.

At 4 p.m., we would have a full dress rehearsal of the routine, and at 6 p.m. the live show would start. They were very long days, as we didn't finish until 9 p.m. − or 9.30 p.m. − in the evening, but they were also very exciting. But just imagine the workload on the day of the final itself: we had five routines to perform, so on that Saturday there were five Band Calls, five dress rehearsals and then the five live performances. Considering the fitness levels I had gained by then, too, I was exhausted physically by the end of it.

During the Saturday rehearsals Karen and I would always make some little adjustments to the routines − some extra fine-tuning, if you like − but by the later stages we were also working extremely hard indeed all through the week.

I remember during the second week of competition saying to Karen that I would be taking one of the weekdays off because I was going to play golf. She told me to enjoy the day because, if we survived in the show for any length of time, it wouldn't happen again. And how right she was. But, then again, we only did the amount of hours we did because it meant so much to us. We were determined to give it our very best shot, and we were enjoying the challenge of trying to win.

Karen has a little boy, and of course I wanted to spend time with my family too, and at first we gave ourselves every Sunday off. But by the time we got to the last few weeks, we were going in to train on Sundays, too. That was how much it mattered.

My stickiest point in the whole competition, in terms of trying to master a particular dance, came in week seven, when we had to perform a rumba. Most of the dances I really enjoyed, but the rumba is so difficult for a man to do, in my view − you feel so effeminate doing it! It is slow, and you have to use your arms and your hips; I felt so self-conscious, and it was the one time that I got a bit tense, so that even the great relationship that had grown between Karen and myself was tested.

I was having real problems with it. I couldn't understand how all the male professional dancers could do the rumba so well and yet still manage to look masculine. Eventually, as I was getting more and more frustrated by my inability to come to terms with this dance, Karen invited James Jordan, the professional dancer, to our training to work with me. James helped me enormously, simply by demonstrating the technique so well and enabling me to copy him. By doing this, I got by.

By the end of my time on *Strictly*, I was being consumed by the challenge and the competition. I think all the amateur dancers who go any distance into it feel the same way. And it can make you very emotional. I remember Jan Ravens, who was dancing with Anton du Beke, getting so wrapped up in the experience – and especially the love of dancing with Anton – that she was very upset indeed when she was voted off.

The reactions and emotions you see on the television screen are not fake. Contestants are absolutely gutted to be leaving the show, because it has taken over their lives and is such fun.

That is why I thought it was so wrong of John Sergeant to walk off the show last year. I know it was controversial, and amusing, the way that the public kept on voting for him and keeping him in. And I know they may have been doing it partly to spite the judges, who clearly wanted to get rid of him. But a big part of the show is the entertainment side – and the public vote reflects this. They wanted him to stay on, and the rules are that you stay on if the public feel you deserve to stay.

John was still there because the public voted for him to come back the next week and he should have honoured that. Everyone else who had been voted off really wanted to stay and, knowing the emotions of being involved, as I do, I felt it was poor on John's part to walk away when he did.

He signed up for the show and he knew the rules at the outset. He became one of the public's favourites – rightly or wrongly – and I believe it was the public who should have had the say when he left.

There is no way that the public would have had him win it – they just wanted him to stay in the competition for longer.

Tom Chambers and Rachel Stevens were always going to be the ones who would end up fighting it out for the actual title but, in my opinion, and knowing how much everyone loves being on the show, John Sergeant should have stayed on for as long as he was being granted the privilege – which it is – of being part of *Strictly*.

CHAPTER 2

FULFILMENT

'The ability that counts is the ability to improve and to continue improving'

– cricketing maxim

I was only three when I held a bat in my hand for the first time. It was a little plastic bat, which Mum and Dad bought for me, and I was soon slogging whatever ball was thrown at me – apparently, the game was to see if I could hit the back windows in our lounge.

But my first proper cricket bat was a Christmas present, when I was six years old. And I can remember dragging my dad outside on a cold Christmas Day to try it out on the driveway. Our house then had a long concrete drive and Dad used to bowl underarm at me with a tennis ball.

My father had a deep love of cricket, generated when he was growing up in Guyana, which has long had a strong tradition of cricket. Considering how small a country it is, population-wise, it has produced an incredible number of world-class cricketers: from the days of Clive Lloyd, Basil Butcher, Rohan Kanhai and Lance Gibbs, there have been the likes of Alvin Kallicharran, Roy Fredericks, Colin Croft, Roger Harper, Carl Hooper, Shivnarine Chanderpaul and Ramnaresh Sarwan.

Dad used to go to the historic Bourda ground, in Georgetown, to watch Test cricket and can remember seeing England play there. He came to England in 1960, when he was 23. Like all West Indians,

49

he likes to talk about the game, too, and his enthusiasm for cricket meant that he was always available to bowl at me on that drive when I was small. I always seemed to be batting, too – I don't think I bowled very often!

What I do remember very clearly is that Dad, who used to be a spinner in club cricket, bowled a variety of off-breaks and leg-breaks at me, so even at that age I had to watch the ball coming out of his hand for clues as to which way it would spin. A simple thing, maybe, but it was a very good habit to get into right from the start. Above and beyond that, though, we were having fun out of cricket. We were just a father and son, throwing a ball at each other.

There have, however, been so many things that my father has given to me, as a cricketer: lots of information about the game, but also solid basics such as how to hold the bat and how to stand at the crease. I've always remembered him telling me how each game is a new game and that even if you've scored a hundred or more in the last match you have to start totally from scratch in the next game – because it is a new day, with new conditions and new challenges.

He told me things like I should make sure I walked out to the wicket slowly so that my eyes could better get used to the light; all his little snippets of information were as relevant to me as a young boy as they became when I moved up the levels of cricket.

Dad has had a massive influence on me, both in terms of cricket and generally. Even now, we discuss cricket and cricket issues a lot. My mum has not had the same sort of influence, cricket-wise, but she has very much influenced the way I live my life. We are a very close family, and I would always go home to discuss with Mum and Dad anything that was important in my life.

When I was thinking about leaving Middlesex, I talked it through a lot with my parents. I chat to them about my game, or if there are issues in the dressing-room or with any of the coaches. I can talk to them about anything, and they have always been very interested in my career. They have also given me their opinion, or feedback, on a particular issue. And when I was young, they also provided the taxi service that is so vital for any young cricketer!

In 1978, when I was coming up to nine, we moved house. This was a pivotal moment in my life because just around the corner from our new house was a park, and in that park was a cricket club – which Dad joined. Initially, I used to go along to watch him play, and also travelled with him to some of the away matches, and soon I was being selected for their colts team and I played a few games for them.

Then, when I was ten, I joined another club. Bessborough Cricket Club had a very strong colts section and, after I had played against them in an Under-15 game in which I had scored about 20 in an all-out total of 42, I was asked by Graham Sainsbury, who ran the Bessborough colts side, if I wanted to join them.

They were a very much more organised club and it was through them that I got picked for a Middlesex Under-11 trial. I was down to bat at number three and had to wait and watch as the two openers put on more than 100 – which in U11 cricket is an awful lot of runs! Finally, I was in, but three balls later I was walking off again for a duck, having been bowled by a swinging full toss. It was the first time I had seen a ball swing like that.

You can imagine that I felt my whole world had been shattered. It was very upsetting, especially as my parents and a lot of other family had come to watch the game. But perhaps I had impressed with the way I had walked out to the wicket, because I was still selected in the squad for the rest of that summer's Middlesex U11 matches and ended up playing half a dozen or so games.

I think Graham Sainsbury had made sure I was included on the basis of what he had seen of me before, and one of the great benefits of being in the county age group squad was that, the following winter, I was also invited to go to nets at the Finchley Indoor Cricket School.

It was there that I began to be coached by an old Middlesex player called Jack Robertson. He had been a very fine batsman, scoring 31,914 first-class runs in his own career, from 1937 until 1959. He had been a very orthodox and correct player, and his coaching instilled in me at just the right age the benefits of playing straight.

He was always immaculately turned out, with slicked-back hair and Middlesex sweater, and I liked him a lot and enjoyed his coaching. In fact, I have got a lot to be grateful to Jack Robertson for, because he put a lot of the basics into my game at an early age. Since I have done coaching myself, I can also see what a huge advantage it is for a young player to get access to the best coaches at an early age. The best habits get ingrained then and it saves a lot of hard work later.

In recent years, it has always intrigued me – and worried me, to be honest – that a lot of young professionals seem to come into the game with poor set-ups at the crease and deficiencies in their technique that obviously then get exposed by the better bowling they face. How has this happened? Should we not make sure that all our young cricketers do not get that far without their techniques being up to the standard required to succeed at first-class level?

Anyway, I only hope dear old Jack will forgive me for going past his own first-class run tally in my first innings of the 2009 season. He is now in 51st place in the list of all-time run-getters, and not 50th! Who would have thought that would be the case when, as an 11 year old, I hung on his every word during those Finchley net sessions?

My cricket, out in the middle, was learned at club level. I didn't go to a private school, and at my comprehensive in Harrow the only cricket we played was the occasional 20-over knockabout stuff, wearing trainers and our black school trousers. And so 99 per cent of what I learned about playing the game was through club colts and senior men's cricket.

At Bessborough I represented the U11, U13 and U15 colts teams, but I was playing men's Second XI cricket at the age of 12 and then got into the men's first XI at 13. The club were brilliant with me, too, because even at that tender age I was encouraged to open the batting, so that I got the maximum opportunity to develop my batting out there where it matters.

Graham Sainsbury was also my opening partner for much of the three years that I played in the men's firsts and to have someone at the other end who I knew and trusted, and who could give me tips on my game as we played, was invaluable. If I was still in after an hour or so, I would be able to accelerate my scoring, but up to then I was encouraged to build my innings and play correctly.

I think it is worth emphasising here, though, that in the 1980s it was more a part of cricket's culture that players – at all levels – were expected to do a lot of the working out for themselves when it came to learning how to play. Yes, at the time I was getting excellent information and instruction from good coaches and senior club players, but I was also expected to take responsibility for my own game and its development.

Nowadays, coaches tend to analyse players quite extensively and then go to the player with their thoughts and instruction. It was different then, and remained that way even when I joined the Middlesex professional staff.

The advantage I had of playing predominantly in adult cricket, and playing competitive league cricket every Saturday, was that I had to work things out very quickly. The faster bowlers were pretty sharp, too, for someone aged 13 or 14, and there were no batting helmets in club cricket then.

By the time I was 15, I was playing for Middlesex U19s and I was fully immersed in the club's youth system. At 14 and 15, I was also playing for England schools' teams, alongside the likes of Mike Atherton and Nasser Hussain, who are both about a year and a half older than me.

Chris Lewis was another fellow future England Test cricketer whom I played alongside at that time. He was a couple of school years older than me, but we played for Middlesex at an U19 festival at Cambridge. One of the most prominent players in the Middlesex U19 side then, however, was Alastair Fraser – the elder brother of Angus – but although he did play for the county at first-class level he did not go on to international honours like Gus.

But, from the age of 15, it was practising regularly alongside the county's Second XI players and fringe Second XI players that made me realise that, perhaps, I could make it at professional level myself. Up until then, despite my representative honours, I was playing my cricket purely for the enjoyment I got out of it. My dad and I had never spoken at home about even the possibility of my becoming a professional player.

At this age, too, I had also signed schoolboy forms with Watford Football Club and so my cricket simply had to fit in alongside the demands of football.

But what I liked about the Middlesex county age group cricket I played, and the England schools' games, was that they were always so well organised. We played on lots of superb grounds, and on good pitches, and I think I was very lucky to experience that as I was growing up. It was very enjoyable cricket to play in.

Cricket, as a game, appealed to me initially because I was good at it. If you are successful at something, you automatically enjoy it. But, as I've gone through my career, I realise I also love cricket for the challenges that it has always thrown up.

I do like the fact that every single game you play is such a new challenge. You have different surfaces to bat on every time, and the overhead conditions change constantly, too. Then there are the challenges posed by different bowlers. I enjoy the hard work that goes into getting yourself in at the crease, and sometimes how you have to struggle early in your innings to get to the next stage, which is to feel a bit more comfortable and to get your footwork moving smoothly.

Then you might have to absorb pressure, either from bowlers who are on top of you or from the match situation itself, before hopefully you can relax more into your strokes and start to progress your innings. Because a lot of my early cricket was played as an opener, I've always enjoyed this process of building an innings.

Every time you walk out to bat you are on 0. And, although over the years that has sometimes not been easy to handle – I think I've been out for a lot of ducks over the years – it has always been a challenge that I've relished. When you see the scoreboard clicking over and recording a decent total by your name, it is a very satisfying feeling. And the fact that you started out on 0 makes it an even better feeling, to my mind!

Steve Rixon once said to me, when he was coach at Surrey, that he felt the reason I have been so successful and so consistent a run-scorer over the years is because I am so suspicious – of bowlers, of pitches, of what might get me out. I suppose he is right. Even if I've scored a hundred the day before, I will never just go out there and try to hit the ball on the up from the off. I need to go through the process.

The very fact that I have now played professional cricket for 23 seasons also shows how much I love the game. A lot of Test players come back into county cricket and don't enjoy it because there is no adrenalin rush and far fewer people there to watch.

But I look at it as a pursuit of excellence, and of a desire to keep improving. My Level Four coaching course has underlined to me how important that is to me. Trying to stay one step ahead of the opposition bowlers who are trying to get you out is, for me, a constant challenge and one that really motivates me. In fact, my game has evolved all the time throughout my 23 seasons as a first-class cricketer, and it will continue to do so.

Take an example from the 2008 season – in the next Championship fixture after I had completed my hundredth first-class hundred. We were playing down at Taunton, against Somerset, and I was thinking about how I was going to play against Charl Willoughby, their former South African international left-arm swing and seam bowler.

Left-arm quicks, who swing the ball back into the right-hander from over the wicket, had troubled me all the way through my career. I always seemed to be falling over with my head, and therefore feeling vulnerable to the lbw, and I just couldn't work out how to combat it. Everyone I had spoken to, including respected coaches such as Alan Butcher at Surrey, had said that they thought my set-up and stance were right and that there was nothing technically wrong.

But I knew that there was and, through the best part of 22 seasons, it had been something niggling away at me. You don't face left-arm pace bowlers in every game, of course, but good county performers such as Mark Ilott of Essex, Mike Smith of Gloucestershire and Paul Taylor of Northamptonshire had always caused me problems and down at Taunton the presence of Willoughby in the opposition ranks set me thinking again.

Willoughby had got me out, too, in the match we had played against Somerset at Whitgift School in Croydon earlier in the season. He had first bowled me an excellent inswinger, which I managed to keep out, but then slanted one across me next ball and I got an edge.

In recent seasons, I have got into the habit of doing throw-downs in practice with Scott Newman, the Surrey opener, who is a left-handed batsman. And, as I was throwing balls at him at practice during this game, I suddenly began to realise that anything I threw at him coming into his pads didn't seem to bother him at all. He was perfectly balanced over the ball.

I realised, too, that in all the matches I had played with him I had never seen him get into trouble with right-arm bowlers swinging it back into his pads. He simply flicked them away through mid-wicket, most of the time. But then, when he was growing up, facing mainly right-arm bowlers as a left-hander was natural for him; for me, however, as a right-hand batsman, coming up against left-armers was far more of a rarity.

Anyway, as Scott was hitting my throw-downs, I found myself wondering how he didn't fall over to the offside when facing right-arm bowling, whereas I did, facing left-arm stuff. I imagined it as a mirror image of myself and tried to work out what Scott was doing in his own stance and set-up.

That evening, in my hotel bedroom, I continued to theorise on this. I know it's rather anal, but when I get a particularly good bat these days I never leave it overnight in an away dressing-room. I always take it back to my hotel room! I don't literally sleep with it, I can assure you of that, but I also don't want to let it out of my sight!

Anyway, there was a full-length mirror on the hotel bedroom wall and so I began to imagine I was facing Willoughby and worked out how I was going to stand at the crease. I thought about the great West Indies batsman Shivnarine Chanderpaul and the way he is very two-eyed at the crease as a left-hander facing predominantly right-arm bowlers from over the wicket.

I didn't want to be as open-stanced as Chanderpaul, but I worked out that if I did open up my stance, so that my front foot was pointing directly at the bowler – and not down the pitch – then I found that a slight movement back and across did not mean that my head was going too far to the offside. I decided there and then to adopt this new stance, to Willoughby, in my innings the following day.

Immediately, at the crease, it felt comfortable, and so I kept on doing it to every ball I faced from him. I ended up scoring 200 not out, too, so it worked pretty well! And, since that mid-August day last year, I have adopted this new stance to left-armers every time. I have now had none of the problems I experienced for the vast majority of my career; it just shows that you can indeed always improve in cricket.

Meanwhile, I am not someone who is always looking in the record books to see where I am now on this list or that list. People will come up and tell you if you have reached a particular landmark, but I am not especially interested in that.

The hundred hundreds was one target for me, however, and when I got to 79 – by the end of the 2005 season – I really began to allow myself to look at it and work out how possible it was. I thought, at the time, that I might have a chance, but that I would probably have to play until 40 at least to get it done. Back then I concluded that it might be a tight call!

But then I had two great seasons in 2006 and 2007, when I scored more than 2,000 runs in each campaign and averaged above 100 both times. In 2006, I made eight hundreds and in 2007 ten. I knew then that it was going to happen, and six more centuries in 2008 took me to 103 by the end of that summer.

I could never have predicted such a rate of production as that, but it was as if all my previous experience came through: I knew when to consolidate at the crease, and I knew when to counter-attack. But, more than the actual landmark of scoring a hundred hundreds, what has been truly fulfilling is that I have been able to continue to show to myself and to other people in the game that I am still a good player.

Since being overlooked by England, from April 2002, I have thrown myself into my cricket with Surrey and I have put everything into becoming the best batsman I can be and doing all that I can to make Surrey successful.

I will always be grateful to Surrey for rejuvenating my career in 2001, and of course I have tried to repay their faith in me, but most important of all I have tried my best both in terms of batting out in the middle and preparing myself for cricket. And the knowledge that I have done my very best is what matters most to me.

When we met up at a pre-season county tournament in Abu Dhabi last March, Graham Gooch said to me that the really good players are those who don't want to be the ones sitting on the dressing-room balcony, clapping the achievements of other people. And he's absolutely right. I don't want to play the shot of the day, I want to play the innings of the day.

I have taken tremendous satisfaction from batting a long time and building a big innings during my career. First-class cricket is the ultimate for me, and always will be, because it is the truest test of all your range of skills as a cricketer. I've always set my standards high, too, and that approach didn't suffer a bit just because I wasn't playing Test cricket for England any more.

The other huge satisfaction to be taken from playing professional cricket is the feelings you get when you come off the field after an innings which has either won a game or set up a winning position, for your team, and your teammates are all there to clap you in and congratulate you. There's no prize of a Ferrari or anything like that for scoring a great hundred or playing a match-winning innings, but I don't think any sort of material reward could ever beat the thrill and satisfaction of getting the appreciation of your teammates.

So, for me, records and landmarks are just a by-product of playing well, and in my case also being fortunate enough to be able to play for a long time at first-class level. Of course, I am proud of my statistical record, but there are other things such as winning the Surrey Player of the Year Award five times in succession, or winning the Professional Cricketers' Association Player of the Year Award in 2006 and then being named as one of the five *Wisden* Cricketers of the Year in 2007, which mean a lot, too.

Ricky Ponting said earlier this year that individual records do not interest him, for the very reason that scoring lots of runs means more than anything that he has been lucky to have a lengthy career, and I agree with that sentiment.

My own fitness has always been good and I have never been above 12 and a half stone in my whole adult life. I look after myself, and don't really drink, and that has been a big help, but I've always looked upon keeping fit as a necessity for batting. It is one of the tools you need for the job, especially to bat for a long time. I am happy to do around 12.5 on the bleep test every year because, although that is by no means outstanding, it is what I know to be good enough for me to reach the standards I want to achieve.

Early in my Middlesex days, I was influenced a lot by a fitness trainer employed by the club called John Neale. His philosophy was that cricketers don't need to do lots of long-distance runs because that just wears out your ankles and knees and hips, but they should concentrate on cricket-specific fitness drills, such as 20-yard shuttles, and only light weights to build up core strength.

A lot of cricketers were not properly fit when I started out in the game – nowadays, if you are not fit, you are very much the odd man out – but John's influence meant that I got into some good fitness habits early on in my career and I am very grateful for that.

As I have got older, it has also become very important to me that my teammates in the dressing-room have respect for me and think that I bring a lot of positive attributes to the group. I would be very disappointed if they believed I was doing anything that could be perceived to be a negative influence.

In my early 20s, I had a bit of a reputation for throwing my bat or throwing the odd tantrum when I got out. That's when I acquired my 'Bloodaxe' nickname at Middlesex. I didn't handle things very well in those days. I wish I had dealt with the disappointments and frustrations of professional sport far better than I did.

To be honest, I wasn't mature enough then to realise how my behaviour impacted upon the group. I was naive and unaware of how it looked to those around me. Having said that, the dressing-room at Middlesex was not the sort of place where it was minded too much, anyway. If you had any personal issues, or frustrations, then people didn't care too much. All they were interested in was how you performed on the field and what you brought to the team in that respect.

I am not for one moment condoning some of my more excessive behaviour, in terms of dressing-room tempers, but it always humours me when I hear cricketers being described as 'a good man in the dressing-room' or 'a good bloke'. What, when you really boil it down, does that have to do with being a good cricketer?

In 2008, we had a great team spirit and a really good level of camaraderie in the Surrey dressing-room, but we didn't win a single Championship match, lost five and went down to division two!

Now, so much effort goes into making the squad a tight-knit group that a lot of emphasis is put on how a player fits in to the environment around him. I think I've always had more intensity in my approach and attitude to the game than most, but in English sport we do always seem to have a problem accommodating single-minded and ambitious people. Do we really appreciate them all, or is it better if they are also looked upon as being 'a good bloke', too?

Having said that, both the Middlesex dressing-room I started out in and the Surrey dressing-room I joined in 2001 were both quite unforgiving places. The players in those teams were all individual high-achievers, or wanted very much to be, and their collective attitude was overwhelmingly that if they went out on the field and performed their skills accurately and well then they would be contributing a lot to the team effort anyway, and so everyone would be happy.

Would I have had a different and less intense attitude myself if I had been brought up in a traditionally more relaxed and low-profile county like Somerset or Northamptonshire, for instance? I don't know, but I think it would have gone one of only two ways. Either it would have calmed me down, if the environment had been more easy-going, or it would have frustrated the hell out of me and I would soon have wanted to move counties!

More to the point, perhaps, is that what I have felt about my game – and still feel – comes from deep inside me. I don't think that it is a characteristic that has come from my mum or my dad, or any other family member. It's why I want to play sport, and why I've always wanted to play.

I played football with the same passion, especially when I was younger and dreamed that I could be a professional player at Watford, or wherever. I also think that growing up in London has also contributed to my character and my approach to my sport.

Reaching full maturity as a cricketer has been a long process and I still feel that I can improve. I really do believe you never stop learning. But the important staging posts for me, along the way, were 1990, 1995, 1997 and then the 2001 and 2002 summers.

As you will read in the following chapters, it was in 1990 that I felt I had made my first big playing breakthrough: I felt I could really play at first-class level and make a good career out of it. In 1995, scoring 2,000 runs in a season for the first time represented another important new level reached. And in 1997, being given the Middlesex captaincy and hugely enjoying at least that first season in charge gave me an enormous boost as a person and in terms of reaching a seniority in the game.

But it was my move to Surrey in 2001 that really led to a maturity for me, both as a player and a person. By 2002, my wife Van and I had two children, and I was discovering then a far better balance between my cricket and my other life.

An awful lot has happened since then, too, and I'm not talking about my 50-plus first-class hundreds for Surrey alone, or the great additional learning experience that starting my Level Four coaching badge in 2005 has brought me, or my other cricketing landmarks or my *Strictly Come Dancing* adventure.

At 40, I am happy to have come through what I have and to feel that it has all made me a better person. I still have ambitions, and the passion to perform still burns in me, but everything is in better perspective now, and there is – after all that has happened to me – a tangible sense of fulfilment.

CHAPTER 3

YOUNG CRICKETER

'Ramprakash, two days away from his nineteenth birthday, took them to within three runs of victory, batting throughout in his cap with confidence, style and a rare charm'

– Wisden Cricketers' Almanack, 1989

I had an inkling that a contract with Middlesex might be coming because I had played in five Second XI matches in 1986, when I was still sixteen, and had held my own. Then, early in 1987, I went to Sri Lanka with the England Under-19 team and performed well – especially in what was termed the third Test against Sri Lanka's U19s, in which I hit hundreds in both innings.

Michael Atherton captained the trip, with Trevor Ward of Kent his deputy. Other players in that England Young Cricketers squad were Nasser Hussain, who also scored a lot of runs, Martin Bicknell and Warren Hegg. I scored almost 600 runs on the tour and after I returned to England at the end of February I was soon signing a summer contract for Middlesex.

Little did I know that as soon as 25 April 1987 I was to make my first-class debut in Middlesex's opening three-day County Championship match of the season.

During the fortnight or so before this game I had taken my England U19 tour form into pre-season matches, scoring three successive hundreds: the first for Middlesex seconds against Durham University, then 180 for Stanmore in my debut game for my new club, and 152 for Middlesex Under-25s against Leicestershire U25s.

Both Chris Lewis and Phillip DeFreitas were playing for that Leicestershire team, and that third hundred was perhaps the most impressive knock I had played up to this point in my youthful career, because it was on a quickish pitch and was against two fairly serious fast bowlers. Don't forget, DeFreitas had already played Test cricket and had just returned from the 1986–87 tour to Australia, in which England under Mike Gatting had retained the Ashes.

It clearly also elevated me in the pecking order, and in the thinking of the Middlesex selectors, because suddenly I found myself included for that opening Championship match of the season, against Yorkshire at Lord's. Gatting, Clive Radley and Roland Butcher were all injured, which had given me my chance, but it was still a tremendous thrill to be picked.

On the day before the game, however, when I turned up at Lord's to join the first teamers for the pre-match preparation, I was late. Not a good start. Someone had told me the wrong time, but I can still remember arriving at the Nursery Ground that morning and seeing all the other players already sitting around on the grass doing their stretching and general warm-up exercises.

Paul Downton, the former England wicketkeeper, called to me to come and join in, and I looked around to see other players such as Phil Edmonds, Wayne Daniel, John Emburey . . . all Test cricketers, too. Anyway, we finished the warm-ups, had an initial net session, went to the Tavern for lunch and then came back in the afternoon for more nets.

On the first morning of the game I sat myself down next to Emburey, who was captaining in Gatting's absence. I will always be grateful for the way he made me welcome in that match and helped me as much as he could to feel settled and relaxed.

In truth, I was in a bit of a daze because there was just so much to take in. Being thrown in at the deep end like that, though, at the age of 17, does mean that you have no time to get really nervous: you just get on with it.

My first ball in first-class cricket came from Arnie Sidebottom – Ryan's father – and although it was a length ball outside of off stump I must confess I didn't see it! It was a very good job it wasn't straight. Then, next ball, Arnie bowled me a bouncer that I didn't see much of either.

I was wearing my Middlesex colts cap and I must have seemed so naive and young to those Yorkshire players as I came in to bat at number four. I also remember that Paul Jarvis, another England fast bowler, played against us in that game. I generally just scratched around before getting out for 17, caught at short leg by Richard Blakey off Jarvis's bowling.

After getting back to the dressing-room I had a chat with Simon Hughes, one of our fast bowlers, and he agreed that I could borrow his helmet for when I had to bat in the second innings. Bowlers like Jarvis were much quicker than I was used to, and again my naivety about the realities of facing such men meant that I had not even considered I would need a helmet of my own.

I enjoyed myself in our second innings, however, with helmet firmly on, reaching 63 not out before we declared. *Wisden* records that I made 'a glowing impression' but what I remember most about my debut match is thinking how quickly the ball came on to the bat. To me, at that time, the pitch was really quick – although to the seasoned professionals, it wasn't. It was like lightning compared to the club pitches I was used to, and I was hitting shots off the back foot because I felt the ball was coming on so much faster.

To have made my first-class debut at Lord's, and to have done well, was a real boost to my confidence and my ambition to make a career out of cricket, but I couldn't get carried away. The day after that match ended I was back studying for my A levels at Harrow Weald Sixth Form College.

In 1988, I again only played the second half of the season for Middlesex because of my A-level work but managed to top the county's Championship batting averages – with an average of 57 – despite only having a top score of 68 not out. But a number of other not out innings helped boost the average, and I was not complaining.

I had also represented England U19s again early in 1988, at the inaugural Youth World Cup held in Australia. Once more the team was captained by Mike Atherton, and both Nasser Hussain and Chris Lewis were included in the squad. I didn't do particularly well, but I learned a lot and it was a fantastic experience. We reached the semi-final before losing to Australia, who then beat Pakistan in the final.

Alan Mullally was playing for Australia's U19s, and Andy Caddick for New Zealand, while the West Indies team was led by Brian Lara. The Pakistan side had both Inzamam-ul-Haq and Mushtaq Ahmed playing for them.

The innings which really brought my name to the public's attention, however, and led Mike Gatting to say that I was a better batsman at eighteen than he himself had been – which was a real tribute, because he was a tremendous player – was in the NatWest Trophy final on 3 September 1988, in which we beat Worcestershire by three wickets at Lord's.

It was two days before my 19th birthday and I had not played in the competition up to that point. Worcestershire scored 161 for 9 from their 60 overs on a difficult, seaming pitch, thanks in the main to Phil Neale's 64, and I came in at number six with our score at 25 for 4. Graham Dilley had struck three times with the new ball and Gatting had been run out for a duck, so it wasn't looking too good.

But I hung around with Roland Butcher until the total reached 64, when he ran himself out for 24 in the 29th over. John Emburey, though, was a great man to come in at that point and together we put on 85 until John was out for 35 in the 53rd over. I had made 56 when I was also out to Dilley, who finished with 5 for 29, with just three more runs required for victory. I was then named man of the match, which made the celebrations even better that night, and received a lot of fantastic publicity for the innings.

The 1989 season was my first full one as a professional and I was pleased with my progress: I topped 1,000 runs and averaged 36, and at the age of 19 I didn't think that was too bad, especially as this was the summer of the 'high seam' ball. The faster bowlers

(Allan Donald, Malcolm Marshall and Wasim Akram finished first, second and fourth respectively in the first-class averages) used it effectively all around the country and for batsmen it was very hard work.

The standard of bowling in the late 1980s and early 1990s was high, and most counties had bowlers of real pace, as well as the traditional 'English' seamers, who always do well when conditions are more in their favour. I was especially pleased to score my maiden first-class hundred, against Yorkshire at Headingley in July. As the summer neared its end, I was being mentioned as a possible England A tourist for the following winter and was appointed to captain the England U19 team against the touring New Zealand U19s.

This was all positive, except that in a Championship match against Nottinghamshire in late August, in between the first and second four-day U19 Tests against the Kiwis, I was hit on the toe by a ball from Andy Pick. It turned out to be broken, meaning I missed the third and final U19 Test in early September, but I wanted badly to play in the second match at Canterbury, beginning on 29 August, as we had lost the first Test at Scarborough.

The New Zealanders, however, led by Chris Cairns, batted well in both innings and we could not prevent the match from being drawn. I scored 47 and 38 not out, but an article appeared in *The Times*, by John Woodcock, in which both my captaincy and my ability were criticised in quite disparaging terms. It was a bit of a shock, to be honest, especially as I had played in quite a lot of discomfort, and it was the first piece of negative publicity I had received. Coming from a writer whom I had never met, and who certainly didn't know me, I thought it was unfair. Perhaps my expectations, following that 1988 NatWest Trophy innings, had been set a bit too high.

Anyway, as far as I was concerned, I was still a baby in cricketing terms. I was still learning the game; I felt that I had consolidated well during the 1989 summer, as I had come to terms with the demands – and quite considerable demands, too, for any young player – of playing week-in and week-out on the county circuit.

I remember well one particular game which not only opened my eyes to how difficult making runs could be in certain conditions, but also led to a piece of advice from an opponent which was valuable to me as I sought to improve my game and my chances of achieving the levels of success that I desired.

We played Lancashire at Lord's in a three-day Championship fixture which began on Saturday, 1 July and resumed on the Monday following a 40-overs-per-side Refuge Assurance League game on the Sunday. We lost both games by some distance, but on a very quick pitch it was still an experience facing the likes of Patrick Patterson, Wasim Akram and Phil DeFreitas. Paul Allott, another international-class fast bowler, also played in both games.

We thought we had done quite well when, after asking Lancashire to bat first on a surface that was also quite well-grassed, we bowled them out for 161, with Norman Cowans taking 4 for 29 and Angus Fraser, Simon Hughes and Ricky Ellcock sharing the other six wickets equally. But by the close we were 66 for 8 and I had been one of the four victims of Patterson, the West Indies fast bowler, who then ended up with 5 for 48 when our innings was finished off for 96 on the Monday morning.

By then, of course, we had been beaten in the Sunday League game, from which Patterson had been rested and Wasim brought in! I had followed up my 9 of the previous day by being out lbw to Wasim for 6. Indeed, I only faced three balls from him: bouncer, bouncer, rapid inswinging yorker – thank you and goodnight.

The worst was still to come, though, because after we had bowled out Lancashire for 196 in their second innings, we were ourselves skittled for a mere 43. And that included a ten-run stand for the last wicket! Patterson and DeFreitas were absolutely fearsome, and the ball was flying through. They bowled unchanged, sharing 21.2 overs, having had a rest overnight on the Monday when we were 12 for 4 and I was on 2 not out.

I made it to 7 the next morning, the joint second-highest score in the innings, when it took Patterson and DeFreitas, who finished with figures of 7 for 21, just another 65 minutes to finish us off. Desmond Haynes had recorded a pair (two noughts) in the match, as had Angus Fraser, and the other three batsmen to fail to score in our wretched second innings were Mike Gatting, Mike Roseberry and Paul Downton.

After the Championship game had finished around that Tuesday lunchtime, however, I wandered down to the Tavern for a quick drink and got chatting to DeFreitas and Patterson. I knew DeFreitas well, as he had also grown up in the Middlesex youth ranks, and he told me that I needed to look at wearing a helmet with a grille. Not only had he been bowling at me on this quick pitch, but he had also seen how I'd gone against Patterson and Wasim, and he felt it was important for me – especially at 19 – to make sure I was properly protected when I was facing bowling of that speed on quicker pitches.

Even in the short time I had been at the crease on those two days I had narrowly avoided being hit by short-pitch deliveries. I remember them whistling past my face, very close, and of course the helmet I was using was completely open at the front. A couple of those short balls could easily have cleaned me up.

DeFreitas said that if wearing a grille was good enough for the likes of Haynes and Gatting, then it should also be something I did, and it was a piece of advice that really stayed with me during the weeks that followed. It was also very much appreciated, especially from an opponent. DeFreitas had obviously seen that the pace and ability of Wasim and Patterson was a bit too much for me at that age and he took time to have a quiet, considerate word.

Many people have asked me over the years whether I have ever been scared out there in the middle, facing the fastest bowlers in the world, and what I would say is that on those three days at Lord's I was as close to being scared on a cricket pitch as I have been. The ball was jagging about, flying through at you at extreme speeds, and being bowled by magnificent bowlers who had great command of line, length and the ability to move it about either in the air or off the pitch.

Physically, you were left wondering if you could actually react fast enough as a batsman to get out of the way and – although I had my youthful reactions on my side – I had rarely at that time

faced bowling of this speed and hostility. It was taking you close
to the edge in terms of your courage and your character, as much
as your ability, and Wasim on the Sunday was really a bit too much
for me at the age I was then.

As a result of that conversation with DeFreitas, indeed, I went
away and practised a lot with a helmet and grille, because it does
take some getting used to when you have never worn a grille in
front of your face. By the end of the following winter, I was totally
used to it and wore one from then on.

Apart from the occasional chat like that with an opposing player
or one of your own teammates, it was the lot of the county cricketer
in those days to work things out for himself. In the Middlesex
dressing-room of the late 1980s and early 1990s, especially, it was
certainly a case of getting your own game sorted out.

Looking back now, I realise just how lucky I was to begin
my professional career in an environment which was so used to
winning. The expectation at Middlesex under Mike Gatting, and
before that under Mike Brearley, was to win trophies. A season
without any silverware was the exception, not the rule.

When I arrived on the scene in 1987, the county had won
ten trophies in the previous eleven seasons, including five
Championships, in 1976, 1977, 1980, 1982 and 1985. In my time
at the club we were also to win Championships in 1990 and 1993,
the Sunday League in 1992 and that NatWest Trophy in 1988.

Don Bennett was already a long-serving coach when I joined
the Middlesex first team, and he was a bit of a godfather – albeit
a kind but firm one – in the dressing-room at that time. Don had
overseen my own development through the junior ranks, too, and
although he didn't say much he was often on hand with a little
word here and there.

It was Gatting who ran the first team, as captain, and who had
the final say in everything concerning the senior squad. But Don
was always there in the background, and he and Gatt worked
closely together. When I turned 17 at the end of the 1986 summer,
I felt I needed to move to a Middlesex Premier League club – and
thus decided to move that winter to Stanmore. It was a club just

ten minutes from where I lived, and it was ideal in terms of my desire to move up and play in a higher league.

But my move created a bit of a stir in club circles, with some people criticising Middlesex for 'forcing' me to move; in fact, they had done nothing of the sort, yet it was the first example, indeed, of me getting into trouble for something that was no fault of my own!

Don Bennett's style as Middlesex coach was very close, in my view, to how Duncan Fletcher operated when he was head coach of England from 1999 to 2007. Duncan was never the most talkative person either, but if he said anything you listened and, like Don, he would be quick to let people know if they were not behaving as they should in any way. It only took a look, actually, to get people back into line.

To me, with my own interests now in coaching, it is fascinating to look at how different coaches have done their jobs. Sometimes coaches can be tempted to talk too much to a player, as if they need to justify their position by doing so. Don and Duncan both preferred to stay a bit in the background, to be consulted by the players and to approach you only if they had a specific piece of information or advice to get across.

They both wanted players to come to them. If you approached Don, for example, he would often answer your question by asking you the question back. He wanted to get you to talk it through, and by doing that to try to deal with the particular issue, technical or otherwise, chiefly by yourself. In what was a very boisterous Middlesex dressing-room, he was also a calming influence. People were not shy about offering an opinion or three, so to have Don sitting quietly in the background was often good for younger players like me.

There are occasions, though, when players don't like the fact that a coach is sitting back and mainly observing; they don't like the fact that they don't know what he is thinking about them. Players can easily start to fret, about an aspect of their game or about their role in the team or whatever. Sometimes as a player you need confirmation that you are doing OK. Often even a quick, 'Keep going, you are doing well,' is all that you need.

Mike Gatting's influence was also a very positive one for me. Being positive was what Gatt was all about, in fact. And not only was he a larger-than-life character, but he was also captain of England when I first walked into the Middlesex first-team dressing-room, an Ashes-winning captain, and a fantastic player. He loved to take on the fast bowlers and he was a wonderful player of spin. To bat at the other end to him was a learning experience in itself, and he was a huge influence on me early in my career.

He really backed me, too, right from when I was coming up through the ranks and in those early seasons, initially when I was still at school, and then when I was taking my first steps as a full-time professional. He backed me 100 per cent, he talked to me about how to approach my batting and my cricket generally, and to have his belief at your back was a tremendous thing for a young lad.

Gatt was also very straightforward in the way he dealt with other players and how he captained both on and off the field. He was upfront and got stuck in. Some players would challenge him, but he would listen, take it all on board and then get on with it in the way he thought was right.

As time went on, it was great for me that Gatt rated my ability because I began to see that players whom he didn't rate to go a long way in the game didn't tend to hang around at Middlesex for very long. But you still had to perform – that was the key to everything.

The Middlesex dressing-room then was a rough, tough place, and it was also highly competitive. Players were highly motivated to do well, both for their own careers and for the benefit of the team. But a lot of those guys were competing for England Test places, too, and getting their individual performance right was all that mattered.

It was a very professional environment, and if you didn't perform, then your teammates soon let you know about it. Looking back, I know now that I was fortunate that there were so many good players in the team during that era that I was able – as a young player – to make a few mistakes and have them covered up by the performances of others. Yet I still knew that I was expected to perform, and to learn quickly.

I was a bit shy and reserved at that young age and so to join this boisterous place with so many top-class players who loved to have a go at one another was something of a culture shock for me! Often, too, to get a point across, players would do it in a mickey-taking way. That is hard for many players to take, let alone someone of my age at the time, and I didn't take to it that well. It wound me up a treat, and as I was the young kid it was easy for them to wind me up.

It was hard to understand why your teammates would want to take the mick if you had just missed a straight one or something, and often the mickey-taking would be about non-cricketing issues as well which, again, was sometimes difficult to handle at a young age.

The Middlesex dressing-room of that time was, however, a very professional place. The team expected to win things, and all those trophies told you everything about the talent in the squad and the drive to be the best they could. It was like, as a young footballer, walking into the Manchester United or Arsenal dressing-room. If you performed, that was all that mattered. If you didn't, whoever you were, your teammates let you know.

The environment in which I learned to be a professional cricketer, then, was a very boisterous one. You sank or swam by your own performances, and by your own actions; performance alone was the bottom line. This is not the way the game is now, by the way, because you are just not left to pick things up as you go along. Now, with more and more coaches and support staff around, you are encouraged to forge togetherness as a team, to build team spirit, to be mates with one another and encourage each other, and enjoy everyone's success as well as your own.

There are a lot of lovey-dovey, idealistic things said in dressing-rooms these days and although that may be preferable for the young players in particular it is not a pre-requisite for success. We also had a lot of fun during that time, but the only way to survive and be in the in-crowd, if you like, was to perform.

Quite a number of players could not handle the way it was at Middlesex in the late 1980s and early 1990s, because they did not gel with others and didn't feel welcomed. Good players such as Graham Rose, Colin Metson, Aftab Habib and Matthew Keech all left the club during this era because they felt they would do better elsewhere.

As for myself, looking back, I just wish someone – quietly – had got hold of me in a friendly, fatherly sort of way and tried to educate me a little bit more about how to behave in certain situations, and how to handle the ups and downs of being a professional sportsman. I was a kid in a grown-up world, really, and I just followed the crowd. I also didn't know it when they were just winding me up. I would react, but I was just the youngster.

With hindsight, I know I would have valued that sort of help because then things would not have festered so much. You had to be self-reliant in those days, because that was simply the way it was done, but I was so wrapped up in my game – and in wanting so badly to do well – that I couldn't see the bigger picture. Nor was I mature enough to see it, and that is where some help could have been given to me.

Yet I don't blame anyone at Middlesex at the time for not doing so. Not only was there the culture of having to work things out for yourself, but I was also an extremely intense character when it came to my batting, and very intense in particular about doing well. I think the coach and others on the sidelines might have been a bit reluctant to come over for a chat because, on many occasions, that would not have been an easy thing to have done.

No one held your hand, no one said, 'Come over here and have a look at this bit of video of yourself,' or this StatsMaster, or whatever, 'and let's analyse what's going on here.' That sort of thing just didn't happen, and you were also in this dressing-room that was full of cricketers with totally different styles as well as personalities. There was Keith Brown, Clive Radley, John Emburey, all with idiosyncratic batting techniques, while someone like Roland Butcher had about eight different techniques even in the time I played with him.

I only played a couple of times with Phil Edmonds, but he was obviously another highly individual character at Middlesex when I was coming up through the club. The dressing-room could often be quite a sight: Emburey effing and blinding, Fraser being his usual cynical self, Wayne Daniel wandering around in just his huge bowling boots and a jockstrap, and everyone with an opinion.

Today, players have so much support for them and so much analysis of their own games as they come through the system that it is no surprise that so many of them feel far more comfortable in their dressing-room environment. The game has changed so much in 20 years.

Is it better now? I'd have to say so, because players are guided and helped. It is a smoother path for individual players to walk. Some old-school players would say that the new generation of cricketers do not think for themselves enough, but I think that management of players has improved, while technical back-up allows players to understand their own games so much more quickly.

As early as my debut season in 1987, which continued after I finished my college term in July, I was given an insight into what can happen on the road in county cricket. I remember it as a tremendous early learning experience, and immensely frustrating at the time!

Called up to play in the Championship, against Essex at Chelmsford in mid-August, I top-scored with 71 in our first innings out of just 166 – the next highest score was Wilf Slack's 20 – and was feeling pretty pleased with myself against an attack which included Neil Foster, Derek Pringle, John Childs and Geoff Miller.

We ended up with a draw, thanks mainly to Mike Gatting's second innings 132, but on a pitch taking some spin I was lbw to Childs for a second ball duck as the slow left-armer went on to pick up 10 wickets in the match. Also, two days earlier, in the Sunday League match against Essex which was sandwiched into the Championship game, I had been lbw to Foster for a duck even though we won a low-scoring affair, so it was with some trepidation that I travelled down to Cardiff on that Tuesday night for another three-day Championship game against Glamorgan, starting on the Wednesday morning.

When we arrived at the ground, we were astonished to see a pitch that was green on one half and closely shaved, dry and dusting on its other 11 yards! Neither Emburey nor Edmonds were playing for us, because they were at Lord's playing in the MCC Bicentenary match, and so Glamorgan had prepared a surface to suit their seamers at one end and the off-breaks of Rodney Ontong at the other.

The umpires duly reported the pitch to the Test and County Cricket Board and, in the end, we almost won the game with both Phil Tufnell and Jamie Sykes, who bowled some off-spin, taking five wickets each in the match as Glamorgan finished up hanging on at 156 for 9. But that did not mean too much to me: I had been caught off Ontong for 1 in our first innings and then stumped off Alan Butcher's very occasional left-arm spin for 0 second time around.

It was horrendous. At Chelmsford on the Saturday I had batted as well as I had ever done in my short career up to that point, posting my then top score in first-class cricket, but in four innings in six days after that – and on totally varied pitches – I had managed to make 0, 0, 1 and 0. I didn't take it too well, either.

Next up was a long drive up to Wellingborough that Friday night for yet another Championship match beginning the next morning, against Northamptonshire. It rained for much of the time there, actually, washing out the Sunday League match and allowing just an hour and a half's play on the Saturday. The third day of the game was washed out too, but on the second day we reduced Northants from 51 for 1 to 127 all out and then I went in with us 12 for 2.

Winston Davis, the West Indies fast bowler, was leading the Northants attack, and although all the other batsmen were complaining that the pitch was too slow and too difficult I found I could hit the ball on the up and that Davis's pace meant that it came on to the bat nicely! It was only a club-standard pitch, but to me at that time it was like the ones I was used to. I was on 31 not out when play ended for the day and I remember Don Bennett asking me how I found the pitch.

That was the end of the game, as it rained all the next day, but I was still relieved to get some runs again. An interesting 11 days on the road, though, ended with me having a massive ruck with Angus Fraser about who was going to sit in the front seat of the car on the way home. Stupid, but that was sometimes what it was like when you were travelling around the country playing day after day of county cricket . . .

At the start of the 1990 season I was only 20, but by then I had played throughout one full season for Middlesex, plus two half-summers, and had captained England U19s. I should have been relishing the new season, but by April I was low on confidence and that was because I had just endured an unhappy winter in Australia, playing club cricket in Melbourne.

I had been keen to go, as I had heard so much about the standards of grade cricket and how strong it was. I thought it would do a lot for my game, and me as a person. Clive Radley, however, when he heard where I was going, said I'd be back home in three weeks. He knew what I was like at that time, and he didn't see me sticking at it.

North Melbourne were my club, and I lasted the full five months there. But I had a pretty horrendous time and, in the end, I did the whole winter only because I wanted to prove to people – and myself – that I wasn't going to quit.

I found the whole experience tough. There were a lot of brash Australians seemingly queueing up with loads to say about me and what I was doing, and some of the pitches we played on were not very good. I remember that our opening batsman had his jaw broken in our opening game, from a ball which flew up off a length.

In six knocks before Christmas (don't forget, grade games are two-innings affairs played over successive Saturdays) I didn't get into double figures once. I was not pleased, and I was also hugely frustrated because I had made runs at every level I'd played at up until then and I was only in Australia to try to bring my batting on. I was moody, and as the weeks went on I was not much fun to be with.

I didn't mix well enough either with the rest of the players in the team and, once again, it was a situation that was crying out for someone to get hold of me and make me see the bigger picture. I thought everything was about how many runs I got, but it was not; it was also about my game in general and in becoming more mature in my behaviour and my outlook.

Initially, too, I lived in a house with two young Aussie Rules footballers. One of them, Wayne Carey, who was then 18, subsequently went on to become one of the sport's biggest stars. At the time, though, they were just two very loud, very brash, Aussie kids and there were bits of half-eaten pizza left lying all over the lounge and beer cans thrown everywhere. We even had ants coming into the house at one stage, attracted by all the mess.

Around Christmas time, I was happy to be able to move out. I had begged a guy from the cricket club if I could move in with him and his parents, and fortunately he and they had agreed. But I didn't make any real friends and there also didn't seem to be any other young English professionals around in Melbourne.

Through knowing Michael Bell, of Warwickshire, however, I managed to get some more cricket with a Sri Lankan team who played on Sundays, but in my second or third game with them I got myself banned for three weeks for striking an opponent! It was a park game, really, and the opposition were unbelievable with all their sledging, which was getting very nasty.

I got to the point where I'd had enough and, as I was by now batting, I just walked over to this particular guy who was fielding in the gully and put one on him. All hell broke loose. Blokes were flying in from everywhere to break it up. The game continued once it had been calmed down, but it didn't save me from the suspension.

Soon after Christmas I did manage to make 96 for North Melbourne in a first grade match, but that remained my highest score, and the rest of the season was blighted by rain and lots of low-scoring games.

I got a job in the sports department of Myers store, working for four days a week from 9 a.m. until 3 p.m., and that kept me going, gave me a focus and a bit of extra money in my pocket. I also spent a lot of time watching Australia's Test and one-day international matches against Pakistan and Sri Lanka on television, as they were the two teams who were touring that Aussie summer. But the overall result of my five-month stint Down Under was that I came back home in March feeling very low on confidence. I was glad that I'd stuck it out, but it hadn't done a great deal for my cricket.

During the first half of the 1990 county season, too, I felt that I was not being consistent enough. I got the odd decent score, but nothing brilliant, and I felt I was not progressing well enough as a batsman.

Then came a run of three hundreds in just over three weeks, in July, which transformed my season and which – in the case of the third century – also helped Middlesex to pull away from our nearest challengers and move towards the winning of the County Championship.

It began on 1 July, at Lord's, on a beautifully sunny day when everything hit the middle of the bat and I scored 147 not out from 90 balls against Worcestershire in the Refuge Assurance Sunday League. There was a short boundary on the Tavern side, and I hit eight sixes. We had batted first, and so there was no pressure of chasing. It was just the sheer exhilaration of hitting the ball, hard and often. It was a bit of a breakthrough innings for me as well as being my maiden Sunday League hundred.

Ten days later, at Uxbridge, both myself and Keith Brown hit hundreds – and his was quicker and better than mine because he took us all the way to victory in a tight NatWest Trophy second-round tie against Surrey in which we chased down their 60-over total of 288 for 8 with just two balls to spare. But I was very happy with my 104, as I had gone in at number three when Desmond Haynes was out for nought, gloving a hook at Waqar Younis in the first over. Waqar was rapid, and it was very pleasing that Mike Roseberry and I – two young lads – were able to see him off and also give us a great platform to chase what was a big total. Gatt was nursing an injury, too, and so only came in down the order, which meant that both Keith and I had the main responsibility of getting those runs.

Yet it was my 146 not out against Somerset, also at Uxbridge, on 24 July which perhaps gave me most pleasure of all. We had been set to score 369 in what proved to be 69 overs and this was a tough ask, even though it had been a high-scoring game and the weather was still hot and the outfield quick.

Haynes made 108 but was out with our total on 215, and Gatt had also gone after adding only 36 to his first innings 170 not out. The last 20 overs began with us still needing another 149 and although I was seeing it really well it looked as if it would be too much for us. By this stage both Brown and Emburey had come and gone too, and Neil Williams, in at number seven, was having a bit of a problem getting the bat on the ball because the pitch was taking quite a lot of spin.

That was when Chris Tavaré, the Somerset captain, came up to me and asked if we would still go for the victory if he fed me some runs. I just said, Yes! We were actually going for it anyway, but it was just that Neil was genuinely struggling to get the ball away. I wasn't going to turn down a chance like that, though, and Tavaré himself bowled an over which I took for 20 runs, including three sixes. It also took me breezing past my century, which was only my second in Championship cricket at that stage. I will be eternally grateful to Tav for his fine gesture. As Dennis Amiss once said to me, it always seems easier when you've reached three figures.

I then hit Harvey Trump, the Somerset off-spinner, for two more sixes and – although Williams was dismissed – we suddenly needed 12 from the last over. Neil Mallender bowled it, and I managed to run three twos before hitting the fourth and fifth deliveries of the over for four. We had won the game, which for me was a fantastic feeling because I really felt I had made a significant contribution; it was also our fifth win in six games in the Championship and kept up our momentum at the top of the table.

Psychologically, this was a big innings for me. I had won Middlesex an important game, carrying the side's hopes through the second half of our chase, and all this at the end of a game in which I had been awarded my county cap, together with Phil Tufnell and Micky Roseberry.

Yet those three hundreds had not come about by accident. My leap in form had coincided with some work that I had been doing in the nets at Lord's with Desmond Haynes. I had been getting out a lot lbw because of a habit of putting my front leg straight down the pitch from a middle guard. Professional bowlers soon work out that if they hit the line of off stump and nip it back a touch then they stand a good chance of getting you, and first-class umpires are also more inclined to give you out even if you are thrusting your front pad down the track.

I experimented initially in net practice with a leg-stump guard, but I kept on nicking the ball on or just outside off stump and I was beginning to despair of ever getting something worked out. Desmond noticed my problems one day and came over for a chat.

He told me to keep my middle guard but to practise hitting the ball straighter, between the bowler and mid-on instead of wide of mid-on. But he said I must not move my head across, and also that I must not hit across the line, and so he and I worked on opening up my front foot in my stance so that instead of standing totally sideways on, as I had been taught and had always done, I freed my front foot to go down the pitch on the line of leg stump and not middle.

This was simple advice, in many ways, but because it came from a player like Dessie Haynes, one of the very best batsmen in world cricket at the time, it meant everything. It was fantastic that he took the time to help me, and that is not meant to be a slight on any of the Middlesex coaches. It was just that I had by then batted with him quite a bit in the middle and as a younger player you naturally look for guidance from those who have played at a higher level – a level you want to reach.

It was also a matter of styles; someone like Gatt stayed on leg stump and looked to hit through the offside, to cut whenever he could. Desmond, like a lot of top players, looked to get across his stumps and make anything straight disappear through the legside.

In a short time, I felt everything clicking into place and I found I was hitting the ball with a full face of the bat, and through mid-on, as Haynes had commanded. I found myself getting into a real rhythm at the crease, and I was not getting agitated and frustrated. My hands were not holding the bat so tightly, and I was not trying to hit the ball too hard. At a pivotal time in my career I was also not getting out lbw so often. And, if you can survive early on, and not get out so often when you are at your most vulnerable, you are clearly in a better position to make more runs. It was a big turning point for me, and Desmond Haynes was magnificent.

What was especially good about the way he tweaked my technique was the way he went about it. Too many players make technical adjustments which actually end up making their problems worse. In fact, after I began to bat with my front foot slightly open, I noticed quite a lot of other players on the circuit trying to do the same. But they made the mistake of turning their shoulders too, which meant that the bat was coming down from gully instead of straight, and they got into all sorts of bother. What Dessie saw in me was the opportunity to make a small change without it affecting anything else in my technique.

The great thing, too, about Haynes, Gatting and Emburey at Middlesex was that they all loved to talk about cricket. There were many times on the road when Angus Fraser, Micky Roseberry and I would go out for a meal with those three senior players and enjoy all sorts of discussions – and sometimes quite heated debates – about various cricketing topics. It was great for us youngsters, but often it perhaps went a bit too far.

I remember, back in 1989 when I was still only 19, absolutely flying into Gatt for agreeing to lead England's rebel tour to South Africa the following winter. I had studied politics at A level and was quite interested in things like that, and I tore into him for accepting what I told him was blood money. I said there were 20 million black people in South Africa who didn't have the vote and all he was doing by going there was helping to prop up the apartheid regime. The dressing-room, as I recall, began to empty a little quicker than usual as I continued this tirade and Gatt came back at me. What had started out as a bit of a wind-up became a furious argument.

Again, looking back, I should have realised that Gatt had not taken the decision lightly and that his poor treatment by England had contributed quite a bit to how the situation developed, but at the time I was convinced I had a point and the way all the players were with one another meant that I didn't hold back, even though I was still a teenager and Gatt was a former England captain almost twice my age. In the end, he stormed off, but we were fine about it soon afterwards. I can laugh at it now, too.

CHAPTER 4

LESSONS LEARNED

'The press boys had labelled Nasser Hussain, Mark Ramprakash and myself as English cricket's "brat pack". This was slightly misleading, but I suppose we'd all acquired reputations in county cricket, rightly or wrongly, for being talented but difficult'

– Graham Thorpe

I was only a fortnight past my 21st birthday when I became a County Championship winner for the first time. But at that age, and at that time of my career, I was just too young to appreciate what it meant.

Middlesex clinched the title against Sussex, at Hove, in our last match of the 1990 season, but we had been favourites to win it since mid-summer and, overall, the culture of winning was so great at the club that I think I took it all for granted. I only made 13 as we beat bottom team Sussex by an innings to take the Championship by a 31-point margin, and that probably didn't help my mood.

When I look back, I was privileged to play in such a fine team when I was so young. In 1990, we also won the end-of-season Refuge Assurance Cup – played between the top four sides in the Sunday League – but I suppose my thoughts at the time were that winning was what we were paid to do and, looking around the dressing-room, it was no surprise that we were regular winners of domestic trophies.

You only have to look at the consistent and high-quality individual performances of the side to see why we took the Championship by such a comfortable margin. Every one of us in the top five played in all 22 matches, too, as did John Emburey. Both he and Mike Gatting, of course, had been suspended by England for touring South Africa as 'rebels' the previous winter, and only Angus Fraser (three Tests) and Neil Williams (one Test) were called up for international duty that summer.

Paul Downton would surely have played in every game, too, but for an unfortunate injury sustained when a bail flew up and struck him in the eye during a Sunday League game at Basingstoke, yet in Paul Farbrace we had a capable deputy behind the stumps.

Phil Tufnell was the leading Championship wicket-taker with 65, from 20 appearances, and most of the other wickets were shared around by Emburey (57), Williams (49), Fraser (41), Norman Cowans (36) and Simon Hughes (28). Emburey and Tufnell bowled a significant percentage of the overs between them and gave us great control, as well as wicket-taking ability. Having two fine spinners that season, when the seam on the ball was reduced as an experiment by the authorities, was another distinct advantage for us.

As for the batting, Desmond Haynes topped the Championship averages with 2,036 runs at 63.62, and then came Gatting (1,685 at 58.10), Keith Brown (1,416 at 54.46), me (1,327 at 44.23) and Mike Roseberry (1,497 at 40.45). Emburey also chipped in with 698, while Downton made 530 in his 15 matches, and it all added up to a very solid team performance.

Haynes and Gatting, as the two senior batsmen, were very different in their style and approach; Haynes would even practise opening the bat face in the nets so he could better manufacture shots in matches to avoid fielders and pick up ones and twos rather than hit a classic stroke and see it cut off. But both were very positive cricketers and their influence rubbed off on the rest of us a lot. Desmond in particular would often challenge the rulebook, and seeing his skill level was a challenge to us to up ours.

Fraser was an especially fine bowler then, before his chronic hip injury problems, and his height meant he got steep bounce to go with a decent pace. He hit the bat hard and often hit the splice. He also gave batsmen nothing, such was his accuracy, and he absolutely hated – and I mean hated – giving the batsman even one run.

Cowans was a much underrated bowler for most of his career. He played 19 Tests between 1982 and 1985, but England never picked him again after the age of 24. Why, I will never know. By 1990 he had lost a bit of his pace, but he was still a fantastic bowler and he often took wickets with the new ball. Simon Hughes had a quick arm, was shorter in build, mixed it up a bit and swung it, while Williams had good pace and swung it regularly. As a four-pronged pace attack, they were as effective a unit as any in the country.

But it was the presence of Emburey and Tufnell in our attack which meant we had all the bases covered. Embers was so steady and dependable, and very economical, while Tufnell was more attacking in style, like his predecessor Phil Edmonds. They made as good a combination and I don't think many people at Middlesex realised how lucky the county was to have had two such potent pairs of spinners for such a long time.

When I joined the Middlesex staff, it was clear that Tuffers was being groomed to take over from Edmonds, but he was quite a sight. He had very long hair, which he wore in a ponytail, and pranced around in crocodile-skin shoes. He was into acid house, rave, parties and dancing all night. He was married at 20, and divorced at 21.

Yet, apart from being a lunatic for a lot of the time, he was a really nice guy underneath and in 1990 he played a massive role in that Championship title win despite still only being 24. He had also probably benefited from the county's decision the previous year to release a player called Jamie Sykes from the staff. Tuffers and he were big mates off the field and they used to get into all sorts of scrapes. The club felt that one had to go, and Sykes, a talented cricketer, was the one deemed surplus to requirements. Middlesex decided that Tufnell offered them the most, and how right they were because he was a magnificent bowler.

My first senior England recognition also came along at the end of the 1990 season, when I was selected to tour Pakistan and Sri

Lanka with the England A team in early 1991, under the captaincy of Hugh Morris.

There was a dramatic start, as the tour schedule in Pakistan was cut short due to the first Gulf War, but Sri Lanka offered us the chance of a longer visit there and for me it was a significant trip. I came of age particularly on that tour as a player of spin, notably in an innings of 158 against Sri Lanka A at Kandy, which took me nine and three-quarter hours of really hard graft against a good attack in hot conditions.

It was a breakthrough innings, in terms of concentration especially, because sometimes you were only scoring 30 runs in a session because it was so hard to get the ball away, but you had to learn to stick in there and then make the bowlers pay when you got the chance. Also, facing quality spinners for hour after hour meant that I soon learned to put into practice what Mike Gatting had told me about allowing the ball to come on, and playing it with soft hands. I also made 91 in the first one-day 'international' against the Sri Lankan A side and felt I grew in stature as a batsman on this tour.

We also had a first sighting of Muttiah Muralitharan in a two-day game towards the end of the trip, when he was picked for an invitational side when still at school. He took six wickets. But we had an excellent side, especially in batting, that included Nasser Hussain, Graham Thorpe, Neil Fairbrother, Ian Salisbury and Richard Illingworth. The Sri Lankan opposition was strong, and in their own conditions they presented a considerable challenge.

The subsequent summer of 1991 was memorable for me, as I was selected by England for the first time and ended up playing in all six Tests of that season, but for Middlesex it was more of a struggle. My Test commitments meant I played in only 12 of the 22 Championship games, scoring 877 runs at 48.72, and despite Mike Gatting's 2,044 runs at 78, and 134 wickets between them by Tufnell and Emburey, we finished 15th.

Unfortunately, the club had for some reason decided to do without an overseas player that season (Desmond Haynes being with the West Indies) and we predictably missed a player who had topped

2,000 runs in 1990. It would never happen in these two division days! Yet it was injuries to the fast bowlers, in particular Fraser, Hughes, Ricky Ellcock and Dean Headley, and the premature retirement during the season of Paul Downton, as a result of his eye injury of the previous summer, which hit hardest of all. With me away a lot, too, we simply began to run out of ammunition.

Personally, I found my first experience of jumping between county and England games very demanding, although I felt in decent form with the bat throughout the season. I remember on one occasion, at Cardiff, getting out and having a huge tantrum in the dressing-room because, as an England batsman, I felt I should be contributing more.

There was also an incident early on that season at Lord's, when we were hammered by Sussex. I got runs in both innings, including a hundred as we were bowled out for a second time, and I got involved in a running exchange of pleasantries with Peter Moores, who was keeping wicket for them. We had several full and frank exchanges of views. I think I was reacting to the additional pressure I felt I was under; I may have been only 21, but I felt I had to play like a senior player – an England player.

A lot happened to me in the winter of 1991–92, much of which is dealt with elsewhere, but suffice it to say that I was not in the best frame of mind by the time the 1992 summer began. Indeed, before the Championship season had even started, I found myself in trouble.

I had been home from the England A tour of the West Indies for less than a fortnight when Middlesex continued their warm-up to the new season with, allegedly, a first-class friendly against Cambridge University at Fenner's. I say 'allegedly' for good reason: to my mind, this was not cricket of first-class standard. Nor did it turn out to be very friendly.

Perhaps I should not have played in that game, and instead had a bit more rest before the Championship programme began. After all, I had been away, first in New Zealand with England, then in the Caribbean with England A, from just after Christmas until early April. But it was clearly felt I needed some readjustment to English pitches and so, on 17 April, we began a three-day game against the students.

After the frustrations and the sheer hard slog of the winter, what with hardly playing during my seven weeks in New Zealand and then facing some very good and hostile bowling in the West Indies, on a number of difficult pitches, the last thing I needed was to come up against two very ordinary off-spinners pinging the ball consistently two feet outside leg stump with seven fielders on the legside.

I scored 49 and 48 in the game but got out again to one of the off-spinners, a bloke called Marcus Wight, when I tried in vain to catch hold of yet another ball speared down outside the line of my pads and top-edged a catch. I was not very happy about this, nor about what had gone before, especially as, in my opinion, Wight's action was not even legal.

As ball after ball was fired in negatively – and this in a pre-season warm-up match, remember – I began to wonder what on earth I was doing playing in this sort of cricket. It was a joke. I was not slow, either, in voicing my opinions to the Cambridge players and anyone else who would listen. And when this guy Wight came out to bat later on the final day in the University's second innings, I let him have both barrels.

Only a couple of weeks earlier I had flown back to England having been tested hugely by the challenge of a month facing a four-pronged West Indies A pace attack of Courtney Walsh, Tony Gray, Kenny Benjamin and either Linden Joseph or Ottis Gibson, plus a classy Jamaican off-spinner called Nehemiah Perry. Now this.

I know it was childish, and I know I should just have taken what practice I could get and walked away, but to me this was not first-class cricket and it was a disgrace. And, I reasoned, if guys like Marcus Wight felt that this was the right thing to do in a first-class game then I was going to give him something else to remember the experience by: the sort of reception that, like it or not, is all part and parcel of top-level cricket. Even by that stage of my career, I'd had a lot said to me on a cricket field and I'd had to take it. I thought it was now time to give some out.

When Wight came out to bat, I certainly had a lot to say to him, and John Emburey, who was captaining us in the game, told me to leave it alone. I told him what I thought, too, and in the end Embers sent me down to field at third man. I should not have behaved the way I did and it was foolish. Then there were words said in the dressing-room after the match and I was fined by the club.

It was an unhappy start to the new season and, unfortunately, I now found out what it was like to have a disciplinary 'record'. And as an international player, I discovered, even something that happens in a non-match at Fenner's, with hardly anyone watching, can rebound on you very hard. I was also naive to believe, at that age, that anything that happened in the privacy of the dressing-room – and said in the heat of the moment, for instance – would remain private. I soon learned that things got reported, almost word-for-word in some cases, in papers like the *News of the World*.

Emburey was quite correct to tell me to cut it out during the Fenner's incident, but I couldn't accept that it was not my right to stick in my twopenny's worth. It was all, looking back, an accumulation of the frustrations and tough times during that previous winter and my desire to start the season well in order to get a recall to the England seniors. I had gone on that England A tour simply because I had wanted to. I had specifically asked the selectors to be included because I wanted to play cricket; I wanted so much to do well.

As a result of this Fenner's incident, however, I had put my name into the public domain in a disciplinary situation, and it was unpleasant. To make it worse, I had no idea of the commotion it would cause because it was tagged to me being an 'England player'.

The England A tour to the Caribbean had finished well for me, with a hard-fought 86 against Walsh, Gray, Benjamin, Gibson and Perry in the third unofficial 'Test' against West Indies A at the Kensington Oval in Bridgetown, Barbados, and overall I had scored 322 runs at an average of 40 in the five first-class matches.

I had joined the tour at the warm-up stage in Bermuda in late February, having initially flown with the senior England side from New Zealand to Australia as cover for the World Cup squad. Allan Lamb was a fitness doubt for a short while, and I remember I was even kitted out with some World Cup gear before being told that I was not required after all. That was when I asked to go straight to the A tour.

We lost the three-match Test series against Walsh's West Indies A team by a 2–0 margin, but that was no disgrace. They had some fine players, with the likes of Clayton Lambert, Carlisle Best, Junior Murray, Roland Holder and Jimmy Adams in addition to a truly Test-class bowling attack.

The first Test was played on a minefield of a pitch at the Queen's Park Oval in Trinidad. We were at a distinct disadvantage against their firepower when Devon Malcolm, our strike bowler and someone who had taken ten wickets in the match when Graham Gooch's England had narrowly failed to beat the West Indies on that same ground two years earlier, suffered a back injury just before the game, which also ruled him out of the second Test.

My own most disappointing moment came in that second game at Arnos Vale in St Vincent when, on a much better surface, I had reached 41 and put on 88 for our second wicket with Hugh Morris when I attempted to hit Perry over the top and was caught at mid-on. I was batting well, but it was possibly the wrong shot and I mis-hit it and slightly dragged it, and Tony Gray, a tall man, was able to jump up and take the catch.

It was simply poor execution, as much as an ill-judged stroke, but a comment from Keith Fletcher, our England A coach, got back to me second-hand and I was not best pleased. Keith had told someone that some of us 'were playing like millionaires' and it was a criticism that stung. It upset me because he had not spoken to me about it and also because this was a development tour. We were not the finished article and that was why we were all on the tour in the first place, a tour I had also taken it upon myself to join simply because I was so desperate to learn and improve.

I had also toured Pakistan and Sri Lanka the previous winter under Keith as coach. Overall he was nice enough to me and we had a decent relationship. This was an occasion, however, when I don't think he communicated with me as I think he should have done. Indeed, when I look back on my early career, there were several times when I believe I needed a coach to ask me a few questions – in private and at the appropriate moments – and get me to talk about my own game and how I was trying to improve it and build it.

Keith Fletcher was someone about whom I had heard a lot of good things, both as a man-manager and especially as a coach, but in my experience I didn't really see that and it was a shame because I was there to learn; I was eager to learn.

Back in England, though, and after the Fenner's incident and the decision by Middlesex to fine me, I was perked up by a century against Lancashire at Lord's in our second Championship fixture and then, against Surrey at Lord's towards the end of May, my maiden double-hundred. I finished on 233, from 319 balls, but frustratingly Surrey hung on for a draw with their last pair at the wicket after being totally outplayed.

Selected for England's opening Test of that summer's series against Pakistan, I made a duck and was immediately dropped. For most of the rest of the season, and despite being picked twice more by England at the end of that five-match series, I was struggling to find any real rhythm with the bat. I was not playing well and I wasn't exactly going about my business with a smile on my face; what overall was a difficult summer had a very poor ending because of another unfortunate incident.

This happened at Uxbridge, on 16 August, and it was especially frustrating and annoying for me because I had just played a decent innings of 58 as we chased down a Yorkshire 40-over total of 194 for 6 in a match that, if we won it, would clinch us the first Sunday League title in Middlesex's history with two games in hand.

It was a very hot day and, because we could win the title after a great season in the Sunday League, there were 3,500 people packed into Uxbridge's compact ground. I had put on 107 with John Carr, but towards the end of our stand Sachin Tendulkar had come on for Yorkshire and the ball had begun to swing all over the place. He bowled clever, non-bouncing medium pace and he was wobbling it both ways. I actually began to think that Yorkshire had done something with the ball, because it had started to swing so suddenly, and then I was stumped off Tendulkar's bowling with the total at 159 and I felt I had let the side down.

In sheer disappointment, I took a bit longer than usual to drag myself off the field and, as the applause for my innings was dying away, someone in the crowd shouted out in a very loud voice: 'Come on, Ramprakash, get off the field you f****** Paki bastard.'

I felt this was out of order and I lost my rag. I shouted 'F*** off' very loudly back, and was aware of everything going very quiet as I walked on through the spectators and into the dressing-room. But I was very angry and was still upset about it as I took my batting gear off and went to get a drink and watch what I hoped would still be a victory for us from the players' viewing area.

Because of the heat, and because I was very hot and sweaty having just batted, I only put on a T-shirt with the arms cut off over my whites. Bob Gale, the Middlesex cricket committee chairman, who was also in the room, told me that what I was wearing was not appropriate and to go and put something else on.

By now, with Carr and especially new batsman Paul Weekes both batting brilliantly, we were winning the game – and with it the title – but I suddenly felt that I could not be bothered with all the aggravation and so I went and got my kit together and left the ground. I missed the trophy and medal presentations, the after-match TV stuff, because Sky were covering the game, and the team's celebrations.

The incident at the end of my innings was obviously upsetting, even if you discount the racial unpleasantness, but I was also upset because of my reaction, and then I had Bob Gale, whom I felt should not even have been in what was supposed to be an area for the players to relax, having a go at me for not wearing a Middlesex shirt. I just wanted to get away from it all.

Back at Uxbridge the following day, for the final day of the Championship game with Yorkshire, I scored a rapid 94 to lead a successful chase for 231 in 46 overs, and that innings and our six-wicket win made me feel a whole lot better. We then jumped into our cars for the drive down to Bournemouth, where another Championship fixture was starting against Hampshire the next day.

When we reached our hotel in Bournemouth, however, I was summoned to see Mike Gatting and Don Bennett. Captain and coach told me that, in the light of what had happened at Uxbridge 24 hours earlier, I was being left out of the Hampshire match for disciplinary reasons.

I was very upset indeed at this suspension because I knew it would be linked to the Fenner's incident and I knew that the media would be pinning the 'bad boy' tag on me again. There was also the public humiliation, and all because of a stupid and offensive comment being shouted out from the crowd and my silly reaction. I knew that I should not have reacted in the way I did, despite the provocation, and I knew, too, that Middlesex had to deal with it in some way following what had happened at the start of the season at Cambridge.

Phil Tufnell was my roommate in Bournemouth that night and I will always be grateful for the way he calmed me down and talked to me. He himself had been through a few disciplinary incidents by then, of course, but he was a massive help to me that evening because my whole world had been shaken by what had happened.

I was so wrapped up in my career, with my frustrations at not being able to nail down an England Test place after two home summers and one winter with the national squad, and I just knew that this affair was going to have ramifications when it came to the selectors sitting down in the weeks ahead to pick the side for that coming winter's tour to India and Sri Lanka. Not yet 23, though, I couldn't release all my emotions nor see that my ambition to succeed was all-consuming.

The next day I was told to play instead for Middlesex seconds, who just happened to be playing down the road at Southampton against Hampshire seconds. I lashed my way to a hundred, and then Bob Gale came up to me in the pavilion afterwards and said that he had spoken to the England selectors. They had assured him, said Bob, that the disciplinary action the club had taken against me would not harm my chances of being included by England on that winter's tour to India.

After that Second XI fixture was over, I duly rejoined the first team squad for their next match and continued on with what remained of the season, hopeful that the whole matter had been put behind me.

On the evening of 5 September, my 23rd birthday, I was at my parents' house when the telephone rang just as we were finishing dinner. It was Ted Dexter, the chairman of England's selectors. And after telling me that he was sorry that I had not made the squad for the winter tour, he outlined to me that the main reason was that England were worried about my disciplinary problems.

My parents hit the roof when I told them the bad news. Why had Bob Gale gone out of his way to tell me the exact opposite of what had then happened? Was it that Middlesex were trying to get me to take my punishment without any further ado and finish the season with everything thus smoothed over? Even with the benefit of hindsight, I don't know – but that's how it looked at the time.

What I would say here is, looking back on that decision by Dexter's committee, it was fair enough merely on cricketing grounds because both as a player and a person I don't think I should have gone to India. The England selectors probably did me a favour. Nevertheless, my dad and I then asked for a showdown meeting with Middlesex at the end of the season. Both my parents came to the meeting with Mike Gatting and a number of club officials, in fact. We felt very let down by the club. During the discussion Gatt said that his opinion was that players should not react to things shouted out to them from the crowd and – it was true – Gatt himself had suffered some terrible abuse during his long career without reacting to it.

He had a thick skin, but he also said players needed to learn not to react as I had done. Of course, he was right in what he said, but I couldn't help thinking that even Gatt himself had still had his moments on a cricket field. My dad said that it might be easy to ignore comments to start with, but it was like a dripping tap eroding something placed beneath it. Eventually – and especially in the heat of the moment, when sportsmen are experiencing the strong emotions that come with performing in the heat of battle – passions will always ignite.

He also had a very good point, but the bottom line of this affair was that I had learned a very tough lesson. And it was a lesson that I simply had to learn. My season had been tainted, and all the pleasure I should have drawn from our Sunday League trophy win had been taken away by this incident. That was also a huge shame.

The summer of 1991 had been, overall, a very good one for me and I had felt that I had made something of a breakthrough in my career, even though I had not put a really big score on the board in my first six Tests for England. But 1992, after such a tough winter, had been a difficult experience both when I was given some more England opportunities and during my time with Middlesex.

Off the field, especially, it had been a testing time and the result of everything was that I had a winter at home to contemplate. In many ways I needed the rest and recuperation, but it was still a big disappointment not to be picked for England's winter tour. It meant that I had dropped out of the Test reckoning again and that I had to regroup, both in terms of my cricket and my behaviour, if I wanted to get back to that level again.

Therefore when the 1993 season came around, I had made the decision that – no matter what – I would not get into trouble again either on the field or with the sort of incident that had blown up in my face at Uxbridge. My main goal, going into that new season, was not a cricketing one. It was to stay out of trouble. And, do you know what, that attitude meant that I had what I will always consider to be my worst domestic season.

Mentally, that priority took something significant out of my game. At the time I was not aware of it – certainly in the first part of the season – but I began to realise that it took a lot of the fire out of my personality and my approach to batting. In many ways, my heart was not in what I was doing. And that, for someone like me, who is so passionate about my game, is quite a state to get in.

I know I have always walked a fine line when it comes to my competitiveness – not just in cricket but in football, too, when I was younger – but it is in my make-up to have that desire and passion to do well. For most of 1993, I was not truly being myself.

Another big change that season was that, for the first time, the County Championship was made up entirely of four-day matches. As someone who had grown up with three-day cricket, this required a totally different mindset. You obviously got many fewer first-class innings per season than before, and so mentally you had to be right on the money every time. You had to be fully focused as a batsman, and I wasn't.

I only had 22 knocks in 16 Championship appearances that season, compared to 38 in 22 Championship games back in 1990. It was a big difference and meant a big adjustment for batsmen around the country.

No Middlesex batsman scored 1,000 runs in 1993 and I ended up with 813 at an average of 38.71, which might look respectable enough but was boosted only by an innings of 140 against Yorkshire at Scarborough in mid-August and then an unbeaten 117 against Lancashire at Lord's in our penultimate match.

By then, too, we had been confirmed as Championship winners and – although the season ended with this flourish and with my sudden recall to England arms in the final Ashes Test at the Oval – I felt, overall, that I had not contributed hugely to our triumph.

Indeed, although there always seemed to be someone who chipped in with the bat at crucial times, only Gatting with 981 runs at 65.40 stood out among the frontline batsmen, and our comfortable 36-point eventual winning margin was very much down once again to the 68 wickets at 18 and 59 wickets at 20 which John Emburey and Phil Tufnell, respectively, took with their potent spin partnership. Angus Fraser would not want me to forget his 50 wickets at 24.38 either!

Looking back now on that Championship triumph, with the perspective of another 16 years in this world, it was immature of me not to have enjoyed it as much as I should have done. Irrespective of my own form, winning the Championship again – for the second time and at the age of only 23 – should have been a fantastic experience.

Yet it was such a competitive environment at Middlesex that I only really took full pleasure from achievement when I had made a significant contribution to that success myself. I also had very high expectations of myself and that summer it didn't really happen for me with the bat for the reasons I've explained.

My lack of a competitive edge also made it a summer that I do not remember with great affection. Of course I was pleased we had won more silverware, but I couldn't see the big picture in those days.

However, with those two late hundreds and with my unexpected Test return, at least I could say at the end of it all that I had achieved my goal and had been ultimately rewarded for it. I had stayed out of trouble, I was a county champion and I was back in the England team!

CHAPTER 5

ENGLAND CALLING

'Ramprakash and Smith offered England the first joy of the day. The young Middlesex batsman displayed a sound technique and admirable temperament. It was a most heartening innings in the circumstances'

– Cricket Year report of first Test
at Headingley, England v. West Indies, 1991

It was to my surprise that I heard I had been selected by England for the first Test of the 1991 summer series against the West Indies – then, of course, indisputably the best side in the world.

Yes, I had enjoyed a good England A tour to Pakistan and Sri Lanka earlier in the year. Yes, I knew that my name was being bandied around in the media during the opening weeks of the new county season, and I had won selection for two of the three Texaco Trophy games against the West Indies in late May. Yes, my batting had certainly come on a lot during the winter. Against an excellent Sri Lankan A team, on spin-friendly pitches and in tough all-round conditions, I had demonstrated method, patience and the ability to carve out big scores. I had learned a lot.

But, back in England and at 21 years of age, I still felt I had it all to do in terms of becoming an established senior cricketer in the county game. I aspired to play Test cricket for England, of course I did. It was just that, looking around me, I saw how many other good players there were in county cricket. I was simply trying to consolidate in 1991 after a decent year and it was hard for me to know at that stage what other people from within the game thought about my cricket and if I was ready for the Test arena.

The new season had begun quite well for me, however. I scored a century in a Championship match against Sussex in early May and, just over a week later, my innings of 38 and 21 for Middlesex against the West Indians in a three-day tourist game at Lord's seemed to attract quite a bit of interest in the media. Clearly, my name was being mentioned in the right places, but I still found it amusing that a knock of 38 should result in my picture being all over the papers the next day!

In my two Texaco appearances, at Old Trafford and at Lord's, I finished on six not out and nought not out and only got in right at the end of each match, which England won to take that series 3–0. Then came the Test selection, and the realisation that I had reached the top level of the game at a very early age, and earlier than I had expected.

It was all a little bit overwhelming, really, and I am not sure that at the time I felt I deserved to be picked. And that feeling was hardly banished from my mind when I drove up to Leeds to join in the pre-Test net practice and check in at the England team hotel later that day.

Walking into an England dressing-room with great figures such as Graham Gooch, Allan Lamb and Robin Smith around was quite daunting. Gooch, as captain, was very reserved in nature and, although a very nice person, he was in his late 30s and of a completely different generation to me.

I am not saying I lacked confidence in my own ability, because at 21 I was very confident with a bat in my hand, but getting to know the other players was not a straightforward task for someone of my age. I was also not the sort of person who wanted to walk up to the local pub in the evening for a drink, as some of the other players did.

Lamb and Smith were both very welcoming to me, and I appreciated their easy sociability in the dressing-room and around the hotel. One of the first things Lamby asked me, though, was if he could have my allocation of lunch and tea tickets for the hospitality areas!

On the eve of the game I remember that there was only a very quick team meeting – none of the in-depth analysis of the opposition that you would get these days – and a team dinner at the hotel at Bramhope. Soon, it was the morning of the match and I was being driven to Headingley by Phil DeFreitas in his white 7-Series BMW with some questionable music blaring out of the speakers.

But it was a very special feeling to arrive at the ground, find my way through the crowds and get ready for a Test debut against the world's number one side. I think it was the fact that it was the West Indies that made it an especially great day for me. My hero, Viv Richards, was captaining the opposition and Desmond Haynes, who had been so helpful to me at Middlesex, was also in their team. It was a truly memorable day.

Naive as I was about Test cricket, and everything that surrounded it, I could still very much enjoy the buzz of the occasion. In fact, as I didn't have very high expectations of what I might achieve as a player in this sort of company, I think I was quite relaxed and not at all daunted by the five days that lay ahead. My mind was quite uncluttered. I was going to go with the flow and see what happened.

What happened immediately was that Gooch lost the toss and Richards quite naturally put us in under heavy cloud cover and in damp, almost misty, conditions. I was down to bat at number five and soon Mike Atherton, Graeme Hick and Gooch were all dismissed and I was walking to the wicket with England in some trouble at 45 for 3.

Allan Lamb was also out fairly cheaply and it was all I could do to hang on in there and survive. I remember, initially, wondering how the hell I was going to get a run. The first balls I faced in Test cricket were from Courtney Walsh and I had no idea about where to get off the mark, although a shortish ball then rose up into my ribs and I managed to get it down wide of long leg for two runs.

The ball was darting around off the seam quite a bit, and the West Indies pace quartet of Malcolm Marshall, Curtly Ambrose,

Patrick Patterson and Walsh were all such good bowlers – as well as being fast – that they quickly realised that in the conditions they had to keep it just short of a length to make it extremely difficult for the batsmen. The one consolation was that the pitch was not overly quick, and so the bowling was not as hostile as it might have been.

Marshall, in particular, was very clever and he bowled a really searching length, which meant you could never get right to the pitch of the ball. He nipped it around both ways, too, and it was quite an experience to hang around for a couple of hours and help Robin Smith, who had come in at six, to put on 65 for the fifth wicket before Marshall got me for 27 to a catch in the slips.

That was disappointing, having done so much hard work, but I still felt I had contributed and could be reasonably pleased with the way I had fought to stay in and build an innings. You only had to look around the field, from Viv, Desmond and Richie Richardson in the slips and Jeffrey Dujon behind the stumps, to the four fast bowlers themselves, to realise that you were up against the cream of the crop. I had no expectation of making a huge score, but I wanted to do my very best and show that I could play at that level. I was determined to dig in and hang around for as long as possible, to soak up the pressure and bat time.

I suppose I had the mindset of an underdog, and my attitude and approach were exactly the same in our second innings when, having bowled out the West Indies for 173 in reply to our eventual 198, I walked in with us struggling again at 38 for 3. Ambrose had shot out Atherton, Hick and Lamb, and the match was in the balance.

Happily, I again hung on and had the absolute joy of sharing a 78-run stand with Gooch before, for the second time in the match, succumbing for 27 – this time to a catch at the wicket off Ambrose, who was to take the first six wickets to fall. Watching Gooch take on the West Indian quicks from 22 yards away was awesome, and he ended up carrying his bat for 154 out of a total of 252. Only Derek Pringle supported him for a long time after I was out, but Goochie was simply incredible; to see someone play an innings as great as that in my debut Test match remains one of the fondest memories of my career.

We ended up bowling them out for 162 in their own second innings and winning by 115 runs – the first home victory over the West Indies since 1969. Gooch's magnificent hundred had been the match-winning performance, but DeFreitas took four wickets in each innings and I had made two important contributions with the bat at crucial times. I had also taken a diving catch at cover to get rid of Phil Simmons in their first innings and had run out Carl Hooper with a direct hit, so I was more than content with my first taste of Test cricket.

Both Gooch, before the game, and Mike Gatting, before I left Middlesex to travel up to Leeds, had instructed me to enjoy the experience and to play my own game, and although scoring runs had been tough in the conditions and against that quality of bowling I had felt under no pressure to keep the scoreboard moving. Often it was as much as I could do to survive, but I suppose it was an attritional type of game anyway, and I had been fortunate to have batted with Smith and then Gooch for most of the time I was at the crease. They were both amazing in the way they were able to take the attack to bowlers such as Ambrose and Marshall.

It is interesting, looking back, that neither Gatting nor Gooch got too technical in their direct advice to me. Gooch also said that if I had any questions at all, not to hesitate to speak with him, and young players were expected to go to the coach or to the senior professional if they had an issue with anything on or off the field. It was good in a way that no one tried to overload players with instructions, but it could also be quite daunting as a youngster – especially in an England environment – to go up to a great like Gooch and have a chat about some little thing or other. Equally, it was thrilling to be able to speak with someone like Viv Richards a few times during the series – growing up, I would never have thought I would get the opportunity to be on the same Test field as my batting hero – and he was very nice to me, but do you just walk up to someone like him and start a conversation? I was a kid, and he was an icon of the game.

John Emburey, at Middlesex, was always going on about the need to talk to the opposition, or quiz other players, as a way of learning more about the game, and perhaps in my first full summer in the England team I did not spend enough time, outside of the game, with the other players involved in the series.

In particular, I remember that throughout the series both Gooch and Lamb would comment generally about the need, against that West Indian attack, to keep looking for the singles as a means of keeping the score moving forward even when conditions were bowler-friendly. They also impressed upon everyone that when a rare bad ball came along it had to be put away. Gooch and Smith were so good at that during the 1991 series – with Smith's centuries at Lord's and the Oval being up there with Gooch's 154 as truly fantastic innings.

Now, I knew that these comments were not aimed at me specifically, but at the same time I knew it was advice that I did need to act upon. As the series went on, I did become more and more defensive-minded and, with the benefit of all my experience today, I know I would have batted slightly differently in 1991 by being busier at the crease and looking to rotate the strike more. Young players, generally, do not look for enough singles as a way of relieving pressure.

Again, looking back, it was mightily instructive for me to see how someone like Smith, despite being hit on the body a lot by the West Indians at Lord's and the Oval, still managed to maintain his aggression towards the bowlers. Those West Indies fast bowlers were so good that they were able to hit batsmen of the calibre of Smith and Gooch on the head or on the body; this was serious stuff.

Whether it was Smith reacting to being hit by taking the attack back to them, or Gooch calmly accepting the regular breaks in play for drizzle or bad light during his superb century at Headingley, keeping his concentration and just sitting quietly in the dressing-room waiting to go back out again, this was a real education for me.

My inexperience, however, meant that I didn't take in as much as I could have done, but it was still incredibly impressive to see how these guys operated at the top level and how Gooch in particular stayed in his own bubble as a way of handling the pressure of leading from the front against the world champions. He knew at Headingley, especially, that the early exchanges would be vital to the outcome of the series and that, as captain and our best batsman, he would be ruthlessly targeted by the opposition.

At the end of the series, which we drew 2–2 by winning the final Test at the Oval, I had made 210 runs from nine innings without ever getting more than 29. Yet only Smith and Gooch were above me in the England batting averages; players such as Lamb, Atherton and Hick had endured terrible times against the West Indies pacemen.

Hick had been dropped for the Oval, as had Lamb, after scoring just 75 and 88 runs respectively from seven innings apiece. Atherton's nine innings in the series brought him just 79 runs, at an average of 8.77. That was how good the West Indian attack was. Yet Gooch had made 480 runs and Smith 416. And the West Indies' batting line-up wasn't too bad either: Gordon Greenidge did not play a Test after getting injured during the one-day series, but a certain Brian Lara still could not find a way into any of the five Test matches!

To make my Test debut against one of the greatest cricket teams there has ever been, and to be part of Viv Richards' last Test appearance, at the Oval, are experiences I will always be proud of. Yet the overall frustration, personally, of not quite being able to push on and make a really significant contribution – a Test fifty, in essence – was summed up by my last innings of the series.

I went in at 80 for 3 as we chased down 143 to square the series, and that soon became 80 for 4 when Robin Smith was caught and followed Gooch back into the pavilion. Alec Stewart joined me, and the situation was very tense. The West Indies knew that another wicket now would give them a great chance of pulling off an unlikely victory, and Walsh and Marshall, plus Ambrose and Patterson, all ran in with renewed determination.

It was a severe examination, but Stewie and I held on and gradually we began to build a partnership. When we had added 62, the scores were level, and we were just one hit away from victory. Stupidly, I then played across the line at Clayton Lambert, who had just been brought on to bowl his dibbly-dobbly medium pace as a concession of defeat. From Lambert's third ball I was lbw for 19 and the chance of hitting the winning runs, and walking off the field triumphant with Alec, had gone.

Ian Botham, recalled along with Stewie and Phil Tufnell for this match, replaced me and hit Lambert's next ball, a long hop, for four. I had hardly got back into the dressing-room, so, sweet though the win was, my dismissal on the brink of glory obviously took a lot of the shine off the moment for me.

When I look back on my first five Tests for England, and being involved throughout that hard-fought series, it is with a similar mixture of pleasure at the memories, a certain pride in my performances and regret that I did not manage to make at least one bigger score. I never really failed, but scores of 27, 27, 24, 13, 21, 29, 25, 25 and 19 tell their own story.

The fact that batting was so tough, and that I went in to bat at, respectively, 45 for 3, 38 for 3, 16 for 3, 138 for 3, 25 for 3, 108 for 4, 71 for 4, 120 for 3 and 80 for 3, merely underlines the degree of difficulty I was facing. Only twice, in nine innings, did I walk in with the situation anything like comfortable – even using that word in this context is relative!

As the years have gone by, I have often wondered about what might have happened had I faced a lesser team in my first series – and in my early Test career in general. These days, for instance, you might get a few matches against Bangladesh in which to be blooded. But even back then it was possible to be more fortunate about which opponents you came up against early on; Mike Atherton, to give one example, was initially dropped by England after playing his first two Tests against Australia in 1989 and missed the following winter's tour to the West Indies. But then he was recalled at the start of the 1990 summer and ended up with six home Tests that season against New Zealand and India, which allowed him to more easily establish himself at that level.

I was frankly in awe of bowlers such as Marshall, who by then had achieved so much in the game. He was clearly one of the greats of cricket history. And for someone like me, at that age, it was a case of thinking that I shouldn't really be attacking him! I know that sounds funny, but in one Test I remember hitting him for a couple of fours in quick succession and almost feeling like I ought to be apologising to him for being so disrespectful! There were also one or two occasions against the West Indians when I got out to balls that didn't really do anything special. It was their reputations you had to contend with, too, as well as the fact that they were fantastic bowlers technically and tactically.

It was not that I didn't believe I could get runs. At that age, my mindset was such that I felt I could score a hundred against anyone. But perhaps, in the situation in which I found myself against truly great bowlers such as Marshall, who had proved themselves beyond any doubt as being among the very best in history, there was that 1 per cent difference between my mentality and the total certainty of theirs. It's always such a fine line in sport.

Moreover, as I've already said, seeing batsmen such as Smith and Gooch being hit also made you think; as a youngster, I had never worn a helmet nor even thought about it. When I was about 15, I remember a guy called David Wiles, who was a fast bowler of some repute at that level, and a year or so older than me, clipping me twice on the peak of my cap in an U16 game. But I didn't start wearing a helmet until I got into the professional game; I remember that on my Test debut I wore my Middlesex helmet with an England A badge stuck on it.

I also well remember during the one time I actually batted with Graeme Hick during the 1991 series the moment that he was hit flush on the helmet by a bouncer from Marshall. He and Gooch both wore white helmets in those days – there were no actual England helmets provided for you then – and the ball hit him so hard that these little white bits flew off it. It was as hard as I've ever seen anyone hit by a cricket ball. But to give Hicky his due, he carried on batting and took the blow without any complaint or fuss.

Graeme and I have been linked a lot throughout our careers – and often not in flattering tones – but in my view we have both shown a lot of strength of character to come through some very tough times. Having said that, I think it is also true that we both could have learned more lessons a bit earlier in our respective Test careers. After the problems of that debut series, though, Hicky went on to have a decent Test and excellent one-day international career with England and obviously – like me – he has enjoyed very significant success in first-class cricket overall.

In the series against the West Indies, however, I felt quite comfortable, whereas Graeme had a terrible time of it – even though he had scored big runs against the same bowlers before, chiefly in his innings at Worcester during the previous West Indian tour in 1988, when he made the hundred which took him to 1,000 first-class runs before the end of May.

But I don't buy the theories about Hicky failing against the West Indies in 1991 because of technical issues. He had already scored runs against their bowlers. Yet while I went into that series with the mentality of the underdog, thinking that anything I really achieved was a bonus, he had to cope with all the publicity of being English cricket's 'great white hope'. He was at an age, too, when he was in his pomp as a player and huge things were expected of him. In every innings, he was under the pump. Every shot he played was endlessly analysed.

Apart from during the Oval Test, when Ambrose hit me hard on the wrist before I had got fully used to the extra bounce from what was a superb pitch, I did not get into much trouble against the West Indian quicks. I recall Mike Atherton saying to me in the dressing-room at the Oval, at the end of the series, that I had batted well but had not had the rewards I deserved for the performances I had put in.

Micky Stewart, too, told me at Trent Bridge that I was doing well and that I should keep going and keep working hard. I appreciated that comment and obviously I could see around me how much others were struggling to stay in for very long, let alone make runs.

In hindsight, I am sure more could have been done with me to develop my game during and after this debut series, but I was very self-contained and intense in the way I approached my batting, and my cricket in general, and at the end of every Test it was just accepted that everyone went off and rejoined their counties – often playing a match the very next day – and so there wasn't the preparation and analysis work done within international squads that is a matter of course these days.

So much just passed me by in those six 1991 Tests, including the one against Sri Lanka, which followed the West Indies series, mostly because of the way things were for younger players then but also because of my own character. I wasn't the extroverted or open sort who would find it easy to ask questions or communicate issues, however insignificant in the bigger scheme of things they might have been.

For example, there was no media training or anything like that, designed to help a young player get to know his way around an international cricket environment. That, indeed, was something I was desperately in need of in my early 20s and it would have been so helpful to me. No young player nowadays comes into Test cricket as naive as I was in 1991 about the wider picture. That awareness is all part of being an England cricketer. I look back on my own experiences as a wasted opportunity to project my real self to the watching public. But it just wasn't done that way then.

Meanwhile, on 22 August 1991, I found myself walking out to bat at Lord's in my sixth Test appearance, with England on 119 for 3 against Sri Lanka. I clearly remember thinking as I walked through the Long Room and down the pavilion steps onto the turf, that this was a massive opportunity for me.

After the West Indies series, and the reasonable impression I had made overall, this was a perfect chance to finish my first summer as an England player on a high. What happened? To my fifth ball, and still on nought, I tried to hit a medium pacer called Chandika Hathurusinghe through the covers and was caught in the slips.

I had felt so comfortable at the crease. I was confident and expecting to do well. Hathurusinghe was only a part-time medium pacer really, as he was mainly a top-order batsman, and he was a cricketer I had already played against, on the England A tour earlier that year. He bowled little away-swingers, with no real venom, and I suppose I felt so eager to get on with things and get those big runs that I desired so much following the hard slog of facing the West Indies that I simply couldn't hold myself back.

After a couple of deliveries from Hathurusinghe I made up my mind that the next one, if up to me, was going to go. I should not have been predetermining a shot like that, but when the ball left his hand it seemed a heaven-sent opportunity to get off and running. After I had been caught, I remember walking back off with a duck to my name thinking that it could not be happening. It didn't seem real. It wasn't in the script that I'd written for myself that day, and I couldn't believe it.

Again, hard experience has taught me that you can never underestimate a bowler and that you must always respect your opponent's ability. Just because it wasn't Curtly Ambrose bowling, or Malcolm Marshall, it didn't mean to say that I could just go out there and score off any ball I liked. It was still international cricket, and you always have to go through a process of getting yourself in, and properly assessing the conditions and the bounce of the ball − all those things. I played the bowler, not the ball. It was a very harsh lesson because I ended up missing out massively in that match.

Although Alec Stewart got a hundred, we didn't make a very big first innings total despite a pretty good pitch and all I could hope for was a chance in our second innings to make amends. Sadly, that chance didn't come. We were 322 for 3 when I might have come in to bat again, with Gooch making 174, but it was decided to send in the left-handed Jack Russell ahead of me for some quick runs before a declaration and also so he could more easily sweep their slow left-armer, Don Anurasiri, who had taken all three wickets to fall and was proving quite difficult for the right-handers to get away. Jack scored 12 not out and the declaration soon came at 364 for 3.

England ended up winning that Test by 137 runs, with Phil Tufnell getting five wickets in Sri Lanka's second innings, but for me personally the win did not mean too much. I had missed my opportunity to ink in my name for the starting XI in New Zealand during the following winter. If I had got a decent score against the Sri Lankans – a 70 or an 80, say – I am sure I would have been given a start against the Kiwis when we arrived for a three-Test series early in 1992. As it was, I was a member of the tour party but told very early on that I wouldn't be part of the Test side.

Micky Stewart pulled me to one side very early on in that trip to tell me not to worry about it, but that I was unlikely to play much cricket on the tour. He said I was to use the tour to get more experience of what international cricket, and touring, was all about and to learn. Sitting and watching is very difficult, though, when you are hardly getting a chance to play yourself, and those seven weeks in New Zealand were very dispiriting for me.

England were also planning ahead for the 1992 World Cup, which was taking place in New Zealand and Australia and began immediately after our Test tour was over. Therefore, a number of selections were made during the Test series that were simply to prepare certain players for the World Cup matches. England, don't forget, were perhaps the best and certainly the most consistent one-day side in the world at that time – as the tournament proved, even though Pakistan emerged as winners at the end of it and beat Gooch's team in the final.

And so there was an element of the management needing to make sure, for England's benefit, that certain players got the amount of cricket they required in the build-up to the World Cup. Dermot Reeve, for instance, played in all three Tests and batted at six or seven – even though his bowling was rarely used. Ian Botham was allowed to join the tour late, due to his television and pantomime commitments, and played in the third Test (his hundredth) after both Derek Pringle and Chris Lewis were forced to pull out due to injury.

The policy of playing six specialist batsmen, as against the West Indies the previous summer, was discontinued, while Alec Stewart was used as a specialist opening batsman, handing back the wicketkeeping gloves to Jack Russell, which in effect also militated against selecting the extra batter.

I did not feel in very good form during that trip, which was hardly surprising given the lack of matchplay and the lengthy break following the end of the English summer. My fate as a permanent drinks waiter was all but sealed when the selectors also decided to try to rehabilitate Graeme Hick on that tour – as much because of his status as a key World Cup batsman as they wanted to get him established as a Test player.

Hick had been dropped from the final two Tests of the 1991 summer in which I had played, but now he was back in at number three. Allan Lamb, similarly jettisoned before the end of the West Indies series, was also recalled at number five; he, too, was a World Cup certainty.

Lamb was in magnificent form during the Tests against New Zealand, but Hick again struggled to impose his obvious talent on the big stage. His three first-class centuries on that tour took his tally to an astonishing 63 (he was then still only 25), but in the three Tests his top score was only 43 and five innings brought him just 134 runs.

I suppose I could be sore about Hick in particular, but also both Lamb and Reeve, being selected ahead of me in that I was, in effect, a man in possession of a Test spot before the tour. And when England scored 580 for 9 declared in the first innings of the opening Test in Christchurch, with the middle-order contributing heavily against a modest Kiwi attack, I might have been even more frustrated and angry.

However, the truth is that I could understand the selectors wanting to pick Graeme for all three Tests. Older than me by three years or so, he was also much further down the road in terms of his cricket career and his maturity. He was a dominant player who obviously could score heavily for England, and they wanted to ease him back in and get him settled into the team. New Zealand was the perfect place to do that, and of course he was also one of the first choices for the one-day side, so it made sense to involve him in both forms of the game.

Perhaps I could have been played in place of Reeve at number six, especially as he did very little bowling, but that would have left only four specialist bowlers. Again, the truth was that I was not in very good form: I didn't bat very well in the net sessions and overall I didn't really look the part.

I also didn't feel part of things on the trip; I wasn't part of the group that went out socialising in the evenings and, at that stage of my career, I wasn't good friends with people such as Stewie, whom I had yet to get to know properly.

I only had five first-class innings on the tour, two of which were not out, and my top score was an unbeaten 19. As I am a player who likes to feel I am in a flow with my batting, it was all very frustrating. It was a very long seven weeks. I also did myself no real favours in the end by going on the England A tour to the West Indies straight after flying home from the senior trip.

In hindsight I should have stayed at home for the rest of that winter and concentrated on getting ready for the new season with Middlesex and tried to get my England Test place back that way. But, again, the management of my early career was not very good. There was no one making considered decisions about how I could develop as an international cricketer, and as a person, and I know I really suffered from that.

A century against Lancashire in early May and an innings of 233, my maiden double-hundred, against Surrey at Lord's later in the month meant I was back in the England Test frame for that summer's series against a very talented Pakistan side. Going up to Edgbaston for the first Test, however, I felt very nervous – quite unlike the previous season.

The match was a high-scoring, weather-affected draw, but even walking in at 348 for 3 I still did not feel comfortable. A decent seamer called Ata-ur-Rehman was bowling, and he was in the Pakistan team only because of an injury to Wasim Akram. To my second ball, I pushed forward and somehow nicked it to the keeper. I couldn't believe it. Of course, we didn't get the chance to bat again and I was subsequently left out of the next two Tests.

My form for Middlesex was pretty good, though, and I was recalled for the fourth Test at Headingley, with England 1–0 down after a close-fought defeat at Lord's. This time I felt better going into the game, but when I got to the crease, to join David Gower at 298 for 4 after Graham Gooch had scored a quite brilliant 135, I found that Mushtaq Ahmed's leg-spin variations were far too much for me. I really didn't have a clue which way the ball was turning.

I should have taken my time, tried simply to survive, and used Gower's experience at the other end. But I was desperate to get off the mark and went for a sweep fine behind square. I missed the ball and was given out lbw. It was one of the lowest points of my life.

Back in the dressing-room, I just went and sat in the shower while the rest of England's first innings disintegrated. I had bagged three ducks in my last three Test innings, dating back to the Sri Lanka match of the previous August. Just what was this Test cricket that I was finding so difficult to succeed in? I couldn't even seem to locate the ball and get a bat on it. In county cricket I was being very successful, but in Tests it seemed as if the ball had a mind of its own. My confidence was being shattered.

Gower remained 18 not out, but we were soon all out for 320. That was still a lead of 123, however, and it was a good job it was. After bowling out Pakistan again, we needed 99 for victory. It looked a simple task, but it was anything but, as Wasim, Waqar Younis and Mushtaq reduced us to 65 for 4. As I walked out to bat, it was impossible to think about the fact that I was facing the prospect of a fourth successive nought.

Happily, I somehow managed to hit a couple of fours and, bit by bit, Gower and I inched England to a series-levelling victory. I know I only made 12 not out, but Gower's unbeaten 31 had taken him two hours and our stand had been incredibly tense throughout. At last, I felt as if I had come through a real test of my mettle.

Batting with Gower for that passage of play was also one of the great pleasures of my long professional cricket life. It was really something. He had broken Geoff Boycott's then England Test run aggregate record in the previous match, at Old Trafford, and he was a truly great player. He had a stature, and he gave you confidence just through his relaxed nature at the crease. I had never really come across anyone with his kind of attitude before, either.

The situation was so difficult when I came in, but he soon wandered down the pitch at the end of an over and said, 'Well, I think it's safe to say that it's doing a little bit!' He was all understatement and dry humour, and he always seemed to have that wry little smile on his face. But he had so much time at the crease, and balance, and his strokeplay was of the highest class. He had played against so many great bowlers, and flourished. He was a special talent.

Like Gooch, he too didn't wear a grille on his helmet. They were confident in their ability not to get hit. They were serious players. But it was fantastic for me, during that stand and with so much pressure on me individually let alone because of the match situation, to have had Gower as a batting partner. So many of those I had batted with before were macho in their approach, but he wasn't at all like that. He was very quiet, and amusing. It helped me a lot. It was good, and I enjoyed what was to be our one real partnership very much.

Any England victory is to be savoured, too, and against a team as good as that Pakistan outfit it was a sweet moment. Walking off unbeaten also lifted my mood; it was great, in a small way, to feel in the middle of things as we celebrated the win.

I was also heartened when we arrived at the Oval for the final, deciding Test that the pitch that had been produced was as good a surface as you could wish to bat on. It was quick and bouncy, but beautifully prepared, and the bounce was so even you could plan to play your strokes knowing that the ball would come on to the bat perfectly.

Once again, though, I didn't get going and had made just 2 when Wasim bowled me an inswinging full toss that I missed and was lbw. Then, in our second innings, when I went in to join a battling Robin Smith with us at 59 for 4 and still 114 behind, I did manage to hang around for a while and to reach 17 – and was actually beginning to feel quite comfortable – when David Shepherd, the umpire, adjudged me out to a bat-pad catch at short leg off Mushtaq when my bat was nowhere near the ball.

Shep came up to me after play to apologise, having seen the replays later, which was nice of him, but it didn't do much for my sense of despair. I had got myself in, the pitch was still excellent and a couple of boundaries had begun to move me forward. Smith was batting tremendously at the other end and would go on to finish on 84 not out as Wasim and Waqar again blew away our lower order, and with a little bit of luck I could have stayed with him for much, much longer. I was desperate to get the sort of score that would get my own Test career properly started – a fifty, at least – and that's when you need the rub of the green.

We lost the game comprehensively, and with it the series, and although there were still a few one-day internationals to come against Pakistan it was the end of my own England summer, as I was not in the one-day squad. I knew I would now struggle to make the winter tour to India, and it was just so frustrating and demoralising.

I wanted to succeed as a Test batsman so badly, but looking back I can see that I was very nervous in 1992 and this did not help me. These nerves were becoming a big problem, and it was a shame because they impeded me as a batsman and did not allow me to show my real talent.

The bowlers I had faced in my first two summers as an England player were fearsome. Ambrose, Walsh, Marshall, Waqar, Wasim were all quick, but also very clever and accomplished. Throw in Mushtaq Ahmed and Patrick Patterson and there were not very many relaxed moments for anyone in the England side, let alone me as a youngster trying to establish myself. However, if I'm honest, it took me too long to get myself used to what Test bowling was about. I've always been big on preparation, and I should have been quicker in tailoring my training and match practice to what I was facing out in the middle. 'Nose and toes' was the phrase that was around at the time to describe what facing up to the likes of Wasim and Waqar was all about. It was tough, but you had to train for that.

When I moved to Surrey in 2001, they would shoot tennis balls at you at 95 mph to quicken up your reactions, and when

I look back it is clear that during my early England career there simply wasn't the depth of preparation done as a team unit that was required for success against great bowlers.

In 1992, in particular, it is my opinion that we didn't prepare well enough as a team against Pakistan and therefore we weren't best able to meet the challenges that they posed. Bowling-machine work against fast left-arm inswing and fast right-arm inswing might have been a start, for instance! But, in that era, everyone was responsible for their own preparation; I needed those with more experience to make up for the fact that I didn't yet have the know-how required at that level.

CHAPTER 6

OUT OF DESPAIR

'There was certainly a fear of failure within him when he played
for England, and it grew as he struggled to do full justice to his
talents'

— Nasser Hussain

My time on the outside of the England Test team ended,
quite suddenly and without warning, just over 12 months
later on 19 August 1993. I was busy practising at
Lord's, before the start of our Championship match against
Northamptonshire, when I was told that Graham Thorpe had
broken his thumb in the nets over at the Oval, where England were
preparing for the final Test of that summer's Ashes series, and that I
had been summoned across London to take his place in the team.

Perhaps the wheel of fortune had turned – if Middlesex had been
due to play away from home in that round of games, I might never
have got the call. As it was, I was soon bundling myself and all
my gear into a taxi and crossing the Thames with a growing sense
of excitement. Hopping out at the front gate and having to walk
through all the crowds just before the start of the Test to get to the
dressing-room was a real experience.

England batted first, and I was in at number seven. It was a good,
hard pitch and I was in at 253 for 5. Mike Atherton, in his second
Test as captain after Graham Gooch had stood down following
Australia's retention of the Ashes, had scored a half-century at the

top of the order, as had both Gooch and Graeme Hick, but I only made 6 before being caught behind off Merv Hughes.

On one occasion during my short innings, though, after I had inside-edged a ball from Hughes for a single, I was informed by the bowler as he walked past me back to his mark, 'You don't f***** know whether you're a curry-muncher or a West Indian, do you?' There was simply nothing I could say to that, as Hughes walked on. It was typical Merv and I certainly wasn't offended: it was just nice to be back in Test cricket!

I was disappointed not to have marked my comeback innings with a decent score, but I'd had no preparation for the Oval, which was so different to the lower bounce that I had become used to again at Lord's, so my failure was understandable. But I was determined just to enjoy the match, as my participation in it was so unexpected, and it quickly developed into a superb cricket match.

As the third day drew to a close, we were more than 250 runs in front but wobbling a touch at 186 for 5 after the loss of three wickets for six runs. I joined Alec Stewart out in the middle and the first priority was to get through to the close, which we did with me on 12 not out. The next day we took our partnership to 68 before Stewie was out and I had the pleasure of reaching my first Test half-century – in my tenth Test – and going on to 64 before I fell again to Hughes.

We ended up bowling Australia out again, with Angus Fraser taking eight wickets in the match, and Devon Malcolm and Steve Watkin sharing the other twelve. For England, it was a great win at the end of what had been a very tough summer. For me, too, it was a big game career-wise. I had been given a chance of a comeback out of the blue and had taken advantage of it. I was now also in with a shout of selection for the upcoming winter tour to the West Indies.

Atherton, with a major say in selection for the tour, chose to go with youth ahead of the likes of Gooch, Gatting and Gower, who announced his retirement from the game when he was not selected. This meant Graham Thorpe, Nasser Hussain and I were all included in the England squad, but in the run-up to the tour, and also in the first couple of weeks, I was still uncertain about what was expected of me in terms of a batting role – if anything.

It seemed as if the management wanted Stewart to open with Atherton, with Robin Smith and Graeme Hick at four and five. This meant, in effect, that the rest of us front-line batsmen – myself, Nasser, Thorpey and Matthew Maynard – were battling for two places: number three and number six.

It was a great opportunity for us, but the West Indies still had a very handy team in early 1994, especially on the fast-bowling front. But I'd enjoyed my trips to the Caribbean before and I felt happy and relaxed in that environment. We had done a lot of work as a squad up at Lilleshall before the tour, yet I still arrived in the West Indies uncertain of what my role was to be in the batting line-up.

You would think that the selectors would have had a specific batting order in mind when they chose the squad in the first place, especially with regard to the number three spot, which is so crucial in any side. Whatever, in the early warm-up games, there did not seem to be any policy emerging.

There was almost a month of cricket in the lead-up to the opening Test at Sabina Park in Jamaica, including – somewhat bizarrely – the first one-day international, in Barbados, three days before the Kingston Test. I got a hundred in a three-day non-first-class match in St Kitts and then played in both four-day games against the Leeward Islands, in Antigua, and Barbados. In three of my four innings in those games, however, I opened the batting.

Thorpe went in at three in both innings of the Leewards fixture, with Maynard at six. But Maynard, who scored only 25 in his only innings in that match, was then omitted from the Barbados game and I batted at three in the first innings.

Maynard was back at six for the opening one-day international, with Thorpe at three, and I didn't play. And, when the side for the first Test was announced, the decision was to go with the same top six, and in the same order, with Robin Smith at four and Hick at five.

Thorpe had at least been batting at three at Surrey during the 1993 season, but he was still very inexperienced at Test level at that time, having made his debut only the previous summer against

Australia; it looked as though England were desperate to protect both Smith and Hick from the new ball, even though they were both far more experienced, and in the case of Hick, in particular, a long-time specialist at number three with his county.

It seemed as if it was between Thorpe and me for the number three position, with Nasser initially not in the best of form on that tour and – like Maynard – more of a four or five anyway at first-class level. When Thorpe suffered a bruised hand in the field after scoring just 16 in the first innings at Sabina Park, on a very hard and almost shiny surface, as England declined from 121 without loss to 234 all out, another decision was made to send in Robin Smith at three for the second innings.

The match was lost by eight wickets after Hick had scored a brilliant second innings 96 from number four and Courtney Walsh had provoked some controversy by peppering our last man Devon Malcolm from around the wicket. Devon was hanging around for 18 and helping Andrew Caddick to add 39 for our final wicket; Courtney did not think he had done anything wrong in the situation by hitting Devon several nasty blows on the body. I don't think that the West Indies in this vital opening Test would have minded too much, however, if Devon, who was a real number eleven, had broken a bone warding off the short balls: he was our strike bowler and the one man we had with the sort of pace to respond in kind to the West Indian quicks.

By the time we reached the second Test, in Guyana, we had played the remaining four one-day internationals (of which I played in the last two) and a four-day match in Georgetown against a West Indies Board President's XI, which was, in effect, a West Indian second team which included Carl Hooper, Shivnarine Chanderpaul and Cameron Cuffy.

Arriving in Guyana for that game was a big moment for me because it was the first time I had visited my father's home country. It was special, and all the more so because Dad was there and was able to take me to see the village in which he had grown up, which was about a 30-minute drive out of Georgetown, and to introduce me to many of his friends and relations.

I also marked my debut match in the land of my father by scoring 154 not out in the first innings of the game against the President's XI, watched by Dad and some of his friends. Growing up, he had seen so much of his early cricket at the historic Bourda ground, so this was a wonderful experience for him too.

Sadly, though, when I played in the Test that followed at the same ground I could only manage 2 and 5, being bowled by a near-shooter from Curtly Ambrose in our second innings. We lost by an innings, to go 2–0 down in the series, despite a first innings 144 from Atherton and 84 by Smith.

At the time I felt it was strange to change our batting line-up after just one Test. Maynard was dropped to make way for me, despite scoring 35 in the first innings in Jamaica, with Thorpe dropped down to six, and I was thrust into the number three role. In both innings, I found myself coming in with no runs on the board, first when Stewart was out to Walsh in the second over and then when Atherton was bowled by Ambrose for a duck to the fourth ball of our second innings.

For an experienced Test number three, this would have been a tough ask, and at that stage of my career I was a bit of a sacrificial lamb. I wonder why Thorpe – as at Sabina Park – or Smith or Hick were not asked to go in at three. At the Oval the previous August, in my comeback game, I had been played at number seven . . . now it was three!

I know that Athers and the England management were showing a lot of belief in me and that they were giving me a huge opportunity to establish myself, especially when I was kept in the side at number three for the rest of the series despite never making any score higher than 23. Also, my unbeaten hundred in the warm-up game for the Guyana Test showed that I was in good touch; in fact, I scored 91 and 67 in the one other remaining first-class game, at Grenada, in between the third and fourth Tests.

But deep down I didn't believe that I should have been playing for England at number three. My expectations of myself in that position, and at that time, were not high enough. I was thinking merely of trying to survive, of hanging in, and not of making that position my own. I knew that I was being used as a buffer between the openers and our middle-order strokemakers, and I believed, at the age of 24, that both Smith and Hick were far better players than me. They were more dominant, with track records significantly better than my own. I was still looking to find myself as a batsman, even at the best of times. An England number three I was not.

It was all very well to be given that job in Guyana and for the rest of the series, but if I was the preferred number three why had I not been included for the first Test? That fact hardly did much for my self-belief. At Middlesex, I was still number four behind Mike Gatting at three. And, there, I had started out at six and had been gradually brought up the order as I became more established and more confident. In my eyes, as at Middlesex, it was right for the senior players to be in the most important positions – such as Gatt at three – and for the younger players to be groomed in areas of the side where there was a little bit less pressure to perform consistently and when it was really needed.

The way Middlesex brought me on as a player was exactly the right way of doing it. My development, as that of the other young players, was managed in that sense, and I realise now that this just did not happen at England level for me. Perhaps if Gatting had still been England captain, or even in the side, during my first few years at Test level it might have been different. As it was, the only Test match in which I ever played alongside Gatt was at Perth in early 1995 – his last.

There is no way that I want to use this book to make excuses for my early failures as an England batsman, but at no stage during this West Indies tour was I ever spoken to about the batting strategy and what my role, at three, was to be. In many ways, of course, it was bloody obvious: get out there, get stuck in and do your best. And, if you survive the new ball, go on and score a big hundred.

Yes, that part of it was obvious. But the change of batting line-up, from first Test to second, was not explained, nor was I ever told that I would get a run of games at four. Consequently, in every match I felt that I was playing for my place as much as anything, which makes it very difficult to stay relaxed. After all, if they could change the batting order after just one Test, then they could certainly do it again.

In the end, I was very surprised to hold my place at three for all four remaining Tests, especially when the evidence suggested that, like Maynard after Jamaica, I should be jettisoned. Mentally, on that tour, I just didn't believe that I could kick on and play the major innings that number three batsmen were there for. My aims never stretched beyond getting to 20 or 30. It is interesting that when Chanderpaul was picked by the West Indies for his debut Test in his native Guyana, he was brought in at six and kept there despite enjoying immediate success and clearly looking a class act.

In my case, and especially in 1994 in the Caribbean, a little bit of encouragement from the England management – and some clarity as to their thinking – would have gone an awful long way. A few encouraging words, perhaps along the lines of, 'We want you to do this, for the benefit of the team, but don't worry because we rate you and this will make you a better player,' would have made all the difference. But there was no communication, and no support.

As it was, we limped off to Trinidad and our top six remained the same. I added 66 with Atherton for the second wicket, making my series high of 23, and was disappointed to get out caught and bowled because I was just beginning to feel reasonably comfortable. Nevertheless, we made 328 for a lead of 76, and at 167 for 6 in their second innings the West Indies were struggling.

Crucially, though, the usually reliable Hick dropped Chanderpaul twice in the slips and he went on to 50, and with Winston Benjamin making 35 we were eventually left to score 194 for victory. It should have been 60 or 70 runs less but, by the close of the fourth day, we were 40 for 8, as Ambrose delivered one of the most destructive spells in Test history. He finished with 8 for 24, and we were bowled out for 46, but it was my stupid run out for 1 which really opened the floodgates on that remarkable fourth evening.

Atherton had been lbw to Ambrose to the very first ball of our second innings, so once again I was walking out with the total on nought. From the fifth ball, I worked one away wide of long leg and set off, shouting at Alec Stewart as we crossed to look for a second run. Before the match we had talked as a team about the need to push for every run, and Walsh at long leg had a poor arm and, indeed, bowled the ball in rather than throwing it. So, knowing that Walsh was down there, I wanted to look for two.

As I turned, though, I was suddenly disorientated because I could not immediately pick out Walsh in the outfield. Did he have the ball in his hands or not? Then, just as I was trying to find him, I was aware of Stewie already coming back for a second. It was my call, of course, but I still didn't know where the ball was. I hesitated, ran, and was run out by Walsh's return. It still wasn't the end of the first over and we were 1 for 2.

It is a dismissal that should not happen at Test level. It was a ridiculous way to get out. I was surprised to see Stewie striding back for the second, but we had not batted very much together at that time; with Graham Thorpe, for instance, I have always had a great understanding – we often only need a look, rather than a call.

Being bowled out for 46 was also humiliating and the series was now lost. We then turned up in Grenada and, of course, the practice facilities there, as was so often the case in the Caribbean, were almost non-existent. I think one of the reasons why overseas players are generally mentally tougher than the average English cricketer is because they grow up unused to having proper practice and preparation facilities; therefore, when they step out onto the pitch for the actual match, they have to concentrate fiercely and learn to survive while they get attuned to the conditions.

I remember going out to bat in that match and having to work really hard due to our lack of preparation. But I also remember that despite my own good performances as an opener we played very poorly against a West Indies Board XI, for whom a local leg-spinner called Rawl Lewis took nine wickets in the game, and we ended up losing by eight wickets.

The general mood in the camp was summed up as Robin Smith and I were preparing to go out and open the second innings. Keith Fletcher, the England coach, came up to Robin and told him to get his head down and play well. Robin answered, in his usual cheery way, 'OK, coach, I'll do my best,' at which point Fletcher, clearly feeling the pressure of our poor cricket, exploded. 'You'll do more than your f***** best, and don't get out again to the leg-spinner.' (Smith had been caught off Lewis in the first innings.) Robin was slightly taken aback at this outburst, but he didn't get out to the leg-spinner; he was lbw for nought padding up to Anderson Cummins in the first over!

And so we went into the fourth Test, in Barbados, on the back of another humiliation and in some disarray. Yet an unchanged team was named, and England went on to win by 208 runs – the first visiting Test side to do so at the Kensington Oval for 59 years – with Alec Stewart scoring magnificent hundreds in both our innings. On the opening day, I came in at 171 for 1, after Atherton was out for 85, and managed 20 before being caught at the wicket off Winston Benjamin.

Once again I had got a start but failed to go on. Whereas Alec had a method and trusted it totally, even when his tendency to go back and across, looking to score off the back foot, got him lbw, I was still doubting my own way of playing. I was still looking for a method to bring me success at Test level.

After further scores of 3, in the second innings at Barbados, and then 19 in our only innings in the high-scoring drawn final Test in Antigua, where England replied with 593 to the West Indies' 593 for 5 declared and Brian Lara's then world record 375, I was very down about my own game. I had played some good shots in my Antigua innings and felt fine, but then I padded up to an inswinger from Kenny Benjamin and was lbw.

I was very disgruntled with life, and as I was sitting quietly by myself in the pavilion Viv Richards sauntered over and said hello. He asked me how I was, and I told him, and he replied, 'You have got everything, to me, but there is still something clearly missing.' I asked him what he thought that was, and he said, 'Belief.' I will never forget that. Viv was my idol, and it was kind of him to have a word with me because he could obviously sense my despair. And, of course, when I thought about it I realised that the whole of his own great career had been based on belief. He actually used to intimidate Test bowlers – not the other way around – with that massive belief and self-confidence.

Perhaps, in those early years of my England career, I didn't like to admit it to myself, but Viv's words were spot-on. I did hear what he said, and appreciated his support and his view, but it took me another four years to get my first Test hundred, so it definitely took me a lot longer than it should have done to find a method, and a trust – a belief – in that method. How that happened I will come to later, but for now all I will say is how disappointing it is to look back and see what a sad indictment it was of the then England management that there was no one on hand to give me the help and advice I needed.

I had the technique and the application – and the desire – to be successful at that level. I often felt comfortable at the crease and felt that I could be a Test batsman, but I still kept on finding ways of getting out. I was immersed in my game and continually practised hard to the best of my ability, but I required the England coach, and his support staff of assistant coaches generally, to prepare me fully for the big games. I needed to organise my method, and I needed someone to talk to about it. But there was nothing being offered by anyone.

Left out of England's plans for the rest of 1994, as a result of my poor four Tests in the West Indies, and also omitted from the following winter's Ashes tour squad, I found myself instead selected as vice-captain to Alan Wells on the England A tour to India in the early months of 1995.

It was a highly enjoyable trip, with some excellent cricket against an India A side boasting the likes of Rahul Dravid, Sourav Ganguly, Rajesh Chauhan and Paras Mhambrey. We won all three five-day Tests and also the one-day series, but I didn't stay in India for the whole tour.

Midway through, after I had scored 99 and 36 not out in a tense opening Test win in Bangalore, I was called up to England's tour of Australia as a replacement for Graeme Hick, who had suffered a slipped disc. We had just arrived in Calcutta, where the second five-day match against India A was to be played, and such was the urgency of the command for me to get to Australia I had to pack my bags again hurriedly and leave without the chance to say my goodbyes to most of my teammates.

It was the start of a nightmare journey, however. I left Calcutta at 10 a.m. on the Wednesday morning and finally arrived in Adelaide, where England were playing the fourth Test of the Ashes series, via a 24-hour overnight stop in Bangkok and a connection in Brisbane, where I was able to watch on television in an airport lounge Mike Gatting complete his last Test hundred with a suicidal single after an interminable time in the 90s! An Indian journalist helped me to get on the flight from Calcutta, as my name didn't seem to be on their computer; I then had to pay £600 in excess baggage for all my gear. I checked myself into the Bangkok airport hotel because they, too, didn't seem to know that a room had been reserved for me.

When I finally got to Adelaide, though, it was in time to field as a substitute on the last day, when Devon Malcolm bowled as quick as I have seen him (I was at leg gully and praying the ball didn't come to me!), and to join in the celebrations of a rare England win. The Ashes had already been retained by Australia, but this was a real boost for the team and the hundreds of Barmy Army supporters who were then just starting to appear on England tours.

At 2–1 down, it was also possible now for England to level the series in the final Test in Perth and, when we arrived there, I suddenly found myself in the frame for selection. England's management decided to field six batsmen, plus Steve Rhodes, the wicketkeeper, and four quick bowlers. And so, on the first day, as Australia moved steadily towards an eventual first innings total of 402, I was called upon to bowl a lengthy spell of my non-turning off-breaks (I was the only 'spinner' in the team) to provide a bit of variety.

Towards the end of the second day, following a slide to 77 for 4, I walked in to resume my Test career again – this time at number six, you'll notice – and by the close I had reached 14 not out. Graham Thorpe, my partner, had just gone past his fifty, and the next day we added a further 125 runs before Thorpey was stumped off Warne for 123. I went on to 72, my highest Test score, before Warne also got me out by going around the wicket and bowling me off both my front and back pads with a ball that pitched about two feet wide of leg stump.

It was a slightly unlucky dismissal, but I was happy to have batted well, and to have expressed myself with some good strokes on a pitch with good bounce and pace. I had gone to the crease determined to enjoy myself and felt little pressure because my call-up had been so unexpected. Craig McDermott bowled really well, especially in the second innings, when we were bowled out for 123 to slump to a heavy defeat, and of course there was Warne and a young Glenn McGrath, who took six wickets in the game but was slapped around by Thorpe in his brilliant century. I think Thorpey was at his very best in 1994 and 1995, when he picked his bat up like Lara, and his pulling and cutting was magnificent. His strokes really flowed from him in those years.

I also made 42 in England's second innings, the top score, after coming in at 27 for 5. It was soon to be 27 for 6 when Atherton was out immediately the following morning, but Rhodes and I added 68 for the seventh wicket to offer at least some resistance. Four days after that Perth Test had ended, though, I was back in India, playing a one-day game for England A at Indore. It would just not happen now.

Yet I really enjoyed that winter, however surreal it seemed at the time to be batting one minute on low, slow Indian turners and the next on one of the quickest and bounciest pitches in the world at the WACA. But it had given me the chance to show that I could adapt to different conditions, and flourish in both, and I finally flew home from Bangladesh (where England A went for a week following the three one-dayers in India, in which I scored 36, 70 and 57) thinking and believing that I had made a bit of a breakthrough.

How wrong I was. Yes, I had something to build on, but in 1995 the West Indies were our opponents once more and, for me, that meant trying to exorcise the demons that came in the tall shapes of Ambrose and Walsh. In all my years in the game, they are the most difficult bowlers I have ever had to face, because there was something about their height, their consistent line and length, and their ability to bowl long spells and keep up the pressure on you that I never came to terms with. Plus, of course, in England in early summer batting was never going to be easy.

Driving up to Headingley for the opening Test in early June, I felt as confident as I'd ever been before an England game; in May, I had played in all three Texaco Trophy one-day internationals against the West Indians, scoring 32, 16 and 29 not out from the middle-order as we won the series 2–1, while the memory of Perth was still fairly fresh in my mind.

In that Leeds Test, however, nothing seemed to get easier. It was a re-laid pitch, quite quick and lively, and I got hit on the head by Kenny Benjamin. Although still batting at number six, I scored only 4 and 18 as England, put in on the opening morning, were bowled out for 199 and 208 and lost by nine wickets. The West Indies attack of Ambrose, Walsh, Benjamin and Ian Bishop shared out our 20 wickets like sweets in the playground.

This was Ray Illingworth's first Test in sole charge of the England team, following the sacking of Keith Fletcher after the Australia tour, but there was still no conversation about my role in the side. We had a lengthy tail, with Phillip DeFreitas at seven and Darren Gough at eight, so at six was I to concentrate on defence in a bid to protect that tail for as long as possible, or attack in the hope of getting as many runs as possible in whatever time I had? Sadly, in both innings, I didn't last long enough to face this conundrum, but the fact that there was no planning again did nothing for my overall mental preparation.

When we got to Lord's for the second Test, I did not feel good. Our top six batsmen were the same, but this time Stewart opened as well as keeping wicket and Robin Smith dropped down from opener to number five. I went in at 185 for 4 in our first innings, and Carl Hooper was bowling. When you played against the West Indies in that era, this was a considerable bonus, but even then I could not get going against them. Eager to get off the mark against Hooper's tidy but relatively unthreatening off-spin, I hit a couple of good strokes off the middle of the bat but straight to fielders. Frustrated, I did what I shouldn't have done and that was try to force things. The result was an edged drive to slip, and I was walking off with a duck feeling that I had thrown it away.

Worse was to come in the second innings when, fighting for

supremacy in a thrilling Test we were eventually to win by 72 runs with Dominic Cork, on debut, taking 7 for 43, I completed a pair at the start of the fourth day after coming to the crease the evening before. It was a shattering dismissal for me, caught off Bishop, and although England went on to win it was difficult to join in the celebrations wholeheartedly because I knew I would be dropped yet again. I had felt vulnerable throughout that Lord's Test, and with a pair to my name the return of this fear of failure had dealt me a grievous blow. My ambitions of Test match success were once again in ruins: my runs in Perth had been but another false dawn.

To put the icing on the cake, I then had to hang around at Lord's, feeling miserable as the other England players went their separate ways, because the Middlesex squad were due to meet there in the early evening to board the team coach which would take us down to Cornwall (yes, Cornwall!) for a NatWest Trophy tie the next day against the minor county at St Austell. We arrived there at about one o'clock in the morning, so we didn't even get a proper night's sleep before we were up again and down to the ground to prepare for the game.

Sportsmen react in different ways to extreme disappointment, however, and my own answer was to try to take out my anger and frustration on opposition bowlers. I resolved to go out and see how many runs I could make in the coming weeks and months. I was driven on by this desire to make up for these latest failures with England and to show that I was far better than a horrible pair at Lord's seemed to indicate.

After a much-needed day's rest following the long journey home from Cornwall, I went into our County Championship fixture against Surrey at Lord's determined to be aggressive. I also had a new bat that I had bought from Cork during the Test; it just felt good when I was fiddling around with it in the dressing-room. I had hardly practised with it, but I suppose I wanted a new start and so a new bat seemed as good a way of going as any.

Anyway, whatever the reasoning behind it, I hit 37 fours with it and scored 214 as we beat Surrey by an innings and 76 runs. Everything suddenly seemed so easy – perhaps because I wasn't facing Walsh and Ambrose! But I also wanted to go out and enjoy myself; I was fed up with my international trials and tribulations. As my choice of bat indicates, too, there was almost a devil-may-care attitude to my approach in those days immediately after the Lord's pair. And, relaxed by that, I found my footwork, my timing and my strokeplay were helped and the runs just flowed.

By this stage of my professional career, too, I had fully absorbed a lesson that Mike Gatting had drummed into anyone who was listening during our travels around the county circuit: never be satisfied by the number of runs you make; 'get some runs in the bank for a rainy day'. Now, after the despair of the Lord's Test, I was ravenous for runs and I was also enjoying batting too much to give anything away. The result was a stream of big scores, including two more double-hundreds and a total of nine centuries (or double-centuries) in fourteen championship innings. That season, I made ten scores of a hundred or more and topped 2,000 first-class runs for the first time, while averaging 93 in the County Championship.

I topped the national averages, won a nice £10,000 award for heading a player-ranking list and was named Middlesex's player of the season. I had never batted better. Apart from those two Tests against the West Indies, my game had gone to another level and the ultimate reward was selection for England's winter tour to South Africa.

Illingworth, the England supremo, went on record before the tour to say that he was going 'to get Ramprakash right'. As it turned out, the only time he actually spoke to me directly during the whole winter was when he sidled up to me as I was waiting to bat in our first warm-up game in South Africa, at Nicky Oppenheimer's private ground, and said, 'We want you to kick on here and do well on this tour,' to which I replied, 'OK, great.' That was it for three months.

For some reason – probably for the same reasons as in the Caribbean two winters earlier – I was soon earmarked again for the number three batting spot, despite the more senior status of Graham Thorpe, Graeme Hick and Robin Smith in the three positions below me. Yes, number three was proving to be a problem for England: since 1987, there had been only six centuries scored there in Tests, and by six different batsmen. But should I really have been thrust into that position again, especially with a pair at Lord's as my previous Test experience, when someone as well established and good against fast bowling as Smith was down at six?

Perhaps, too, there should have been a proper discussion with me about my role in the side. Perhaps I should have demanded it. But, as throughout my career, I have been happy to do what I have been asked to do. As a player, it is very difficult to refuse to do something in a team game where all your teammates are depending on you to do the job you have been allocated.

Athers actually came to me at the end of the tour and said he felt I had been negative about the chance to bat at number three. I felt he was covering himself. At the time I think he should have tried harder to understand what it was like to be in my shoes, still trying to establish myself in the England side after a number of years. In my position, in effect the more 'junior' of the middle-order batsmen in that squad, what would he have wanted for himself?

Perhaps he didn't want to go up to one of his senior players – like Smith or Hick – at the start of that tour and tell them that they had to do number three. It's a little bit like the situation England were in at the start of the 2009 summer. I know Ravi Bopara came in against the West Indies in the opening Test and scored a hundred at number three, but at the time it was my opinion that Kevin Pietersen – as the number one batsman in the land – should have been told he was the best option to go in at three.

He should have been challenged to become England's Ricky Ponting; in other words, go in at three and dominate because you are the best player and you can best shape the game from that position. Then I would have had Paul Collingwood at four and either Bopara or Ian Bell at five – assuming that Matt Prior was at six because of the need still to field five front-line bowlers due to the injury absence of Andrew Flintoff.

Back at the end of 1995, though, when I got the nod to bat at three in the opening Test at Centurion, I decided to treat it as another golden opportunity and I did try to be positive. South Africa were a tough side to play in their conditions and in Allan Donald, Brett

Schultz and Shaun Pollock, making his Test debut in this game, they had a high-quality pace attack.

Our main strike bowler was Devon Malcolm who, famously, had routed the South Africans with 9 for 57 at the Oval in August 1994. But here in South Africa, and despite being described early in the tour by Nelson Mandela as 'the destroyer' when we met the great man at a game played in Soweto, Malcolm's confidence was all but shattered by the attitude towards him of Illingworth and Peter Lever, the bowling coach. Devon was working his way back steadily from a knee operation, but Lever and Illingworth seemed determined to change his action and it led to a huge confrontation. I don't remember there being much wrong with Dev's action when he scattered South Africa's batting at the Oval.

I was rooming with Devon during one of our warm-up games in East London and I remember one evening that he was on the phone for hours to his wife, Jenny, discussing what he should do. Devon himself was thinking about flying home because he was so upset at the management's general attitude to him, but he didn't really know what to do and Jenny said she would support his decision to leave the tour. As it was, he stuck it out, but his relationship with Lever and Illingworth never improved and, from my perspective, it was a remarkable own goal by the England management to upset their number one strike bowler even before the series had started.

The first Test, though, which Malcolm missed, was completely ruined by rain, with the last three days all washed out, and there was only time for us to reach 381 for 9. Hick made a superb 141, in what was probably his best Test innings, but on a slowish pitch I got an edge to a ball from Donald and was out for 9.

It was frustrating not to get a second innings opportunity, and despite a few runs in a three-day game against Free State, I was feeling on edge again as we arrived in Johannesburg for the second Test. I didn't feel comfortable with life, but I was named again at three in what was the same top six as at Centurion.

The result was a struggle to get to just 4 before being bowled, by Donald, and in our second innings – which will always be remembered for the way that Mike Atherton scored 185 not out and, with Jack Russell's obdurate 29 not out in four and a half hours, saved the match – I was bowled off an inside edge for a second-ball nought as I tried to drive Brian McMillan. I was attempting to be aggressive, but yet again it just didn't happen for me.

It was another chance of a run at Test cricket squandered; as against Pakistan in 1992, after the West Indies tour in early 1994 and against the West Indians once more in the summer of 1995, I could not take that chance. Dropped for the third Test in Durban, it was one of the very lowest points of my life. The rest of the tour passed very slowly and it was tough to motivate myself to practise my cricket – something which I'd never experienced before. I went out running, and kept myself fit, but I just couldn't face many nets. Perhaps it was unprofessional, but I was in a dark place.

Yet, just when I was least expecting it, something happened that not only lifted my spirits, but also, in time, rejuvenated my whole career and led – in 1997 and 1998 – to my best years as a Test batsman. It also changed my approach to batting and at last gave me the trusted method I had been seeking ever since my Test debut in 1991.

It is sad to relate that the vital information that I was looking for came from a member of the South African opposition – and not from the England management. Then again, that is to take nothing away from the man who gave me what I was looking for because it just shows what a great cricket man he was, as well as being a world-class coach. He was also an Englishman.

Bob Woolmer, who is sadly no longer with us, spoke to me just when I needed someone to do so. As coach of South Africa, he technically had nothing to do with England's players, and I didn't really know him either, despite the time he had spent as a coach in English cricket with Warwickshire.

It was during the fourth Test, at Port Elizabeth, that I happened to be sitting in the shared players' viewing area – doing my 12th man duties yet again – when Woolmer caught my eye and asked me how I was. I said that I was feeling pretty demoralised, and a bit deflated, and I sat down near him. He commiserated with me and said that things had clearly not gone my way. He then asked, adding that his comment was based only on what he had seen of my batting that winter, whether I was watching the ball as closely as I could.

After a couple of minutes' chatting, I realised what Bob was driving at. He was asking, was I watching the ball in the bowler's hand? Then, was I watching where the seam was in his hand? And, more than that, was I watching where the gold writing was on the side of the ball?

What he was really thinking was that my mind was too cluttered when I was at the crease, that there were too many other things getting in the way of what was most important of all: watching the ball. I had to watch it out of the hand, through the air and almost onto the bat itself. I had to free my mind of everything else. I had to concentrate so intently on the ball that nothing else could intrude into my thoughts.

Bob, as a great coach, could see that I was worrying about too many things. I had to get back to this basic discipline and commit 100 per cent to it. There were many highly successful players in the game's history who did not have orthodox techniques – such as Sobers and Viv Richards, for instance – but they all watched the ball right onto the bat and that enabled them to succeed and to be true to their talents.

We only spoke in all, I suppose, for about five minutes, but I thanked him for what he had told me and it had a huge impact on me. The information he had given me really made me think; one of the first things it made me do was get back into the nets and practise. It had given me food for thought and I wanted to test it out, to feel how it worked for me.

I realised that, in five years at international level, I had never really watched the ball closely enough. Later, when Justin Langer came to play at Middlesex, I realised that he – like a lot of other top players – was massively into this discipline, too. No pun intended, but Bob's words were a real eye-opener for me and they also gave me a huge amount of encouragement. I decided to take his thoughts on board and I got myself back into a positive frame of mind, and actually played in a couple of the one-day internationals that ended the tour to South Africa.

I was also called up on standby for England's World Cup quarter-final defeat against Sri Lanka in Faisalabad in March because of an injury to Neil Smith, but I didn't play and – although it was to be another 17 months before I was involved with England again – I began the 1996 season much heartened by the work I was now doing to improve myself as a batsman capable of succeeding at Test level.

At 26, I had taken a lot of blows, but I had also had a lot of experience of what playing international cricket was all about. Thanks to Bob Woolmer, too, I had something else to take with me into the next phase of my career: a nugget of information as valuable as if it had been pure gold.

CHAPTER 7

PEAKS AND TROUGHS

'Ramprakash made 48, which was worth at least double, and began at long last to bat for England with the certainty he showed for Middlesex'

— *Wisden* report of sixth Test, England v. Australia, 1997

The Oval, in August 1997, marked the start of my rebirth as an England batsman. And, this time, it was to lead to the sort of success and consistency of performance that, as a kid, I had dreamed of achieving.

The first thing that happened to me after my recall, which came on the back of runs scored for Middlesex, was that David Graveney, who that summer took over from Ray Illingworth as England's chairman of selectors, came over to me at the pre-Test practice nets and had a chat. He was very friendly and encouraged me to do well, and I was impressed. I know it doesn't sound much, and it wasn't an in-depth conversation, but I still felt valued in a way that perhaps I had not before. It certainly helped me to settle back in.

As for the match, it was a thriller. Australia had already retained the Ashes again, but England's win in this final Test of the series pulled the scoreline back to 3–2 and gave English cricket a much-needed fillip. Everyone was expecting a traditionally hard, fast Oval pitch that was good for batting, but it was incredibly dry at the start and so very quickly it dusted up and the ball began to go through the top a little. We didn't make many in our first innings and I was out for 4 to Glenn McGrath. With the pitch obviously not going to get better, I feared I might have missed out.

Phil Tufnell, though, bowled truly magnificently on his own return to the England side to take seven wickets in Australia's first innings and limit their lead to 40. I have seen a lot of fine finger spinners in my career, but few who could seemingly hang the ball in the air like Tuffers; when he was on top of his game, as here, it seemed as if the ball was on the end of a string. He teased and tormented the Australian batsmen and showed what a class bowler he was.

We were only 52 for 4 when I came in again, but Graham Thorpe was playing brilliantly in the conditions and we managed to put on 79 for the fifth wicket, which put us back in the game. The night before I had gone out to dinner with Alec Stewart – to a restaurant in Chelsea, obviously – and he was also very encouraging. He said I just had to go out and play my normal game, and to be positive.

Like Graham Gooch, whenever I had worked with him in the nets, Alec simply underlined the basics. It was a message I needed re-emphasising, though, because I was still someone who was looking for a magic ingredient in Test cricket and it was over-complicating things. As it was, I went out there determined not to let the situation dominate me and, even though the ball was turning square, I cut my first ball – from Shane Warne – for four and then quickly swept him hard for another boundary.

I knew I had to be aggressive and take every scoring opportunity, and my chat with Alec and the match situation simply underlined everything and made it crystal clear. I was looking to score first, and to defend second, and although that was only a subtle change in terms of attitude and approach it was an important one in this particular innings. Those two early boundaries also meant I was off and running straightaway, and it gave me confidence.

After Thorpey was out for 62, I went on to reach 48, before being stumped off Warne trying to hit a few more before the tail was blown away, and we had given England a bit of hope. Australia required only 124, but in those conditions it was beyond them, as Andrew Caddick, with 5 for 42, and Tufnell, with 4 for 27, combined to bowl them out for 104. What was interesting, too, was to see some great Aussie batsmen now suddenly looking very ordinary and vulnerable.

As for myself, it was great to celebrate such a victory knowing that I had made a significant contribution. After the Oval in 1993 and Perth in early 1995, I had completed a hat-trick of late call-ups to an Ashes series – and each time I had come up with a decent score.

Nevertheless, I did not think it was enough to get me selected for the following winter tour to the West Indies – especially as Mike Atherton, still England's captain, had seen me fail against the same opposition four years earlier and also in 1995. But I was selected, and in the early net practices I felt good and on top of my game.

The night before the opening tour match, however, against Jamaica in Montego Bay, I was in my room when Athers knocked on the door and asked if he could come in. I was disappointed at the news he brought: I wouldn't be playing the following day nor would I be selected for the other warm-up match before the first Test, against a West Indian A team.

As in 1994, the only batting places up for grabs were numbers three and six. Again, as in 1994, Atherton and Stewart were to open and, this time, it was Nasser Hussain and Thorpe who were nailed on at numbers four and five. Mark Butcher, John Crawley, Adam Holioake and I were therefore competing for two remaining berths.

In shades of my first winter abroad with England, in 1992, I had arrived on tour seemingly the man 'in possession' of the number six position, following my decent showing in the final Test of the English summer, but I had again found that this had not counted for much.

But what can you do? You have to respect the management's decisions and, in the form of David Lloyd, England now had a head coach whom I found very approachable and whom I liked. Nevertheless, after the opening day of the Montego Bay match, I became embroiled in the first of two off-the-field incidents involving the team's new fitness trainer, Dean Riddle, which spoiled the first half of that trip for me.

On both occasions, I felt I had been unfairly treated and, indeed, that the incidents were entirely not of my making. The first occurred after Riddle had overseen some training during the lunch break. We had also done some running and I had had 12th man duties as well. It was a hot day and, when the minibus arrived back at the hotel, I was looking forward to getting to my room. Instead, I was told to report to the gym in ten minutes.

I replied that I would rather not. Riddle said I had to. I replied again that I didn't have to and that I was tired and I would decide if I wanted to go to the gym or not. He told me he would have to see David Lloyd about it. I said that was fine by me.

When I got to my room, however, I felt even angrier about this situation. I have always looked after myself fitness-wise, so I felt this was a stupid incident and something that had been created out of nothing. To work off some steam, I decided to go to the gym after all.

I had only been there five minutes when Riddle walked in and told me Lloyd wanted to see me. We went together and I told Lloyd that I had done all the running and training that had been asked of me during the day and that I had been in the gym before coming to that meeting. Lloyd said he wanted me to work with Dean, and that I had to accept that for players not involved in matches there would be a specific fitness programme. I said that if that was explained to me, so that I could embrace the programme and understand it, then that was fine. I had managed my own fitness up to this point of my career.

The whole thing was just a silly incident, but worse was to come during the first of two Trinidad Tests, the second of which was organised to replace the scheduled first Test in Jamaica, abandoned because of a dangerous pitch which allowed just 10.1 overs to be bowled.

At the end of one of the days' play, Riddle came up and said that he wanted me to run back to the hotel with Mark Butcher, who was also not playing in the Test, as Crawley had been chosen at three and Hollioake at six. I said that was fine, as this was not an unusual occurrence. But when I found Butch, he said he could not join me as he had a meeting arranged with one of the media guys and had to wait for that to happen.

So I jogged back to the hotel myself and headed for a shower and a rest in my room. After about 15 minutes, there was a knock at my door. Dean Riddle stormed in. He was obviously upset and asked me why I had not done what I had been told. I replied, initially rather bemused by what was happening, that Butch had needed to stay on at the ground, so I had run back myself. Perhaps he didn't believe me, or whatever, but he had another go at me and I didn't back down. In fact, things became heated and I was so angry at what I perceived to be another silly injustice that I kicked the hotel door off its hinges behind him as he stormed off.

You have to remember, too, that at this stage of the tour I was also right out of contention for a Test place myself. I was therefore feeling quite aggrieved, and the last thing I needed was to be accused by the fitness trainer of insubordination when I had done nothing of the kind. Indeed, I had done exactly what I had been asked to do.

When Riddle had gone, I was beside myself. I even began to think seriously about asking for a ticket home, such was the state I was in. The suddenness of this incident also shocked me, and I felt that my whole England career was being dogged by aggravation that I didn't need. I was also one of the fittest players, and I didn't drink or smoke. There had to be quite a number behind me when it came to fitness issues!

All sorts of illogical thoughts were swirling around my head, so I went for a walk to try to calm myself down. At reception, just by chance, I bumped into Mike Selvey, the former Middlesex and England bowler who was then working as a cricket correspondent. He was great. He clearly saw that I was upset and he sat me down and we talked in a quiet corner. He calmed me right down and made me see the bigger picture. He said the pitch in Trinidad was not good for batting and that I should be patient because there could well be some fallout from the two Port-of-Spain Tests.

The next day I was called in to see John Emburey, who was acting as assistant coach to David Lloyd on that tour. Riddle was also there, but of course Embers had been a long-standing Middlesex teammate and he took a very balanced view of this latest silly incident. He spoke well, and actually I was trying not to smirk when he said that Dean Riddle had an important job to do because, as a player, Emburey's view was that if you didn't have muscles then you couldn't pull them! But he also told Riddle that I had a good track record of personal fitness and that he needed to be sensitive to the fact that some players did not like being out of the side. It was basic man-management stuff, but it shouldn't have gone this far in the tour before it was sorted out. To his credit, Riddle started to understand my situation a bit better.

England's stay in Trinidad had also been quite eventful, on the pitch. The West Indies won the first game, thanks to a brilliant innings from Carl Hooper, but England – now with Crawley at three, Hollioake dropped and Butcher in at six – bounced back to win an equally tense second match by three wickets. Angus Fraser took 20 wickets in the two Tests, so helpful were the conditions for his brand of naggingly accurate fast-medium, and he said he'd like to bowl there for the rest of his career!

The West Indies' manager, the former batting great Rohan Kanhai, had told me I would get my chance when he commiserated with me for being left out of the opening Test in Jamaica. I had been a bit down when I was left out of that match, especially as Jack Russell's late withdrawal because of illness led to another batsman being called in to the starting eleven – which turned out to be Mark Butcher, meaning that I was now even further down the pecking order than I might have thought.

Mike Selvey had also predicted that the England batting line-up would not stay the same for the remainder of the series. Both Kanhai and Selvey were now proved right, as the tour moved to Guyana, initially for a three-day first-class game and then the fourth Test at Bourda.

I felt like it was home from home for me, as several of my dad's friends were at the airport to welcome me when the England team flew in. I had enjoyed being in Guyana four years earlier and those memories came back as we arrived in Georgetown. I had also been selected in the team to play Guyana, at the Everest Cricket Club ground, and so had a chance to press my claims for a Test place.

With Butcher having played well to guide England home in the previous Test, it was a straight fight between Crawley, Hollioake and me for the number six batting position, the place which I perhaps should have been given right at the start of the series. The Everest club pitch was OK, but it was still not easy to score runs on a surface that helped the spinners on both sides. I came in at 56 for 3, and early on I pushed forward to Guyana's excellent slow left-arm spinner, Neil McGarrell, and got a very thin edge to the keeper. Everyone appealed, but I was given not out. Both umpires did know my dad, by the way . . .

Anyway, given that little bit of luck in what was my first innings in the middle for five months, I went on to make 77. It was the highest score of the game and suddenly I was being told I would be batting at number six in the Guyana Test. Things had, indeed, changed very quickly.

One of the new support staff that David Lloyd had introduced into the England set-up was Steve Bull, a sports psychologist. I had gradually got to know him, and before the Guyana Test we sat down together at the Pegasus Hotel and had a very good chat. Steve did not give you a magic formula for success, but what he did do was encourage you to put in place a formula for preparation that you were happy with and which would hopefully work for you.

He got me talking about my approach to batting, about what I was thinking in the lead-up to an innings, what my mental preparation was and how I could improve it. I opened up to him, and by talking I found I was better able to understand what I was feeling at every stage of the process. I had dedicated so many years to hitting balls in practice, but I had never really done much work on my mental preparation.

We began to break it down into what I wanted to do the day before a game, what was best for me the night before a game, and then the morning of the game, plus waiting to bat and actually walking out to bat. Those of you reading this might think this is all getting a bit too deep, but in fact when you are a professional cricketer there are so many things going through your mind before a big game that it is important to have a strong mental approach.

For instance, quite apart from the physical preparation and the analysis of the opposition, there is the feeling that you don't want to let yourself down, or let your family down. All your dreams since being a child have been about succeeding at cricket. You also have to deal with the scrutiny of the media. Being criticised, and seeing that criticism in the public domain, can be very difficult to handle, and personally I felt I had gone through the mill in this regard. As I sat there, so close to my latest Test match comeback, all these things were swirling around my head and it was good to talk them through with Steve.

At the end of our chat, he gave me a framework and a structure to take into my final preparations for the Test. Included in this, I was to look specifically at the challenges each opposition bowler presented and practise accordingly, to look at the pitch the match was to be played on and visualise myself playing shots – attacking and defending – against every opposition bowler. The night before the game I was to go through that visualisation process once again. It had to be real: the sounds of the place, the noise of the crowd, the feel of the conditions, putting on my helmet and my gloves when the wicket fell, which meant I was in, what to think when I was walking out and actually taking guard . . .

What was vital about this visualisation was to familiarise myself, mentally, with the situation I was about to face, so that I was fully ready to play the innings. The Bob Woolmer instruction to watch the ball – to really watch the ball – was also second nature by now, but I told myself that if a delivery was off line then I was looking to score, and I knew the areas where I was looking to do that.

We went through everything I did when I was waiting to bat – be it having a little look at the bowling, both from the dressing-room viewing area or on television, or having a stretch or a chat or listening to my favourite music – and again we talked about the best process for me to deal with the nervous energy that every player gets before an innings.

Overall, we quickly got to the stage where, when I did actually walk out to bat in the first innings of that Guyana Test, I found that I was far more in control of my thoughts and I felt far more comfortable knowing that I had done all the preparation that I could. The relationship with Steve was a working partnership, and I was the one who had to be happy with whatever structure we put in place, but he was excellent at providing guidance and being someone you could bounce ideas off. And that's what I needed at that time.

When I was 21, and starting out with England, I just did what came naturally; I knew nothing else. But in 1992, against Pakistan at Edgbaston, I wasn't at the races mentally; it was similar against the West Indies in 1995, and again in South Africa at the end of that year. I had been through so many downs at international level that, by early 1998, my self-belief had really suffered.

I also found talking to myself, to keep things at the front of my mind, helped a lot. Robin Smith used to do that, too. And so I would actually say to myself things like: 'If you're off line, I'm going to punish you.' Cricketers should work on their mental approach in the same way as they work to perfect their cover drive. When I went to Perth in the winter of 1996–97 to play club cricket and to coach, I discovered that Western Australia colts players as young as 14 and 15 had already been drip-fed drills to improve their mental preparation.

Steve Bull's input was great for me, and I wish it had been available earlier. He talked sense, but he didn't push things. He gave the players he worked with an ownership of the process, and in that Guyana Test I immediately felt much more confident when, at 65 for 4, I walked out to bat. Soon we were 75 for 6, and right up against it after the West Indies had won a crucial toss on a pitch that quickly began to crumble and scored 352.

Again, early in my innings I had a stroke of good fortune when I nicked a sweep to the keeper off a Jimmy Adams no ball just before the close of the second day. Having survived, though, I was joined in a useful stand by Robert Croft and hit out when last man Phil Tufnell came in to join me. When Tuffers was out for two, I had reached 64 not out and we had at least avoided the follow-on.

We were never going to hold out for a draw, as the pitch got worse, but I felt that I had made an impression on my comeback, and in our second innings I again top-scored, this time with 34, after coming in at 28 for 4. Scoring those runs also backed up and made even more valid the work I had done with Steve before the match. From a personal point of view, my belief in my own ability and my belief that I could succeed at this level was very much reinforced. I felt relaxed in this feeling, too, and you always play better when you are relaxed.

Little did I know, however, as we moved on to Barbados for the fifth Test, following a three-day fixture against the island's team, that I was about to achieve my lifelong ambition. Deep into my seventh year as an international batsman, and after so many knock-backs and knock-downs, I scored my maiden Test century. In my previous twenty-one Test appearances, and thirty-seven innings, I had passed fifty only three times.

I have always enjoyed going to Barbados, and I have many friends there. During that Test there were around 8,000 England supporters packing the stands alongside the locals at the Kensington Oval, so the atmosphere was superb.

The pitch was good, but a little damp at the start, which is why Brian Lara, the West Indies captain, quite rightly chose to put us in to bat. I had done the same pre-match preparation, both physical and mental, as in Guyana, but I didn't expect to be in quite as soon as I was, before lunch on the first morning with the total at 53 for 4.

What is more, Graham Thorpe suffered a back spasm when he had made only five and after lunch Jack Russell came out as my new fifth-wicket partner while Graham stayed in the dressing-room for treatment. Jack, though, took on his Gloucestershire teammate and friend Courtney Walsh, who for some reason decided to keep feeding Jack's pull and cut with some short balls, and our innings began to gain a bit of momentum.

When Jack was out for 32, to leave us 131 for 5, Thorpey was able to continue and it was a fillip to me to see him emerge from the pavilion. Conditions had by now eased considerably and, gradually, Graham and I began to get on top of the bowling in hot sunshine.

We added 205, and it was fantastic that Graham should be batting with me when I brought up my hundred.

Before that, though, I had to endure a night on 80 not out after we had reached the close of the first day's play at 229 for 5. I went out to dinner that evening with my wife Van, who had come out to Barbados, and there were a lot of England supporters at the restaurant who wished me well. Of course, I was well aware of what a huge opportunity I had to fulfil my ambition of a Test hundred, and Van and I had a bit of a discussion about whether she should come to the ground the next morning or not. Only once before had she come along to a game when I was on the verge of a century and on that occasion I had been out for 97 when playing in a match for Middlesex. So, this time, we decided that she should stay away. I didn't get a lot of sleep that night – whenever I am not out, no matter what match I am involved in, I find that my mind is ticking over about my innings.

The following morning I discovered that my new mental preparation before going out to bat was becoming more natural, even in that situation, and when I got to three figures the emotion that was released was the best feeling. I had finally got there and the noise from the crowd when the ball hit the boundary rope, to bring up my hundred, was staggering. I could hardly hear myself think.

Brian Lara was the nearest fielder to me as the ball went over the boundary and he came over to shake my hand and congratulate me, which was a very nice gesture and a great memory for me. I also kept looking up at the scoreboard to make sure there really was a three-figure total next to my name. I suppose I had to keep looking at it to believe it.

Scoring that first Test century was so satisfying for many reasons. The match situation demanded an innings of substance from me, for a start, and I had delivered. For too long I had watched the likes of Atherton and Smith get big runs when they were needed and, at last, I had also made a hundred with the pressure really on. I was determined to keep going, too, once I had celebrated the three figures, and after lunch on that second day I began to go for my strokes, as I reached 154. It is amazing how much easier batting seems to become once you have a century against your name.

I had a lot of messages – around 80 or 90, I remember – when I got back to the team hotel that evening. My parents, who were on holiday in Antigua and had been listening on the radio, sent a message of congratulations. Even now I get people coming up to me to say that they were in Barbados watching that Test and how glad they were for me that day. It is a special memory.

The shame of the match, however, was that prolonged light drizzle on the last day (I have never seen a day like that in Barbados before or since) meant only 18.3 overs of cricket and that spoiled what was going to be a fantastic finish. West Indies were 71 for no wicket overnight, needing 375 in total for victory after our second innings declaration. But there was time for them to reach only 112 for 2. With the pitch beginning to turn, Phil Tufnell would have been in with a real chance of spinning us to victory.

That, too, would have meant the series being levelled at 2–2 going into a decider in the final Test in Antigua, but, still at 2–1 down, it took a lot of wind out of our sails. As it was, we performed poorly there and I got a second innings duck as we collapsed to defeat when a draw looked certain. Atherton resigned from the England captaincy in the dressing-room after the game, and there were some emotional scenes. I was particularly surprised by how tearful both Nasser Hussain and Angus Fraser were, being normally such hard-nosed characters, but Athers had put a huge amount into his four years in charge and it had clearly taken an awful lot out of him.

I also played in three of the five one-day internationals that ended our Caribbean campaign, though I was not included in the one-dayers that began the following summer's itinerary against South Africa. But I knew that I was going to be selected for the Tests, as Alec Stewart, named as Test captain in succession to Athers (with Adam Hollioake continuing to do the one-day international job), made it clear to me that I figured in his plans.

That summer was memorable for the way that we battled long and hard to beat South Africa 2–1, the first win in a five-match Test series for England for 12 years. They were a good, strong side with their usual mix of deep batting and a formidable pace attack. England were being written off for most of the summer, in fact, so it was especially pleasing to show the critics that we were made of sterner stuff than was popularly believed.

I did not score a huge number of runs in the series, although I had to battle hard for 49 in the drawn first Test at Edgbaston and made 67 not out in the first innings of our win at Trent Bridge. There were a number of 20s and 30s, too, but overall I felt part of the set-up. I threw my wicket away for 12 in the second innings of the opening Test, too, trying to answer Stewie's call for quick runs. Then the final day was washed out, anyway, but playing for the team is what you have to do when you are asked.

In the first innings of the second Test at Lord's, my England troubles at my home ground continued when Darrell Hair, the umpire, gave me out on 12 when a ball from Allan Donald brushed my elbow on its way through to Mark Boucher, the wicketkeeper. As I walked past him, on my way to the pavilion, I said, 'You are messing with my career, Darrell,' which was meant only as a sort of ironic aside – and something I'm not even sure Darrell heard. But the Sky cameras picked up on it, as they had a close-up of my face, and then they kept on replaying it and it became a major issue.

At the end of the day, I had to go to see the match referee and was found guilty of showing dissent and fined £850. I was also given a suspended one-match ban. I felt quite aggrieved at the way the incident was blown up out of all proportion by the television camera's intrusion. Then, in the second innings, I received what was perhaps the best ball I ever faced in Test cricket – a reverse away-swinging yorker from Lance Klusener – which cleaned me up for nought. No, it was never going to happen for me at Lord's, much as I wanted it to.

The draw in the third Test at Old Trafford was a triumph for Stewie, who had scored a brilliant hundred to lead a gutsy rearguard action, and the win in Nottingham was followed by a pulsating victory in the final match at Headingley, where 10,000 supporters turned up for what transpired to be half an hour's play on the last morning. I did a lot of fielding at short leg in that last game, a job I never enjoyed, but I must say it was a pleasure to be that close in as the South Africans folded to 12 for 4 and then 27 for 5 before Jonty Rhodes and Brian McMillan forged a fightback that, in the end, took South Africa to within 24 runs of their 219 target.

Mention of Rhodes reminds me of perhaps one of the silliest comments I have made to an opposing player during my career and the quite interesting follow-up. Early in his brilliant counter-attacking innings of 85, I was getting quite excited at short leg and, as he was settling over his bat, I shouted out, 'Come on, lads, we all know what happened to the Christians – they got eaten by lions!' This was a terrible attempt at humour, based on the fact that Rhodes was one of those South Africans who seemed to wear their faith on their sleeves and we England players all had lion motifs on our shirts and caps. It was a crass thing to say, and it was very unpleasant. I was just getting carried away in the excitement of the situation. It wasn't meant to be deep and meaningful.

But Rhodes pulled away from his stance and, bat over one shoulder, he just glared at me. And then, at the end of the match the following day, as we were all shaking hands with the South Africans, I was pulled to one side by Hansie Cronje, the captain, who looked so upset at his side's defeat it was as if the world had ended. 'Ramps,' he said, 'during this series have we ever referred to your racial background? No, so we don't think you should talk about our religion. We think you were out of order with what you said.' I simply replied that I was sorry, that no offence had been meant, but clearly it had not gone down well either with Rhodes or the other strong Christians in the South African team.

I had averaged 31 in the series, which was not as much as I would have liked, but I was certainly enjoying the team's success and – at last – feeling like I was having a decent run in the side. I also scored 53 and 42 in the one-off Test match against Sri Lanka at the Oval which ended the international summer, batting for four hours in the second innings in a despairing effort to ward off Muttiah Muralitharan, who took 9 for 65 on a dustbowl of a pitch (to go with his first innings 7 for 155) as we were beaten in a remarkable match. We had scored 445 first up, but the Sri Lankans then replied with 591 and we were bowled out for 181 second time around to leave them with just a few runs to knock off.

That was deflating, especially after the elation of the South Africa series, but we were still in good spirits as a team when we set off for Australia a couple of months later for the 1998–99 Ashes series. From a personal point of view, too, it was another ambition realised: Australia was somewhere I'd always wanted to tour and I'd had a little bit of success against the Australians already in my one-off Ashes appearances in 1993, 1994–95 and 1997. Also, I loved conditions there, as pitches were usually good and you could trust your technique.

England should have drawn that Ashes series 2–2 – and would have done, in my opinion, if Michael Slater had been given out in Australia's second innings in the final Test at Sydney, as he should have been, when we ran him out for 35 from a direct hit from the deep by Dean Headley. Television replays could not be used to confirm the decision because the crease line was hidden by players – in those days there were fewer cameras available. Anyway Slater, who was two-thirds of the way back to the pavilion as he knew he had not made his ground, was given the huge benefit of the doubt and went on to score 123 out of an Australian total of just 184.

In the end, on a turning pitch, we were 98 runs short, which meant that the extra 88 runs that Slater scored after being given his life were the difference. To lose 3–1 in that manner, especially after the way we had come back with a brilliant victory in the fourth Test at Melbourne, was heartbreaking.

It was very exciting, however, to play throughout a five-Test Ashes series and I really enjoyed the whole tour. My form was very good, too; I topped the England batting averages with 379 runs at 47.37 despite a top score of only 69 not out. But I passed fifty on four occasions and batted consistently. My only regret was that, in two innings in particular, I didn't go on and get the hundred that I felt was achievable. Certainly, if I had made it to three figures in at least one innings during that series, it would have been another massive boost to my Test career.

Overall, on that tour, I scored more first-class runs than any of England's other batsmen – 845 at an average of 52.81 – and by the end of the Test series I had moved up from number six to number four in the order. I felt established in the team, felt that I'd made a bit of a journey and that I now belonged at Test level.

The amazing last session at Melbourne will be an abiding memory of that tour and not just because it was – ridiculously – four hours and three minutes long by the time we clinched our 12-run victory by bowling out Australia for 162. Watching videos of that last day now, I still get embarrassed by how pumped up and fired up I was in the field, especially after I took the best catch of my career to get rid of Justin Langer for 30 and began Australia's demise from 103 for 2.

I remember how agitated and frustrated I felt in the field when Australia initially looked as if they were making serene progress towards their victory target of 175. I felt powerless, to be honest, and I simply decided to channel all that emotion into my fielding. When I took the Langer catch at square leg, my reaction was just a release of that frustration and anger. But, then, as Headley bowled brilliantly to take 6 for 60 and Darren Gough claimed three key wickets at the other end, it was fantastic to see us turn the screw on Australia and them begin to capitulate under the pressure. That win gave us a lot of pride. I just wish the Slater run-out decision had gone our way in Sydney.

Despite the progress I had made in the Tests, I still wasn't kept on for the one-day international leg of the tour and, with seven other players, flew home after the Sydney Test.

Back in England in early 1999, I then unsurprisingly did not get selected for the World Cup squad, and so it was not until 1 July that my England career resumed, at Edgbaston, in the first of four Tests against New Zealand. I was out for a duck in my only innings, although at least England won the match by seven wickets in what was Nasser Hussain's debut as captain.

During the previous few weeks I had also had the honour of effectively being interviewed for the job of England captain. The decision had been taken, following England's terrible showing at the World Cup, that Stewart should be stripped of the captaincy and David Lloyd sacked as coach. That was despite Stewie having done a very good job in his only two Test series as captain, at home to South Africa and away in Australia.

But the desire for change was all-consuming and Alec paid the price. And so it was that both Nasser, who was Stewie's vice-captain, and I were summoned to Lord's for what was actually billed as an informal chat with the England and Wales Cricket Board (ECB). Well, my 'interview' lasted five minutes, while Nasser was in there for an hour. We were both asked for our opinions about the England set-up and what we would do if we were in charge, and obviously Nasser had a lot of views and no hesitation about putting them across. As for me, I didn't really have a lot to say. I actually didn't think I should have been there. I didn't feel in any position to have much to say – especially having not played in the one-day team since the end of the West Indies tour more than a year earlier.

As for the resumption of my England career, I very quickly got the impression that anything could be around the corner. I felt uneasy about things, in a way I hadn't over the previous year or so since breaking back into the Test team in the Caribbean; my duck in the opening Test against the Kiwis did little to quell that unease.

Scores of 4 and 24 at Lord's, in the second Test, continued my unhappy record there. In our second innings, I chased a wide one from Nathan Astle, a part-time seamer, and edged to the keeper.

I also had a half-jokey spat with Stewie in the dressing-room about whether the volume on the television should have been up or down (I wanted it on mute). The next day there was a mention of it in the media, which really concerned me because it had been nothing, and especially because only those present in the dressing-room at the time could have known about it.

Anyway, we arrived for the third Test at Old Trafford and I was astonished when David Graveney – now in temporary charge of the team until Duncan Fletcher took over officially from Lloyd at the end of the summer – said he wanted a chat with me and mentioned this incident, as if it was a reason (or part of the reason) for what he really had to say to me: I was being left out of the final XI.

I was stunned. Not only was Hussain missing this match with a broken finger – Mark Butcher was the man who had been asked to stand in temporarily – but I had been England's most successful batsman in two of the previous three Test series and I had scored more than 1,000 runs at an average in excess of 40 during that time. Now, after just two poor Tests, I was out.

Or was I? As it turned out, England decided to go with six specialist batsmen after all and I won a late reprieve. You can imagine how I felt when, with us at 83 for 4 and with both Chris Cairns and Dion Nash bowling well in helpful conditions, I walked out to join Graham Thorpe. Soon it was 104 for 5, when Graham fell for 27, and as wickets continued to tumble around me I was left trying to protect the tail, as well as my own place in the team, while also gathering as many runs as I could before we were bowled out.

In the end, I managed to finish 69 not out, with England dismissed for 199. On Sky's coverage, Bob Willis apparently said with some disappointment that I could not now be dropped. New Zealand then ran up almost 500 in reply and only rain saved us from defeat. I was next man in when the match was abandoned as a draw.

Retained at number six for the final Test at the Oval, I found myself in a similar position in our first innings. I came in at 87 for 4 and soon saw the side slump further to 94 for 6. The innings was falling apart and I again had only the tail for company. Andrew Caddick did hang around for 15 while we added 47, but Alan Mullally then came and went fairly quickly and I was left with only Phil Tufnell and Ed Giddins as partners. Without wishing to decry their batsmanship abilities, all three of Mullally, Tufnell and Giddins usually only bat at number eleven because cricket teams don't stretch to twelve.

I did not have to hit out. I could have pushed a couple of ones and come in unbeaten again. But, on 30, I decided I had to do what was best for the team and had a slog at Cairns and was caught. Then, as a low-scoring match went from bad to worse for England, I was out first ball in our second innings to a horrible shot. I was expecting an inswinger from Nash but ended up fencing at a widish ball that

I should have left alone and was caught behind. I knew there would be some fallout from this defeat, which gave New Zealand the series 2–1 and pushed England down to the bottom of the new Test Championship table; I also believed that my name would figure in the fallout. And I was right.

I must say I felt pretty unloved, and very frustrated. My 18-month run in the team had largely gone well, and in recent years the way England have stuck by the likes of Ian Bell, Paul Collingwood and Andrew Strauss when they have endured lengthy lean spells with the bat has made me wonder how much more relaxed and secure I would have felt during my time in the England set-up had the same kind of support been offered to me. It might well have made a huge difference to my international career.

I didn't have the whole of the 1999–2000 winter at home, though. Just before Christmas I received a call, asking me if I would fly out to join the England squad in South Africa, as cover for Michael Vaughan, who had made his Test debut earlier in the tour but was suffering from a badly bruised finger. It was made clear that, almost certainly, I would get no cricket and would only come into contention if there were other injuries. I definitely would not play in front of anyone originally selected.

The call came at a very sensitive time. It was only a few days before Christmas; I had a young family and was looking forward to being around them. But I decided to sacrifice both Christmas and New Year at home and I accepted the standby duty. As expected, I did not get to play, but I think my willingness to go out there did me no harm. I also think that Duncan Fletcher, on his first tour in charge, was impressed by my attitude in practice and by the way I batted in the nets.

One thing stands out from my short time in South Africa and it concerns the developing captaincy style of Nasser Hussain, also on his first tour in command. In South Africa, I think Nasser sometimes went a bit too far in trying to set out his stall, although it must be remembered that he came into the captaincy job at a very difficult time and provided firm direction, and a firm hand on the tiller, just when England needed it most.

Alex Tudor, who was and is a good friend, was still not at the team bus one morning with the minutes ticking by until 9.15 a.m., when we had been told we were leaving for the ground. Because every other player was on board and Nasser wanted to go, he told the bus driver not to wait the couple of extra minutes until 9.15 but to drive off. And so Tudes, even though he would have technically been there in time, was left behind. When Alex later turned up at the ground, Nasser had a bit of a go at him, expressing his displeasure in front of the rest of the players.

Later, all the players were talking about it. I remember Vaughan saying to one or two of us that he felt Nasser was completely out of order and that it was not the way to speak to or treat your players as captain. That is interesting to recall now that we know that Vaughan, then very inexperienced at international level, went on to become such a great England captain himself. Again, what I would say is that this was only one relatively small incident on a long tour, but it shows just how passionate Nasser was about leading England and getting it right. The job consumed him. In my own captaincy experience, at both Middlesex and Surrey, I also demanded high standards from all the players and wanted them to buy into that.

Knowing Nasser, as I do, from when we were both very young, I always find it amusing to imagine how Nasser the player would have coped under Nasser the captain! I remember, in the West Indies in 1994, that he was not exactly the life and soul of the party on a trip where he was out of the team and playing little cricket. In Australia in 1998–99, when he was left out of the one-day side, he didn't speak to Graham Gooch, who was then England manager, for a couple of days! Actually, Nasser and I are very alike in that we both didn't like being out of the team, simply because of our huge desire to do as well as we can.

But in Nasser's world, as captain, he wanted everyone to conform and muck in, and if he had something to say he would say it; he was very clear about how he wanted his players to go about playing for England and he certainly got that message across. It was also definitely the message England players needed to hear in those pre-central contract times, when we were a bunch of county cricketers

The young footballer, winning a cup with Belmont United Under-12s, my local club in Harrow (courtesy of the author)

Batting for Bessborough Cricket Club's Under-11 side, aged ten. I don't know what has happened to my right pad, but I am proudly wearing my Tony Greig-style batting gloves and wielding my Stuart Surridge Jumbo bat à la Viv Richards (courtesy of the author)

Batting for Middlesex at the age of 17
(© Getty Images)

The Middlesex squad in 1987. I am in the back row, on the far right. Mike Gatting and John Emburey sit in the middle of the front row, either side of the 1986 Benson & Hedges Cup, while Phil Tufnell is third from the left in the middle row. Angus Fraser is the tall young lad in the middle of the picture, and Simon Hughes is in the back row, far left (© Getty Images)

With Mike Gatting, the Middlesex captain, after our 1988 NatWest
Trophy final win against Worcestershire at Lord's

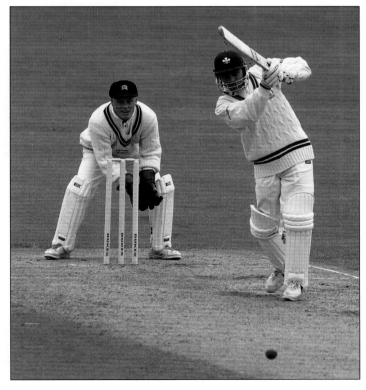

Down the pitch
to drive for Surrey,
against Middlesex
(© Getty Images)

England win the series against South Africa in 1998, and the Headingley crowd floods the outfield (© Getty Images)

South Africa always have some genuinely fast bowlers, and our 1998 series against them was no exception (© Getty Images)

One of my favourite cricket photographs: leaping for joy after completing my maiden Test hundred, for England, against the West Indies in Barbados in March 1998 (© Getty Images)

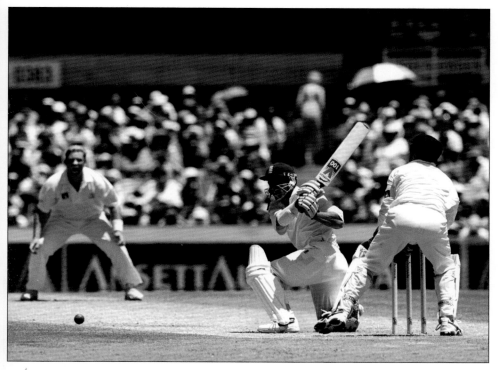

Batting against Shane Warne, on the Ashes tour of 1998–99 (© Getty Images)

Celebrating an Ashes hundred, against Australia at the Oval in 2001 (© Getty Images)

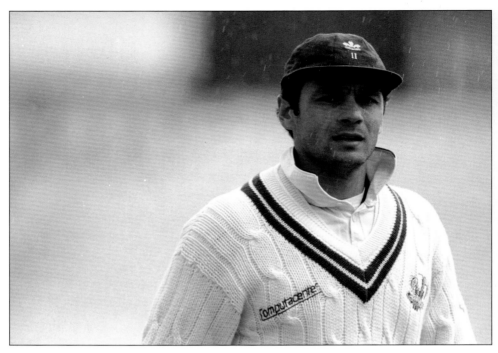

Wearing the Surrey cap with pride (© Getty Images)

Receiving the 2006 PCA Player of the Year Award from Andrew Flintoff
(© Getty Images)

Swimming with my two
daughters, Cara (left) and
Anya (courtesy of the author)

Anya (left) and Cara
(courtesy of the author)

With my wife, Vandana
(courtesy of the author)

In action with my partner
Karen Hardy during our
Strictly Come Dancing adventure
(© BBC Photo Library)

Lifting the *Strictly Come Dancing*
trophy with Karen, while Bruce
Forsyth looks on
(© BBC Photo Library)

coming together to play for our country. And, to be fair to him, he was so focused as captain – so determined to succeed – that this direct approach was really just a by-product of the way he did the job. In many ways, he was often quite close to suffering from stress because of the intensity with which he poured himself into being England captain.

Meanwhile, back in England, I was contacted by Fletcher in April to be told that he wanted to recall me to the squad and that I was being put on one of the new ECB central contracts that were being introduced that summer. He also wanted me to be Mike Atherton's new Test opening partner in a shake-up of the side following the experiments of selecting Darren Maddy, Chris Adams and Gavin Hamilton on that tour and the fall from grace of Mark Butcher, who had opened in South Africa.

To say I was surprised at this turn of events is a bit of an understatement, but at the same time I was pleased to learn I was literally at the forefront of Duncan's thinking and – when it comes to England – I have always been willing to put the cause of the team before any personal preference. Athers said he was not perturbed either about me becoming his 12th different opening partner at Test level or that our styles of batting were too similar. I was simply to bat normally, and if we got England past 40 or 50 without loss then that was great.

There were also two Test matches in early summer against Zimbabwe, at Lord's and Trent Bridge, before the main business of a five-Test series against the West Indies, so I would have – in theory – four innings against moderate opposition to get my feet under the table as England's new opener. This was the least that I needed before coming up against Ambrose and Walsh yet again: I had not opened the batting since my schooldays, apart from once for Middlesex as a stand-in.

England won the opening Test by an innings, but I had reached only 15 when Heath Streak had me lbw. Nine Test innings on my home ground had now brought me only 79 runs, yet worse was to come on that score. However, before that, I did get to 56 in the first innings of the second Test in Nottingham, in a partnership of 121 with Atherton, and felt sure I was in for a hundred only for Neil Johnson, the fast-medium bowler, to get me caught with a ball that popped up alarmingly from nowhere. As I've said before, I'm a big believer in fate and this delivery flew at me from just short of a length when nothing in the pitch had suggested it was possible. Nor was Johnson particularly quick.

In our second innings, opening now with Nick Knight because Atherton was suffering from stomach trouble, I was out for four to a loose drive. As a result, I approached the first Test with the West Indies hardly chock-full of confidence, but the England management were still saying they saw me as a longer-term option at the top of the order.

When the first Test at Edgbaston began, the pitch was damp, and predictably we had been put in to bat. It was also overcast, and I would defy any opener in the history of Test cricket to have found life anything other than comfortable against Curtly Ambrose and Courtney Walsh in those sort of pitch and atmospheric conditions. As it was, Athers played out four maidens from Ambrose, who was like a bowling machine in his ability to hit exactly the right line and length every ball, and I was to try to keep out Walsh at the other end.

We fought our way to 26, which was a minor triumph in its way, before Walsh finally got me out for 18. I had always found him a difficult proposition, with his height and his ability to angle the ball in and straighten it off the pitch. Because of that you always found it awkward to know what deliveries you could leave alone; Walsh bowled a deceptive length and could get you lbw with the one that kept coming in or caught off the edge to one that was a bit wider than you thought. For myself, I prefer bowlers who bowl from closer to the stumps because your eyes are then automatically in line with the ball and your set-up is normal. But Walsh could also seem to find a bit of extra pace when he wanted to, and he could rough you up.

I was seemingly destined to be stuck for an answer to the problems Walsh – and Ambrose, for that matter – posed. In England's second innings, as we were bowled out for 125 to lose by an innings and plenty, I was lbw to Walsh for nought. Going to Lord's for the second Test was not really what I wanted in such circumstances.

Being out for nought and two there was the very worst experience of my Test career. It was a magnificent, no-holds-barred match, with a truly thrilling finish – and also one of the most important Test victories in England's recent history – but at the end of it all I could hardly bring myself to join in the celebrations. I now had only 81 runs to my name in 11 Test innings for England at the home of cricket – the ground on which I had grown up as a county cricketer – and it felt as if I couldn't break what seemed to be a pre-determined fate.

In the first innings, I had gone out to bat determined to try to assert myself. My mindset had been: if I get out early, then at least I do so while trying to take the attack to the two great West Indians. My disappointment at being dismissed, caught in the slips off Ambrose, was such that I simply couldn't drag myself off the pitch. I knew I was out, but I just stood there because I didn't want to go. In the end, the umpire had to put his finger up, which was ridiculous, because it was obvious I was out. But I wasn't trying it on or anything; I just couldn't believe reality.

Then, at the end of the second day, just after Caddick, Gough and Cork had bowled fantastically well to bowl out the West Indies for just 54, leaving us 188 to win, I found myself going out to open again with the light very poor. Thankfully, it was not long before we were offered the light, and went off, but any sense of having been reprieved and looking forward to what the next day would bring soon disappeared when, in the sixth over of our innings, I was bowled off an inside edge by Walsh.

I knew then and there that my latest Test reincarnation was over. I had tried to do a job opening the innings, but now I was back in county cricket with no idea when the call would come again, or even if it would come again. Had Duncan Fletcher, or anyone in the England hierarchy, spoken to me during those two Tests about the specific requirements of opening? No, I can't recall that they did. And why was Nick Knight, a specialist opening batsman, picked in the lower middle-order for that match at Lord's while I, a career middle-order man, continued to open? I don't know the answer to that one.

It was especially difficult for me to think positive thoughts about Lord's, and any cricketer will tell you that there are certain grounds where you always seem to find it hard to get going. Why it had to be Lord's for me in Test cricket, above all others, when I had played so much other first-class cricket there, is simply another mystery. Perhaps it was just fate, or the will of the cricketing gods!

As it turned out, a mountain of county runs – and my move to Surrey – reinvigorated me and got me back into the selectors' thoughts by the beginning of the next season in 2001. Had I not suffered a hamstring strain, I would have made yet another comeback (the seventh and last of my England Test career) in the opening match of that summer's Ashes series, at Edgbaston.

The result of that injury ironically meant that my recall came at Lord's, where – despite falling to a magnificent ball from Brett Lee for 14 in our first innings – I managed 40, my highest score in 13 Test innings at Lord's, second time around and joined Mark Butcher in an excellent stand of 96. This made sure I held my place for the third Test and, subsequently, for the rest of the series. Only Butcher finished ahead of me in the series averages, too, which was mainly due to his brilliant match-winning 173 not out at Headingley in the fourth Test, after Adam Gilchrist had declared in a bid to keep Australia on course for a 5–0 whitewash.

Scoring my second Test hundred, against Australia at the Oval in the final Test of the series, is another of the real highlights of my life. That 133, made after coming in at 104 for 3 and ending when I was eventually ninth out on the fourth morning of the match at 424 for 9, gave me a huge amount of pleasure. The Australian attack of Glenn McGrath, Jason Gillespie, Shane Warne and Brett Lee is one of the best quartets ever to play together at Test level. Warne finished with 7 for 165 in that England innings. He didn't get me, though – I was caught behind off McGrath – and the next best England score was Marcus Trescothick's 55.

Looking back, it is a source of great pride that I managed to take that Australian bowling line-up for a hundred and, again, I believe that it goes a long way to answering the criticism of my suitability for Test cricket. There are plenty of highly rated batsmen from around the world who never scored a century against McGrath, Warne and company.

Later in 2001, in India, I felt relaxed in an England shirt and had several opportunities in the three-Test series there in December to add another very big score to my Ashes hundred. Sadly, I did not get past 58, in my only innings of the final Test at Bangalore, and in the second Test in particular, in Ahmedabad, I missed out on a golden chance to get to three figures again. I was on 37, and batting very comfortably on a flat pitch, when Sachin Tendulkar suddenly produced a googly out of nowhere, which I didn't read, and bowled me.

I had been picking Anil Kumble's googly with no trouble, after spotting that he slightly changed his grip when he was going to bowl it, and had hacked him over mid-wicket for six on one occasion when he bowled it. This was with a 3 lb bat that I had bought in a sports shop in Ahmedabad, by the way, in order to counteract the incredibly slow, low pitches we were encountering.

I was so disappointed to get out to Tendulkar, even though it was a very decent ball, because I had done all the hard work and I was in. As it was, Craig White went on to get a fine hundred in conditions that remained good for batting all match. Then, in Bangalore, I again fought hard to get past fifty, only to edge a straight ball to the keeper. I had shared a nice partnership with Michael Vaughan, who I realised then and there was a special talent, but once again I didn't cash in.

I'd had a reasonable tour overall, but those failures to convert good starts into at least one big innings would come back to haunt me in New Zealand, where we also played three Tests in March and early April. I never got going on that trip – probably because I had been one of a half-dozen or so players not required for either the six-match one-day international series back in India in January and early February or the five one-dayers that began the New Zealand trip immediately afterwards.

My tally of 77 runs in five Test innings against the Kiwis also became my last contribution as an England player, as I have never been selected since. I did not retire from international cricket, mind you, I was just jettisoned after that tour and not selected again. At 32, that was it.

It was a terribly anticlimactic way to go out and a lack of preparation for those three Test matches – plus those failures to get a big score in India – ultimately counted against me. I'm not one for having regrets, generally, but on that New Zealand tour I do think I should have prepared myself more thoroughly for the Tests, even accounting for the fact that the weather and the facilities were so poor.

Between 19 December, when I scored 58 in Bangalore, and the start of the first Test against the Kiwis in Christchurch, I'd only had three first-class innings – and two of them were on a shocking, green flier at Queenstown, where I might have scored 42 in the second innings against Otago, but which was completely useless as Test match preparation as it was simply a case of whacking a few as quickly as possible before you received an unplayable ball.

Then, in the second and final three-day warm-up fixture, against Canterbury, it rained for virtually all the first day and we ended up having just one innings – in which I scored 5. Going into the Christchurch Test, I didn't feel ready, but I had got to 31 when Asoka de Silva, the umpire, gave me out caught at the wicket off Nathan Astle's gentle medium pacers when I had not touched it.

I managed 24 in the only England innings in the second Test, at Wellington, and in the last match I was all over the place, scoring just 9 and 2, as we lost by 78 runs to be pegged back to 1–1 in the series. Perhaps I should have funded myself to go out to New Zealand earlier, to acclimatise and get some match practice – as Andrew Strauss did before the 2007–08 tour there, which completed his successful return to international cricket.

The seven weeks or so between the end of the India Test tour and my arrival in New Zealand did nothing for my game, or my chances. It was possibly my fault for not managing myself better, but also the England management's for not ensuring that we played on better pitches in the lead-up to the New Zealand Tests.

A lot was also made of the poor fitness levels of those of us who had been back in England in between the two Test series, as it was reported that we had been on special fitness programmes and had been carefully monitored. Well, I got precisely one call, from Graham Dilley, the assistant coach, asking me if there was anything I needed – to which I replied 'not really'. That was it in terms of monitoring. The forty-hour journey out to Dunedin did not help, either, with a seven-hour wait in Dubai.

I feel we were unfairly criticised as a group after the initial fitness tests. However, the bottom line was that I went into the series short of where I needed to be and paid the penalty. Lack of preparation for a Test series is still a relevant topic today, with teams often performing badly in early Tests due to a general shortage of proper practice time.

When we got back to England in April 2002, I found some good early season form with Surrey and was hoping I might keep my Test place. During our match with Lancashire, at the Oval in early May, I scored 119 not out to lead the team to a narrow win against an attack led by Andrew Flintoff and Glen Chapple. It was probably the best innings I've ever played for Surrey.

I was 71 not out overnight, at the end of the third day, and went into the pavilion after play to have a chat with Duncan Fletcher, who had been watching the cricket. He asked me how I felt I had done during the winter and I said I had to be honest and told him I should have done better in India with the starts I'd got, but that I had found it very tough in New Zealand because of the lack of match preparation.

I finished up by saying that if I'd had my time again, I would have gone to him for more help with my preparation. He didn't say a lot in reply, and that was it. A line was never officially put through my name, but my association with the England team ended the moment Duncan shook my hand and left.

CHAPTER 8

MIDDLESEX DIVORCE

'The harsh realities of modern county cricket finally caught up
with Middlesex after difficulties on and off the field in 2000.
It was a sorry enough time when the end of August brought
the unexpected departure of two icons, Mike Gatting and Ian
Gould. But the loss of Mark Ramprakash in the New Year, to
join traditional rivals Surrey, cut much deeper'

– Wisden Cricketers' Almanack, 2001

Finishing fourth in the County Championship in 1994, and
then second in 1995, would have represented two very fine
years for most counties. For Middlesex, however, so used to
regular success, with fourteen trophies in the previous two decades,
it was something of a disappointment.

One-day form was generally poor and at best only patchy, and by
the end of 1995 there was very much a sense that a great era was
coming to a close. Desmond Haynes played his last season for the
club in 1994 and although he did not score a mountain of runs that
summer his influence both on and off the field was still huge. His
was a very big hole to fill.

Dion Nash, the New Zealand all-rounder, was the new overseas
player in 1995 and, with 51 wickets and only 351 runs, he more
often than not flattered to deceive. By 1995, we had also lost Micky
Roseberry, who took up the captaincy of his native Durham, and
Neil Williams, who moved to Essex.

Richard Johnson was an extremely promising young seamer, with 36 Championship wickets in both seasons at a cost of 26 and 16 runs apiece, respectively, but he also struggled to stay fit. Angus Fraser and Phil Tufnell were both still international-class acts, while Mark Feltham and Paul Weekes chipped in with useful wickets and, especially in the case of the latter, a decent number of runs.

But it is pertinent that, even in his last two seasons, and in his early 40s, it was John Emburey who finished as the club's highest first-class wicket-taker. In 1994, he had 52 at 27, and in his final summer he bagged 74 victims at just under 22 runs each. During that 1995 runners-up year Emburey and Tufnell bowled more than 1,300 Championship overs between them and took 142 wickets.

Emburey was such a massive player for the Middlesex teams of the late 1970s, the 1980s and the early 1990s. He was ultra-consistent with the ball and could tie up an end even when not taking wickets. He made important runs in the lower middle-order and, as long-serving vice-captain, virtually took over the side in the field on occasions when Mike Gatting fancied a bit of a breather. He was almost like a joint-captain with Gatt by the end.

As a cricketer, and character, Embers was incredibly astute, shrewd and hard-nosed. He was also a great team man, and I think that his retirement from playing in 1995 really marked the end of Middlesex's great years. Gatting may have still been in charge when we rocked up for the 1996 and 1997 seasons, but Emburey's departure left the whole team, let alone his spin partner Tuffers, without a crucial steadying influence – in addition to his huge value as a front-line wicket-taker.

With Gatting averaging 60 and 54 in 1994 and 1995, with John Carr and Keith Brown always solid and occasionally spectacular, and with Jason Pooley doing much to offset the losses of Haynes and Roseberry by scoring almost 1,200 runs at just under 50 in 1995, we were seldom short of runs. My 1,261 at a shade under 55 in 1994, meanwhile, was only a warm-up for an incredible run of form in 1995 following the despair of my Test failures against the West Indies.

Scoring nine centuries in fourteen innings, I finished up with ten in all Championship matches and an aggregate of 2,147 at 93.34, including three double-hundreds: 214 against Surrey in late June, 205 against Sussex a month later and then 235 at Headingley against Yorkshire in late August. It was the form of my life; the only shame was that we couldn't catch Warwickshire, the eventual champions.

We slipped down to ninth in 1996, as the signs of decline increased, although my 1,406 Championship runs at 52 was a fair individual return. But John Carr's decision to retire early at the end of the season, to take up the post of cricket operations manager at the newly formed ECB, meant that during the following winter I was asked to become Gatt's vice-captain for 1997.

It took me by surprise, to be honest, and when Gatt decided at the end of May to stand down from a captaincy position he had held for fourteen years – after only four first-class matches of the season – I was appointed Middlesex captain. In many ways, it was a strange feeling, as Gatt was still intending to play on and, while he was in the team, I'd always assumed he would be the captain. Don't forget, I had known nothing else.

But, as well as feeling honoured and proud, it was also excellent timing for me because I had avoided all the pre-season hype that would have accompanied my elevation if Gatt had decided to give up the job a month or so earlier. I was able, in effect, to slip into the job with hardly any fuss; with a Championship fixture against Northamptonshire starting at Lord's only two days later, both myself and the team had to keep our eyes on the ball.

As it was, I couldn't have wished for a better start. I won the toss, in my first action as captain, decided to bat and both myself and Gatt scored hundreds, as we put on 187 for the third wicket. After topping 500, we then bowled Northants out twice to win by an innings and 57 runs.

One of the reasons why Gatt had decided to stand down was so that he could concentrate a little more on his new job as an England selector. But, as he continued to be a part of the Middlesex team, I found that I could also tap into his experience and leadership knowledge whenever I wanted. I must say that Gatt was absolutely superb during the rest of that season; he encouraged me to do the captaincy job my way, but he was also a big help and never interfered in what I was doing. He was not an overbearing presence at all, although of course I frequently consulted him on tactics, team selection and general issues.

The other bonus for me as captain that year was the fact that Jacques Kallis, then a fast-rising 21-year-old all-rounder who had already represented South Africa, was our overseas player. He was a very gifted cricketer, but what stunned us all was just how quick and effective he could be with the ball. There was one early match against Derbyshire, at Lord's, when Gatt said that Kallis bowled as fast as Wayne Daniel had done in his prime for Middlesex. He also swung it.

The South African authorities had allowed Kallis to play county cricket only on the understanding that he would not be overbowled, and I was quite happy with that because it made up my mind pretty easily that I had to use Jacques solely as a strike bowler and save up his ration of overs for the most important times. So, whenever the opposition's best batsman came in, I threw the ball to Kallis. I remember in my debut match as captain that he really worked over Rob Bailey, their captain and number three, in the Northants second innings before finally getting his man.

It was an interesting season, all round, because I had started it just thrilled to be the club's official vice-captain and soon I was leading the team in what turned out to be a fair run at the Championship. We finished fourth in the end and I enjoyed it immensely. With Kallis, we also had a perfectly balanced bowling attack in which Fraser, Johnson and the emerging Jamie Hewitt – who took 57 wickets – carried the rest of the fast-bowling workload and in which Tufnell was still a top-class spinner.

The summer ended with me scoring more than 1,200 runs at 54, with five centuries, and I also enjoyed making an England return in the Oval Ashes Test. All looked rosy, but little did I know as I left that winter for the West Indies tour that everyone at Middlesex was about to undergo a massive culture change that came with the appointment as first team coach of John Buchanan.

Don Bennett's 29 years as coach had come to an end in September 1997 and, as I had with Gatting's excellent but relatively low-key support, I appreciated Don's quiet presence in the background, and his technical know-how, as I went about my captaincy duties during that summer. There might have been a different captain in charge, but the Middlesex way of going about things hardly changed in those first four months of my leadership. I wanted Fraser, Brown and other senior players to feel that they could come to me with suggestions whenever they wanted, as we had all done with Gatt, as long as it was at the right time – which, again, was the environment in which we had all grown up.

What is more, I didn't want to change things. Why should I? We were a successful county, we had enjoyed success on a consistent basis over two decades and a lot of people had worked hard to put in place a structure, for practice and preparation and club ethics, that had stood the test of time. Indeed, I saw it as my job to simply build on that solid structure and not to tear it down. Wholesale changes were not needed; any changes needed to evolve.

When I sat down at the end of the 1997 season, I felt that there had also been a positive reaction to my captaincy, especially out there on the pitch. Everyone knew their role, and our progress towards fourth place in the Championship had been very encouraging. In the likes of Johnson, Hewitt, Owais Shah and David Nash, we also had a crop of young talent which, we felt, was continuing the tradition of the Middlesex system in producing its own cricketers of substance.

Paul Downton, who was then on the committee, had a chat with me when the summer was over to ask me specifically about the question of who should be appointed to succeed Don Bennett. The name of Buchanan came up, and I have to say here that at that time I was 100 per cent behind the club approaching him. It didn't bother me that he was Australian and therefore someone who would be very much an outsider coming into the tight-knit Middlesex world. In fact, I believed his experience of success with Queensland would be good for us and that he would bring some fresh new ideas to the table that could only be a further positive.

There is one other thing I think it is important to say here, too. During my early time as captain I remember Alan Moss, the Middlesex chairman, taking me out onto the balcony at Uxbridge and making the point very strongly that being captain was not just about the number of runs I could score for the team. He was very firm in his assertion that my responsibility now was to run the cricket affairs at the club and to provide a lead on all aspects of cricket performance.

However, it was a message that I hardly needed to hear. I was very strongly of the opinion myself that Middlesex cricket was a dynasty. It was a little bit like how Liverpool Football Club were perceived when I was growing up. Expertise and leadership were passed on down the generations: for Shankly, Paisley and Fagan at Anfield, you could read Brearley, Gatting and Emburey at Lord's. And, what is more, I am making no idle comparison. Middlesex's many successes now stretched over many years: I had come up through this system and I appreciated fully why things had worked out the way they had.

As the new captain, and especially as someone taking over after 14 years of the Gatting era, I was very keen indeed to make sure the new generation came through and won trophies and were as professional as those players who had been so successful in the 1970s, 1980s and early 1990s.

I'll give you one specific example. When I was capped by Middlesex in 1990, it was a very big deal for me. It had been a big target, and a big incentive to perform well, to improve and to be consistent. I knew it had to be earned, and when I got my cap – and my first team sweater – it was a huge moment in my career.

Ever since I had been aware of cricket – and the fact that I had grown up in a county with a big club, who won things – I had been aware that Middlesex were regarded as something of a machine. Becoming captain at twenty-seven was the end of my first ten years as a member of this machine, and now I wanted to be the one who led the club forward into their next ten years. I had enjoyed growing up in a dressing-room in which you looked around and said, 'Yes, I fancy us to win this game,' and I wanted that to continue. Other counties might have looked at us and said we had a bit of a swagger, but I reckoned we had earned that right because of the trophies in our cabinet.

When I returned from the West Indies tour, however, I soon found that things were very different. What didn't help, in retrospect, was that I was kept on in the Caribbean – quite unexpectedly – for the one-day international leg of the tour that followed the Test matches. Our last match, in Trinidad, was on 8 April and that meant I was back in England only for a week before we played our opening County Championship fixture, away against Kent at Canterbury.

In effect, I had barely a few days' rest, and during that short time at home I went up to Finchley, where the Middlesex first-team squad were training, to have my first meeting with Buchanan. But instead of a one-on-one chat, which is what I would have expected John to have wanted, I found myself called into a general squad meeting in which he began to outline the way in which he wanted us to do our jobs.

This included things like the dress code, that he was going to do away with the capping system in which only those who had been capped were entitled to wear first XI caps, shirts and sweaters. We had always dressed in jacket and ties at Lord's, but he said from now on it would be chinos and a Middlesex polo shirt. On the field, too, we would all wear the same gear. On top of this, Buchanan said that the first team would be required, on virtually all occasions, to travel and meet at 2 p.m. on the day before a game in order to practise and prepare at that venue.

Now, this last point was a big deal for players living in London, and particularly those with young children. We had always travelled late the evening before, so as to miss the London afternoon and rush-hour traffic, and checked into our hotel around 10 p.m. or so. Practice was then done on the morning of a match. This was the accepted Middlesex way, and it was done for a practical reason. Also, those players with young families did not want to leave for a game 24 hours before it started, as it would severely decrease the amount of precious spare time they had at home during what were always hectic summers.

The decision on the dress code was a big thing and I instinctively felt that it was wrong and inappropriate. In fact, overall, I was stunned at what had happened. Buchanan had not run through any of this with me, and even if I had agreed with it I would have wanted the chance to go through it with him before it was presented to the rest of the squad. I was shocked, to be honest, and immediately felt I had been undermined.

It was not until early August, when we had a big showdown meeting, that I knew that Alan Moss told John during the winter that he would be in total charge of first-team affairs. Presumably, Alan had changed his opinion since he had told me to the contrary the previous summer. I can understand that John felt he was in the right to make those initial decisions, but that was never explained to me, neither by him nor the club.

The captain–coach relationship is crucial at any level of cricket, but here was a situation I didn't agree with, developing right in front of my eyes on the very first day I had met Buchanan. It was undermining the traditional, and highly successful, role of the captain at Middlesex and he didn't even want to consult with me. From that moment on, there was little or no proper communication between us all summer.

I accept that I must also take some blame for that lack of communication, but, remember, I only played in nine of the seventeen Championship games that season due to England commitments, as it was also a vitally important time in my international career. I had just scored my maiden Test century in the West Indies and I was determined to hold on to my place in order to be selected for that coming winter's Ashes tour of Australia.

Buchanan, as an experienced coach, should have taken a lead in opening up the lines of communication with me, and although we must share the guilt for what was Middlesex's worst-ever Championship finish, 17th, I think it was his responsibility – as someone coming in from outside and taking over a team that had just finished fourth – to liaise more with his captain and vice-captain. Keith Brown, my deputy and a highly experienced and respected player, was even more old school than me in his thinking about how things should be done, including dress codes and caps, and he also had three young children, so you can imagine what he thought about giving up a lot of his days off to travel to away matches early.

As it happened, the second game of the season, against Lancashire at Old Trafford, brought an early example of just how contentious Buchanan's 'new culture' was in actuality. On the day between the end of our game at Canterbury and the start of the Lancashire fixture, we were told to be at our Manchester hotel in time for a team meeting and then dinner, starting at 7 p.m. That meant, of course, travelling up during the day and ahead of all the rush-hour traffic around Birmingham and on the M6 in particular.

We were all in the bar in good time when a phone call came through. It was Buchanan, who, with new overseas player Justin Langer also in his car, was stuck in horrendous traffic near Birmingham! Of course, our two Aussies had set off at 3 p.m., thinking it was a four-hour trip to Manchester. They had no idea of the realities of travel across England during the day. You can imagine the comments in the hotel bar when the news was relayed to the lads.

I can understand him wanting to come into the English game with fresh ideas, but this was just another small example of how theory and practice can be so different when you don't know the new environment well enough. Buchanan seemed to lack an understanding, and, from what I saw, he simply came to England with a rigid plan that he was determined to stick to regardless of what was in place at Middlesex and why.

Langer's recruitment, to replace Kallis, was very much down to me, and Justin proved to be a fine servant to Middlesex. I had played against him in the final Test of 1997, at the Oval, and we had got chatting in a corner of the Australian dressing-room when the England team went in to congratulate them on retaining the Ashes – although we had actually won that last match.

I had hardly spoken with him before, but I found that we quickly got on and seemed to have very similar philosophies about cricket and how to go about playing the game. At the end of this chat, I happened to mention that Middlesex were going to be on the lookout for a new overseas player and Langer said that he would be very interested. Indeed, before we left to go our separate ways, he handed me a piece of paper with the telephone number I had requested, plus the words 'keen for the opportunity'.

I was very pleased during that winter when the committee agreed to approach him. We needed a top-order batsman and, from what I knew of Justin and from the impression he had made on me during our Oval chat, I was confident that he would help to set exactly the right example to the younger players on the staff.

A couple of draws and wins against Somerset and Glamorgan, both at Lord's, meant that by the beginning of June we were looking quite comfortable, and both Langer and I had made a number of big scores. But while I was away at the opening Test against South Africa, we lost a nail-biting contest against Durham at Lord's by just one wicket and the season started to go downhill from then.

Moreover, I remember Buchanan taking Gatting out onto the balcony for a chat during one of the early season games and, in effect, according to Gatt, telling him that he should retire from the one-day team and then questioned his commitment to the county. Now, Gatt was continuing his role as an England selector, but he was still a decent player; in fact, he went on to top 1,000 runs at an average just above 43 in what was to be his final season – his 24th – for Middlesex. But it seems Buchanan was really saying that he thought he should go immediately and, as I understand it, he said it in very blunt terms.

Gatt, not surprisingly, was very upset by this. He was holding down the number three position when I was not playing, and number four otherwise, and he – and I – felt he still had an important role in the side, especially with youngsters Shah and Nash both in the middle-order.

The last thing I wanted, as I came and went during the South Africa Tests, was a disgruntled Mike Gatting. I just couldn't understand why Buchanan would not want to get Gatt onside and to help set the tone for what was wanted from the younger players. Instead, Buchanan apparently wanted him to retire there and then.

Jamie Hewitt was struggling to reproduce the form of the previous summer, and Tufnell was also struggling, and it was obvious that teams were blocking Fraser at one end in the knowledge that they could score the runs they wanted off other bowlers. Shah was having a few issues playing around his front pad and, understandably, was discovering that opposition bowlers had a few plans for him in what was essentially his second season.

But, as the season went on, it became more and more painfully obvious to me that Buchanan did not seem to be doing any actual coaching. He was good at laying out cones for pre-match drills, he was always in front of his laptop during matches, sitting there day after day inputting stuff into the computer, and he had made his decisions about how we should dress and what we should wear on the field. He even wanted to start a team song, but what he definitely did not seem to be doing as far as I was concerned was getting into the nets and giving technical advice to those who clearly needed it. At the very least, if he couldn't do it himself, he should have got someone else in to work with the batsmen, or the bowlers, but in my opinion he simply did not address those issues.

I should have got together with my senior players, Fraser and Brown and Langer especially, and thrashed things out with John, but I suppose not being around for half the time did not help me to see things as clearly as I needed to see them. I was also immersed in the South Africa Test series, and the team meetings we had when I was around did not achieve a great deal. Buchanan also continued to upset certain players: once, when Tuffers was bemoaning his lack of luck in a game at Leicestershire – about not being able to bowl as well as he wanted and what did we think – John turned to him and said, without a hint of humour, 'Well, why don't you retire then?' That was another senior player alienated!

One of Buchanan's 'initiatives' was to produce wagon wheels of every batsman's innings, from his own computer, so that we could analyse where we had scored our runs. When I was dismissed for a first ball duck in one match, I disappeared off into the showers to, literally, cool down and when I came out I found one of his wagon wheels on my seat. I couldn't believe it. There, on this piece of paper, was the following information: total runs 0, balls faced 1, total fours 0, total sixes 0, minutes in 2. At first I thought it was a wind-up, a joke. But no one was around, sniggering. And it soon became clear that Buchanan had printed out this paper in all seriousness. You couldn't make it up.

Buchanan was also beginning to make decisions about players' futures, as we got past the midway point of the season. I regret, looking back, that I agreed Jason Pooley should be released at the end of the summer. At the time I felt backed into a corner and perhaps my lack of a relationship with John meant that I agreed to it without really putting my case over properly.

Everything came to a head at the end of July, when we were crushed by 144 runs by Hampshire in a NatWest Trophy quarter-final at Lord's. Keith Brown had rung me up a couple of days before, as I was in Nottingham helping England to beat South Africa in the fourth Test, and said he thought that the players should be given a day off on 27 July, the day before the game, as they had just come through nine days of cricket out of the previous ten. I agreed to this request. The players would benefit more from a day's rest and we would meet early at the ground and practise hard before the game. I felt nothing would be achieved by getting all the players into Lord's for a net session on the 27th, which would also involve more than two hours of travelling for some of them, when they were all tired anyway.

I soon got to hear that Buchanan, predictably, wanted the players to go in, though he relented when both Brown and I said no. Unfortunately, after I had won the toss and decided to bowl first, we had a nightmare. Hampshire scored 295 for 5 from their 60 overs, and at 65 for 5 in reply we had nowhere to go. Langer and Keith Dutch then put on a bit of a partnership, but it was mere damage limitation. It was a huge disappointment.

On the following day I received a phone call to say that Buchanan had given a no-holds-barred interview, with David Lloyd of the London *Evening Standard*, in which he slagged off the Middlesex team and severely criticised the senior players for not doing what he wanted, for not embracing his ideas. He also mentioned the lack of practice on the day before the game, when he had wanted to bring the players in.

I was outraged by this because, in my eyes, the worst thing you can do is go to the press to air your grievances in public. If you have something to say, of that magnitude, then you say it in private. The press will obviously speculate – that is their job – but in my opinion John had stepped over the line.

Soon after this, we had a big showdown meeting. Paul Downton was there, as well as Buchanan and myself and several of the committee. It lasted for two hours, and at the end of it Downton asked both John and me whether we were prepared to start again and work together for the following season. I said I was, given certain understandings, but I assume that John was not prepared to resolve his differences with me because he resigned soon after.

I had grown up at Middlesex with the captain as the main man in charge and Don Bennett very much in the background, and although 1997 had shown me how effective that kind of relationship could be I am certainly not of the opinion that the coach has always to defer to the captain. Don had his influence, even if his profile was low, and if the captain was all-powerful then what would be the point of having a coach at all in a management capacity?

The Kevin Pietersen–Peter Moores affair of winter 2008 is a good example of how the captain and the coach must have a relationship based on mutual respect and the ability to compromise in the decision-making process, but to present a united front to the rest of the team, and to the outside world. Pietersen has huge strengths as a player and is very professional, but part of being captain is compromise and communication. To a lot of people in cricket, Moores may not be the best coach in the world, but he has worked hard to become a better coach and has achieved a lot. I think there was quite a bit of snobbery in the England camp because Moores had not played Test cricket, but you don't have to be a great player to be a great coach.

Also, Pietersen doesn't know everything there is to know about cricket. He is only in his late 20s. I simply don't agree with all those pundits who keep on about the captain being the person, in cricket, who has to run the whole show. It's an old-fashioned idea, in my opinion, because today's game, and the demands of it at international level, is so different to how it was in days gone by.

Ironically, when Buchanan did not return, the club turned to the man who had always been earmarked as the next coach, Mike

Gatting. He had retired as a player at the end of the 1998 summer and had been given the post of director of coaching. Should he have been given this job, even on a player–coach basis, in 1998? I'm not sure, ideally, that Gatt wanted to go straight from playing into coaching, or management, but with Bennett still in the background to offer technical advice when necessary I suppose the club could have saved Buchanan's salary and even spent it on acquiring a couple more players. In my view, we were a bit short on the playing side in 1998 – and in the next couple of seasons, too, for that matter.

Buchanan's short reign brought a lot of division and upset, and his outburst in the *Standard* in particular was damaging to the club and demoralising for the players, as well as undermining my authority as captain. The club also gave me the impression during that period that they accepted the criticism he had put into the public domain and believed everything that he was saying. Nowadays, too, people say Buchanan must be a great coach because of what Australia achieved when he was in charge of them. But the skill levels of the players he had at his command during those years were incredibly high; in the whole history of the game, indeed, it is arguable that they were the best team there has ever been.

Unfortunately, my lasting impression of him is of someone who seemed to work on the periphery of things without getting into the nitty-gritty of actual coaching – for example, going into the nets and working with players on technical aspects of their game. What we needed was a coach who could help players to bat better and bowl better. That's how you win cricket matches. Also, his apparent disregard for some of the traditions of Middlesex cricket – things that had helped us to be one of the most successful counties for two decades – was ill-judged. He even turned up for cricket committee meetings in the pavilion at Lord's in shorts, cricket socks and floppy hat. Everyone else sitting around the table was wearing jackets and ties – because that was how it was. John might as well have had corks hanging from his floppy. He looked like he had just strolled in from the outback; he didn't see why he should even think about making an effort to adapt and accept a Middlesex tradition.

It is interesting that when I met John again midway through the 2009 summer, during his spell here working with the England coaching set-up, he was very civil to me and I think he would also acknowledge now that he could have done things differently when he was at Middlesex.

I also remember, at the end of that embarrassing NatWest Trophy defeat, wandering down to the Tavern for a drink and having the club's cricket committee chairman, Andrew Miller, launch into me for, in his opinion, undermining everything the club was trying to achieve and not doing my job properly. For a start, this was not the sort of thing to be seen – and heard – in a public place, and also where was he getting this opinion from, as he was never in the dressing-room, and why would he not even listen to anything I wanted to say? I thought his behaviour that evening was extremely poor, for someone in his position. I lost respect for him, and it also went a long way towards contributing to the impression in my own mind about the way the club as a whole was heading.

Cracks were thus beginning to appear in my lifelong relationship with Middlesex, and sadly they were not to be healed – despite the appointment of Gatting for the following season. Again, it seems strange that Gatt himself had not taken a stronger lead against Buchanan within the club, especially after the early season conversation they had had out on the balcony. But Gatt had other things developing in his cricket life at that time. I think he just decided to take a back seat and concentrate on what was his last summer as a player.

Perhaps I should have spoken more clearly and passionately to the club's committee about what I thought was going wrong. But, at 28, and with my own England ambitions also uppermost in my mind, I was not educated enough in the workings of a county cricket club to play those sorts of political games – even if I had wanted to. I was a cricketer, not a politician, and what had happened reinforced my belief that it is vital for a county captain to have a good head coach, or team manager, or whatever you want to call it, working alongside him.

Anyway, Gatting's new appointment was not universally greeted with unrestrained joy by all the Middlesex players. A number of them expressed caution, wishing to reserve judgement, because although Gatt is larger than life, massively experienced and has a track record as a captain and player that is out of the top drawer, he was never going to be the sort of quiet, in-the-background, organising-and-planning coach that Don Bennett was.

If you want someone to lead you out of the trenches, then Gatt is your man. There is no doubt he can inspire and knows his stuff. But he still wanted to be in the thick of things as coach. The mickey-taking culture that had been central to his long years as captain did not go down so well with the younger players who were now coming through on to the staff and, unlike me, had never seen Gatt in his pomp as a great player. When Gatt talks cricket, I am listening, because I have seen at close hand just how good he was. But some of the young guys found it difficult to take, especially when he was sometimes a little bit late or disorganised in practices.

We had Langer back as overseas player in 1999, but the only other signings were Mike Roseberry, who returned after four seasons at Durham, and Richard Kettleborough, an opening batsman who had been on the fringes at Yorkshire. The only fresh blood on the bowling front was Simon Cook, a medium pacer who had come through from the junior ranks and made his first-class debut in our opening Championship fixture of the season. Keith Brown had also retired.

It deeply concerned me as we went into the 1999 season that despite such a poor year in 1998 the club had made no significant signings. The batting relied heavily on Langer and myself, and the bowling on Fraser and Tufnell. It was no surprise that, once again, we struggled and eventually finished 16th.

But what did anyone expect when we were often taking the field with as many as five or six uncapped players? Some of the youngsters, like Shah and Strauss and Nash and Ben Hutton, might have had talent, but they were still kids. It didn't help either that Richard Johnson was out of action for ten weeks of the season with injury, or that we got through seven different pairs of openers during the Championship campaign. On one occasion, some wag in the dressing-room said that I should get padded up and go and wait by the pavilion gate because I was bound to be in very soon after the start of our innings!

The summer of 1999 was also a difficult one for me, England-wise, but going away again regularly to play in the four-Test series against New Zealand did not do very much for my attempts to get on top of the problems we were having at Middlesex.

There were, in the end, many reasons why I decided to resign from the captaincy, but chief among them was the fact that I thought it unfair in the extreme for people at the club to still have high expectations of what we should be achieving. My view was that you only had to look down the teamsheet to realise that we were no longer a force to be reckoned with in the county game.

I'm sure that Gatt, too, would probably accept some of the responsibility for our performance as a team during that summer. He was a big personality who had been brought in to do a big job, but did he strike the right balance between trying to gee everyone up and providing a calming influence in the dressing-room? Some of the best coaches I have known are calm and considered personalities who keep their emotions under wraps, especially in the dressing-room environment.

Overall, I wasn't enjoying my cricket – and the difficult England series against the New Zealanders was horrible to play in, too – so by September I had made up my mind to give up the captaincy. After batting in quite a carefree manner at Lord's to score an unbeaten 209 in our second innings to help us secure a draw against Surrey, who had just been crowned champions, a watching Don Bennett came up to me and said quietly, 'You've made the decision, haven't you?' He just knew, from my body language, I suppose, that I had cast off the burden.

It was still a big decision for me to make because I loved being captain of Middlesex. My last game in charge was at Worcester, and I ended up 87 not out as we batted out for another draw in a rain-ruined contest. I had announced my resignation just before the start of the match, in which Ed Joyce made his county debut, and, looking back at the scorecard, I see that five of our top seven were uncapped players – as was Tim Bloomfield, one of the quick bowlers.

The County Championship was also split into two divisions after that 1999 season and so we were condemned to start the 2000 summer in the second tier. Immediately, that meant we were one of nine counties who could not aim to be county champions. It was not a nice feeling to be dubbed 'second class' in all but name.

Shah and Nash were capped early in 2000, both, I thought, prematurely, as they had hardly established themselves as permanent fixtures in the side. Nash had inherited the keeper's gloves from Keith Brown simply because there was no one else to do the job when Keith retired, and Shah had another poor season and was actually dropped from five of the last six matches. To me, the decisions to award them caps at that stage of their careers was a kick in the teeth for every capped Middlesex cricketer who had preceded them and another example of how standards had lowered since my early years at the club.

One of the other reasons I stood down from the captaincy was that I had been awarded a benefit year in 2000, and I thought it best for me and the club if I was no longer in charge. Benefit summers are often so difficult for players with regard to juggling playing responsibilities and benefit commitments.

But the bottom line was that I was getting very disillusioned with Middlesex and the constant problem of not being able to compete. You would have thought, wouldn't you, that many other professional cricketers around the country would have loved to come to Lord's and play their cricket at the home of the game? Well, we didn't seem to be attracting any. There was no structure and no plan.

I had wanted to bring in Dominic Cork for the 1999 season, as I knew him well and believed that he would be just the sort of all-round cricketer, and especially strong with the ball, who would make a big difference to us on the field. I also realised that the 1999 season would be a real watershed because of the decision to split the Championship into two divisions; I felt we had to do all in our power to ensure we finished at least in the top nine. I went to the committee during that winter with a list of 17 names, all of whom would have added something to our side. Nothing came of it. And so, as I sat there in the autumn of 1999, dropped by England, as well as having given up the Middlesex captaincy, it was all very depressing to contemplate my 14th season at the club in 2000.

In light of Duncan Fletcher's decision to try me as an England opener that summer, I also opened for Middlesex in our first few Championship games, with limited success. But it was after I was dropped again by England, following the Lord's Test against the West Indies, that I began to settle into an excellent run of form (back at number four) that saw me end up at the top of the county's Championship batting averages. After me on 64, and Langer on 61, the next best average was Strauss's 33. Tufnell, Fraser and Johnson took more than 160 wickets between them, but there was little else from anyone in either the bowling or the batting. Nothing had changed. We were still a very poor side, and we finished second from bottom in the new division two.

Langer, who had taken over the captaincy, was now the one facing all the problems that had driven me to distraction, and he put his heart and soul into trying to drag Middlesex around. He and I have always got on very well and it was hard for me to watch him going through the same process as I had suffered. Gatting and Ian Gould, the coach, decided to resign from their posts at the end of August, which completed the sorry picture.

By then, I had become aware of the mutterings about me leaving – although, to be quite honest, the rumours began to appear before I had really begun to contemplate it. Richard Johnson was also thinking about leaving and I recall having a chat with him about it on one occasion because he was at a more advanced stage than me in his planning. In the end, he went with his gut instinct and left for Somerset – as did Keith Dutch.

At the end of the season, I was called into a meeting by Downton. Vinny Codrington, who had just finished his first year as secretary, was also there, as were Angus Fraser and Phil Tufnell. We had a long chat about things, and part of the reason I was there was that the club had decided on a policy change and would now be offering players only two-year contracts as a maximum.

Ever since establishing myself in the team I had been on a permanent three-year contract – in other words, as you finished one season, you automatically had another year added on. I was astonished, and not a little angry. I had just averaged 64 and I wasn't a kid! I couldn't understand, especially given the speculation in the media that had been swirling around me about my future, why they were not snapping me up on as long a deal as they could. Middlesex weren't exactly blessed with proven, experienced players.

Anyway, the result of our further discussions was that the club officials turned round and said I could have the three-year contract I wanted. In a way, this was even more disgraceful. It felt as though they were making it up as they went along. As if they didn't know what they were doing.

At the end of the meeting, Codrington said, in answer to my expressed concerns about the immediate future of the team, that I should not worry because with all the good youngsters coming through we would be a good side in five years' time. I couldn't believe that, either. What was I supposed to do? Carry on for five more years of my career and be content for Middlesex to bring up the rear? We had had three bad years and I couldn't see any change in our fortunes at all; I couldn't see any light at the end of the tunnel. And what would happen when Fraser and Tufnell were not around to take the majority of the wickets? They weren't getting any younger, and although Angus was being lined up as captain in succession to Langer, who was not coming back as the overseas player for 2001 because of Australia's Ashes tour, he, in particular, surely did not have long left.

The tin lid was put on it when Codrington shared a taxi with Tuffers and me back to Lord's, from the restaurant in which we had held the meeting, and he proceeded to tell both of us that, if it were up to him, he would sack Paul Weekes (who had endured a very poor season) there and then. I was outraged. He wasn't paid to have opinions on the make-up of the playing staff and, anyway, didn't he know that Weekes was a very good friend of mine?

It was all pretty obvious how the club were thinking, and as a professional with a limited number of years at the top I didn't want to be messing about. Every time I went to practise in the nets, or to train at the gym, or to bat in the middle, I was trying to improve myself and get the best out of my ability. But it was now a shambles at Middlesex. There was no direction and no possibility of us even getting promoted from division two, let alone challenging again for the county title.

The more I thought about it, the more I knew I had to move. I did speak to both Kent and Essex in addition to Surrey, but Surrey were always my first choice. I knew all their players and was good friends with a lot of them, and they had won the Championship for two years running. I also did not want to have to move away from my London home, especially with Cara having been born in 1997.

Friends like Martin Bicknell, the Surrey opening bowler, and Keith Medlycott, their former spinner, who was first-team coach, both indicated to me that Surrey would be interested (although neither believed that I would actually leave Middlesex), and I also rang Adam Hollioake, the captain and another good friend, who was on holiday in Hong Kong, to ask him if he thought I would fit in at Surrey – if I were to move.

Having heard nothing to dissuade me otherwise – and technically, of course, Surrey were not allowed to make an official approach unless Middlesex released me from my existing contract – I made my decision. I asked for a meeting with Middlesex, and I sat down and wrote a letter to outline my reasons for looking to move. This was important for me, because I didn't want to leave that meeting without saying everything that needed to be said – I also wanted Middlesex to have the chance to respond to what I had set out on paper.

Phil Edmonds, the club chairman, Vinny Codrington, the secretary, and Angus Fraser, the captain-elect, were present to meet me at Lord's, and I took with me a lawyer friend, as I didn't want to be on my own at such a meeting. I felt I needed an ally in there, which again tells you a lot about how my relationship with the club had broken down.

When we got into the meeting, I gave all three of them a copy of my letter, which set out, clearly and concisely, my thinking behind the decision to ask for a move. I listed the reasons I wanted to leave Middlesex, including such factors as I didn't feel the club were being ambitious enough, I wanted to play division one Championship cricket and that I wanted to play for a more high-profile team who were going to challenge for honours. I also said that a change of scenery would be good for me, and that I wanted to learn from playing with different players.

Once they had read through it, Codrington was the first to speak and, in a perky, upbeat voice, he said, 'Well, I suppose that's it then.' In my opinion, this was unprofessional behaviour. I wonder how he has remained in that job for so long now. What was he doing, saying that, when both the chairman and the captain of the club were there?

Edmonds, quite rightly, said, 'Hang on, are you sure about this, Mark? Are you convinced that moving away is the right thing for you to do?' I replied that I had thought long and hard about it, and that it was a huge decision for me to make, and that there had been so much to weigh up. Angus, meanwhile, never once looked up and, as my conversation with Phil continued, he just kept looking at the piece of paper. I don't think he looked up at all, in fact, and he didn't say a word.

After a few more questions, Edmonds said that my request would go before the full committee and the matter would be discussed. I left, and later I was told that the committee, having debated it, had refused to release me from my contract. I wondered what I should do and thought about writing again directly to the committee. But a few people at the club, whom I trusted and respected, said to hold on and to relax and wait.

Easier said than done, of course. But when the committee met again on 31 January it was discussed once more, and I reckon the delay was that they were playing for time because there were rumours that they wanted to do a deal with Surrey, in which Ben Hollioake would come to Middlesex in a sort of exchange arrangement. Perhaps, though, they were just being bloody-minded.

Anyway, there was never a chance that Ben would want to go to Middlesex, or that Adam Hollioake and Surrey would agree to him going, for that matter, but the upshot of that 31 January meeting was that my release was agreed.

The very next day I was at the Oval, signing my Surrey contract. Paul Sheldon, the chief executive, was worried because the club's budget for 2001 had already been set out and they would have gone over that if they had paid me my agreed annual salary for the year. I simply said I was happy to sign the three-year deal they were offering and that they could make up the balance of my 2001 salary in years two and three.

That was swiftly agreed. Everything was done with total professionalism. Everyone at the Oval was immediately and genuinely welcoming, and I knew right away that I had done the right thing.

CHAPTER 9

SURREY REBIRTH

'Mark brought great qualities to Surrey – his preparation, his work ethic, the runs he scores and the example he sets. Ramps is an outstanding talent with an exceptional record in English county cricket'

– Alec Stewart

I have always been very disappointed indeed, to put it mildly, with the response that my move to Surrey provoked in a good number of Middlesex supporters.

On the many occasions I have been back to Lord's since, there has been the boo-boy element who seem to want to treat me as some sort of 'Judas' figure. Obviously, that was more to the fore during the first few years when I went back with Surrey, but it still persists to this day. This is only a small minority of people, but they are so ignorant and ill-informed.

I accept that my move generated a lot of debate and discussion, and this was not unexpected. Once two divisions were introduced at County Championship level, it was inevitable that more players would look to move to try to guarantee themselves first division cricket.

In my position, at the time, I was determined to do all that I could to regain my England place. In the winter of 2000–01, remember, I had to reflect on losing my Test place again and yet feeling that I still had an awful lot to offer at international level.

Moving to Surrey, even without my disillusionment at Middlesex, made a lot of sense simply because they were the number one team in the land; in other professions, you see people moving jobs to enhance their careers all the time.

Middlesex members and fans who were upset with my decision to go across the Thames should have directed their anger at the club, not at me. Of course, they did not know all the things that had happened behind the scenes to bring me to my decision, but it did not take a genius to work out that there were reasons behind it.

I was someone who had joined Middlesex colts at nine, had helped the club to a number of successes in my first seven years in the first team, and had put in fourteen seasons of hard effort. How could I have become so disillusioned that I wanted to leave a club that was in my blood?

Moreover, the very fact that something happened that should never have happened – in terms of me leaving – meant that more questions should have been asked by Middlesex supporters about how the club was being run.

The day that I arrived at Surrey I knew I had done the right thing. Everything just seemed so much more professional at the club. Yes, they were county champions on the field, but off it things were done properly too. That made an immediate impression on me.

One of the first things Keith Medlycott, the coach, said to me was that a lot of the younger Surrey players were going out to Perth for some West Australian sun and some winter training under Adam Hollioake the captain, who had a home there. He asked whether I was interested in joining them, as a way of kicking off my Surrey career in a low-profile setting, although he stressed to me that the training and the practices were going to be pretty full-on, so he didn't think I should just go out there thinking I was on holiday.

The more I thought about it, the more it made huge sense. First, I could meet a lot of the younger players. Second, I felt I would enjoy getting away from England – especially after all the commotion surrounding my move – and, third, I decided to take

Van and Cara, who was then three. We were there for five weeks, we lived in a hired apartment and Cara attended a local nursery. We loved it.

As Medlycott had outlined, the training was quite intense. We were up early three mornings a week for runs on the beach, and we had nets and other practice sessions. But I didn't mind any of that. I just enjoyed getting to know some of my new clubmates, in a relaxed environment, and I also felt the training and netting did me good.

Once again, as the new season started, I felt that fate had directed me into this new challenge and I felt ready to meet it. At 31, I felt my whole career was being rejuvenated. I learned so much about myself and my cricket by moving to Surrey when I did.

At Middlesex I had been floundering around, not really knowing what to do. Leaving was a massive decision for me, but once I had moved it definitely elevated me as a cricketer in the minds of those who mattered, including the England selectors, of course. Soon – after I had quickly settled into the number three role and started to make runs for what was already a very strong side – I knew that my career was back on track and that international recognition was possible again.

The fact that I had just received a Middlesex benefit in 2000 also rankled with some of their supporters, of course, but I have never understood why. I was portrayed in some quarters as a man who had taken the money and run, but I had put so much into my Middlesex career throughout 14 seasons. What I had achieved in all that time for the club was the reason I had been granted a benefit. I felt I didn't owe them anything in return for it; it was itself a reward for the service I had given and was there, in the record books. Benefits, by definition, aren't there to reward any future service.

What disappointed me hugely, following my departure to Surrey, were the comments made by Angus Fraser, Phil Edmonds and Vinny Codrington, which hinted that the reason the team had not done well was because of me. The gist of these comments was that I was moody and difficult in the dressing-room, that I was interested only in myself, and that they were better off without me.

After all my efforts for the club, this was a real kick in the teeth for me. I was the scapegoat, but I suppose attacking me threw a veil over the real reasons why Middlesex had performed so badly in my last few seasons there.

Other statements made by Angus also hurt me, in the Middlesex review book of the 2000 summer and in club letters to members. He seemed to take it personally that I had left.

He didn't ask me for my reasons at the time and didn't seem to appreciate that it was a decision made in the best interests of my career – especially in terms of getting back into the England team. Angus did apologise to me later about the things he said, however, and he also said on *Test Match Special* that it was right for me to make the move I did.

I give a lot of credit to Angus for apologising, and I appreciated it. It meant a lot to me because we get on well, and nowadays we often find ourselves reminiscing about the early days of our respective careers at Middlesex when we were just two young players with ambition.

In 2003, meanwhile, when I was back playing at Lord's for Surrey, I was walking around the ground when this young lad called out to me that I was 'a Judas'. I went over to him and asked him why he was saying that. He said that his dad had told him I was a Judas. I replied that I had given 14 years of my life to the club as a professional and that it should count for something.

But that young lad was by no means the only one. At times, it has seemed that to be a Middlesex supporter you have to hate Ramps. I know it's not exactly been the same as Sol Campbell leaving Tottenham for Arsenal, but it's still not nice to have to listen to it all. Richard Johnson, who left Middlesex for Somerset at the same time as I moved, was always welcomed back by the supporters whenever he returned to Lord's or Southgate or wherever. It was bizarre.

In fact, I remember playing in July 2002 at Southgate in a one-day league game and there were about forty or fifty blokes in one section of the crowd who had been drinking most of the day and were determined to give me a hard time. Every touch of the ball I had in the field was loudly booed, and when I went in to bat later they were baying for my blood.

Luckily, I managed to get myself in and – as the game moved on and it was inevitable that we would win easily – I told myself that I was going to enjoy walking back to the dressing-room unbeaten and with the match won. This I duly did, with 87 not out to my name and with Surrey triumphant by eight wickets, and it was to an eerie silence from what remained of the crowd. All those blokes had disappeared.

Later, after I had taken off my pads and showered, someone asked me if I would go around to one of the tents and present a raffle prize. I said I would and when I got there a number of Middlesex people came up to me and said they wanted to apologise to me for the behaviour of elements of the crowd during the game.

They also said that a group of them were intending to write a letter to Vinny Codrington, the secretary, complaining about the booing and the behaviour, which they duly did. He then wrote to me, saying that the club were working hard to make sure that sort of thing never happened again when I was playing against Middlesex.

Well, every time I've gone back since, it happens – perhaps not as much as on that day, but enough. And although in cricket it is so easy to pick out the people concerned, and to get their names, Middlesex have never done anything about it. It simply reinforces to me that I did the right thing in moving to Surrey.

I have also never reacted to the abuse I have received – all I do is channel my feelings into my batting. I have made quite a lot of runs against Middlesex in the nine seasons I have been at Surrey, and I am very proud of a number of those innings. My best one-day knock for Surrey, and my best Twenty20 Cup innings, have both come against Middlesex, and I also scored 110 at Lord's in June 2003 in my first Championship innings back there after my move, and then 252 in a four-day game at the Oval in 2005.

Perhaps it is the scarcity of players, historically, who have moved between Middlesex and Surrey which is at the heart of this bad feeling. I don't know, but perhaps it was more the fact that the statements being made about me by people at Middlesex at the time of my move – things that were derogatory and negative about me – simply stoked up a lot of that feeling among the club's supporters.

Whatever, it's hard to take that this is what they think about a player who is second only to Denis Compton in terms of a career batting average for Middlesex!

Surrey gave me a different feeling from the very start: a new environment, and atmosphere, and a management team in Medlycott and Hol, who both said to me straightaway that they wanted me to play my natural game from the number three position. I knew them well, of course, but they both also impressed me very much as soon as I started to work for them. They were clear in their thinking; they were used to winning, as county champions for the previous two seasons; and they were used to dealing with a team full of big players.

What struck me most of all was that, because this team were full of established internationals and big characters, I could simply go out and play my own way. The team didn't depend on me for big scores. I realised I had become a bit inhibited at Middlesex because of the team's reliance on me to make runs. Immediately, I felt freer at Surrey and, I suppose, the shackles were off.

I made my Surrey debut in the Championship game against Kent at the Oval in late April and quite early in my innings I hit Mark Ealham back over his head for six. That surprised quite a few of my new teammates, who thought I was more of a blocker! But I felt good, and my strokes flowed. I made 146, which was then my 52nd first-class hundred, and I was happy not just to have scored those runs but also to have done so fluently and aggressively. I have not looked back since.

The other thing that helped me to settle in so quickly at Surrey was that I knew the majority of their players very well indeed. I had roomed with both Alec Stewart and Adam Hollioake on the 1998 tour to the West Indies, and I knew Alex Tudor and Mark Butcher well. Players such as Martin Bicknell, Alastair Brown and

Graham Thorpe I had known since we had played U12 cricket against each other!

Surrey's supporters were also extremely welcoming, and it didn't seem to matter to them that I had come from Middlesex. Paul Sheldon, the chief executive, and the club's communications department got everything sorted off the field and that definitely helped me to perform better on the field.

The other factor in me feeling at home was the Oval pitch and the ground in general. I had always felt comfortable there, and had got runs consistently both for Middlesex and for England. I liked the way the ball came onto the bat and the even bounce.

In mid-summer, too, I had the pleasure of going back to Lord's for the Benson & Hedges Cup final, in which we beat Gloucestershire – then the most successful one-day team in the country – by 47 runs. I made 39 and, although I didn't go on to a big score, I really enjoyed the innings and felt I had batted well. I also felt very proud to be back on what, on cup final day, is always a big stage – and to be there as a Surrey player. We left two internationals out of our starting XI on that day.

It was my first taste of winning a trophy since Middlesex's 1993 Championship success and sitting in the Surrey dressing-room – at Lord's – after the game was a great feeling. It confirmed to me, if I needed any final confirmation, that I had made the right decision the previous winter.

There have been many highlights of my years at Surrey, even though in recent seasons we have struggled to manage the transition of losing so many influential players – either through retirement, or in the case of Ben Hollioake a tragic accident that robbed the club of one of the most talented young internationals in England, and which also had such an awful effect on Adam, his brother.

I was in New Zealand with England, in March 2002, when the terrible news of Ben's death in a car crash in Perth, Australia, came through. We just couldn't believe it. Ben had actually been with the England one-day squad in New Zealand earlier in the tour and now he was dead.

Obviously, I had played a whole season with Ben in 2001, but what I felt was wrong was that two of his other Surrey teammates on that England Test tour – Mark Butcher and Graham Thorpe – were not allowed to leave New Zealand to go to his funeral. Instead Nasser Hussain, as England captain, and David Graveney, the chairman of selectors, attended on our behalf. Butch and Thorpey should definitely have gone, in addition to Nasser and Graveney.

Everyone at Surrey was absolutely devastated by Ben's death at the age of just 24. He was loved at the club, for his personality and for the fact that he was such a confident young buck with talent coming out of his ears. He was the future of Surrey, in many ways, and his death hit hard.

No one, however, was hit harder than Adam. Ben's death changed him massively and, as a player and captain of the club, it brought a premature end to his own career and to his reign. Before Ben died, he was utterly committed, he was incredibly fit and the way he captained the team and played his cricket was inspirational.

Adam should still have been England's one-day international captain at that time, too, in my opinion. He had been captain back in 1997 and 1998, and was at the time being groomed for the 1999 World Cup captaincy, but the England selectors lost their nerve after the 1998 tour of the West Indies, even though he had won the Sharjah tournament earlier that winter, and in the end it was Alec Stewart who led England into that ill-fated World Cup campaign – and was sacked as captain of both the one-day team and the Test side soon afterwards.

If Hollioake had been given the England one-day job long term, he would have made a success of it. He was a talented limited-overs cricketer, too, and our successes at Surrey in winning both the inaugural Twenty20 Cup and the National League in 2003 showed that he had lost none of his effectiveness as a one-day player or leader even by then.

But Adam's biggest triumph, and yet such a bittersweet one for him, was in leading Surrey to the 2002 County Championship title. He actually missed the first part of the campaign, as he remained in Australia after Ben's funeral to help to sort out family affairs, to get over his brother's passing and to be at home himself when his wife Sherryn gave birth in June to a daughter, Bennaya.

Ian Ward captained in his absence, but when Adam returned, playing his first Championship game in early July, it was immediately obvious that he was treating his cricket as a release from his grief. His batting, in particular, was remarkable and by the end of that season he topped our averages with 738 runs at 67 from nine matches, plundered from just 812 balls with 86 fours and 24 sixes.

He played with total abandon and, although it worked spectacularly, I don't think he really cared what people were bowling at him. He batted aggressively, and with real power, at the best of times – but this was something else. His batting and leadership gave us so much extra momentum during July and August that the Championship title was clinched before our last two matches in September, which were both won, too. In the end, we won it by a margin of 44.75 points.

I would have to say that the Surrey side of 2002 was perhaps the best I have ever played in at county level. Indeed, I often think about a match between the Middlesex team of 1990 and the Surrey of 2002 – both champions and both packed with big-match players and big personalities.

In 1990, you had batsmen of the quality of Desmond Haynes and Mike Gatting, plus the likes of Keith Brown and Micky Roseberry, a fine keeper-batsman in Paul Downton and a bowling attack of Angus Fraser, Norman Cowans, Neil Williams, Simon Hughes, John Emburey and Phil Tufnell.

But that Surrey team had batting to burn: ten different players got hundreds during that Championship campaign, while Alec Stewart's top score was 99! He and Graham Thorpe only played four matches because of England commitments, but players such as Jon Batty and Nadeem Shahid stood in solidly when we lost Stewart, Butcher and Thorpe to England calls. Youngsters Scott Newman and Rikki Clarke also made significant contributions that summer.

The bowling was strong, too, with Jimmy Ormond's signing from Leicestershire adding real quality to a seam attack based around the excellence of Bicknell, a fit and young Azhar Mahmood, Tudor and Ed Giddins.

Perhaps it was the spin partnership of Saqlain Mushtaq and Ian Salisbury that was the real strength of this team, though, and possibly an even more potent combination – certainly on flat pitches – than the Middlesex duo of Emburey and Tufnell. Saqlain and Salisbury could both turn it both ways: Saqlain was a genius who mastered the art of the off-spinner's 'doosra', while Salisbury's googly was a tremendous asset that got a lot of very good batsmen out – and completely baffled a lot more tailenders!

What is more, all Surrey's frontline bowlers – with the exception of Giddins, who only played in six matches – could bat. Azhar was a genuine international-class all-rounder, and Tudor, Bicknell, Salisbury and Saqlain could all be classed as that at county level, too. In that respect, Surrey batted deeper.

So who would win between Middlesex 1990 and Surrey 2002? Could I play for both sides? I'd certainly want to! I have to say I couldn't call it. The only way I could begin to split them would be to say that Middlesex would be favourites if the match was played at Lord's, and Surrey would be favourites at the Oval. But both, believe me, were great sides with great leaders in Gatting and Hollioake, classy batting and bowling for all seasons and all conditions.

Adam's seven seasons as Surrey captain ended after the 2003 season, and that was almost the best summer of all for him and the club. He had always wanted to be aggressive in his approach to the game and in 2003 we played some great cricket in both Championship and one-day cricket.

The Twenty20 Cup win, in the competition's remarkable first year when county crowds went through the roof, was testimony in itself to Adam's leadership qualities and tactical grasp, his own brilliance with bat and ball, and the team's overall talents. The National League title was also added, and we could easily have won the Championship again.

We led from mid-May until the end of August, but then lost two and drew one of three successive matches against Leicestershire,

Lancashire and Kent. That proved the end of our title hopes, as we ran out of steam and eventually finished third.

It was also obvious by the end of a season that had seen Alec Stewart retire and injury hit many of the players that it was not just the side that was running out of steam. Adam Hollioake had clearly lost his will to continue as captain. He agreed to carry on for 2004, his benefit season, in order to help support Jon Batty, his successor, but you could tell his mind was no longer on his cricket.

When he had Ben around, he had to be a role model to his brother, who was six years younger. Part of his role as captain of the club was to bring Ben on. Now, with Ben gone, he found it difficult to motivate himself and do the hard, disciplined work off the field that had characterised his approach in his first five seasons as captain, in fact his whole career to that point.

I suppose the Twenty20 Cup title was really Adam's last great achievement and gift to Surrey. As a team, we immediately set standards in this new-look form of the game. And Twenty20 was made for a cricketer like Adam Hollioake. He played without fear, but also thought clearly about how to win games; for instance, he liked to take wickets with the new ball – rather than just try to be defensive in the first six overs, when you could only have two fielders outside the ring – and in the final against Warwickshire it was the new ball strikes of Ormond and Azhar Mahmood that proved to be the difference.

And so the end of the 2003 season was a watershed for Surrey. Adam played on for one more season, but I don't think he enjoyed it and it wasn't really a good idea. Keith Medlycott had resigned as head coach at the end of 2003 and Steve Rixon, the Australian who had coached New Zealand, was appointed in his place.

I think Rixon was a bit unlucky in his time at Surrey. He inherited a side which all of a sudden was losing a lot of leading players, such as Stewart, Hollioake, Saqlain, Ward and Tudor, but we did manage to reach the final of the Twenty20 Cup again, this time losing to Leicestershire, and also to finish third once more in the Championship.

In 2005, however, everything began to go wrong – including getting an eight-point penalty for alleged ball-tampering which, ultimately, was to cost us relegation to the second division by a single point. Injuries to senior players who remained, especially Butcher, Thorpe and Bicknell, made life even more difficult and the season was summed up when Ormond put his hand through the dressing-room door in a temper at Guildford in late July – and fractured it.

Batty, the captain in 2004, and a top professional and highly regarded, had to give up the job after realising that he could not do that as well as being the opening batsman and wicketkeeper. Even Stewart had found that sort of workload too much. Rixon had appointed Mark Butcher to the captaincy for 2005, but Butch missed three-quarters of the season with a wrist injury that never seemed as if it would heal and I found myself the captain in the field for most of the season.

I wrote a book about that season called *Four More Weeks,* which was published soon afterwards, and the title neatly sums up my abiding memory – and frustration – of that summer. I took the job on initially for what I was told would be four weeks: 'I'll be four more weeks' were exactly the words Butch said to me at the start of the campaign. He then missed 12 of our 16 Championship matches and only returned to the side in August.

Honoured though I was to become the first person to captain both Middlesex and Surrey, it was a summer that I found massively draining. Only Batty and Alastair Brown played in all our Championship fixtures, and although I topped the batting averages and was proud to score more than 1,500 runs at an average of almost 75, it was a deflating experience to be relegated – especially by such a miniscule margin.

The ball-tampering affair is also covered in *Four More Weeks.* Basically, no one in the team for the match in question, against Nottinghamshire at the Oval in early May, would own up to a raising of the ball's quarter seam and we were later docked the eight points by the ECB that were to cost us so dear. The incident happened while Notts were amassing 692 for 7 declared, and as they went on to win by an innings and 71 runs it wasn't as though the offence did us any good even in the match itself.

For me, though, the story of that season came down to a pivotal game at Guildford in late July, against Kent. The early part of the match was overshadowed for us, despite our rapid progress to 452 for 8 declared on a magnificent Woodbridge Road pitch, by a row out in the middle between Graham Thorpe and Alastair Brown.

Thorpe and I had put on 133 for the third wicket, taking us to 238 for 3, and when I was out for 97 Brown came in. Thorpey was nearing 70 when my wicket fell, but Brown immediately began to thrash the bowling all around the park, as only he can, and soon began to catch his partner up.

Like all top batsmen when they get into a golden patch of form, Brown suddenly became very adept at nicking a single off the last ball of the over and, suddenly, Thorpe was seeing very little of the strike. Indeed, Brown was into the 90s before Thorpe himself, and it all came to a head when Thorpe refused to take yet another single from the final ball of the over.

Unfortunately, Thorpe then got out for 95, bowled by Min Patel, and he was not happy. Brown did get his hundred, but was out soon afterwards, and the row continued in the dressing-room. Sadly, this incident did not help the mood among the rest of the players, and when Kent replied our fielding fell apart. It was a disgrace.

Mohammad Akram, our opening bowler, got the hump when he didn't get the end he wanted to bowl from initially and sent down medium pace until I took him off. Then, when I did put him on at the other end, he was as quick as I'd seen him. But Kent scored 572 in their first innings, and we collapsed from 240 for 2 in our second innings to 350 all out, leaving Kent to knock off the 231 they needed in double-quick time. We lost by six wickets – and Ormond was so annoyed he put his hand through that door.

Steve Rixon wanted to resign from his position as head coach there and then, and I persuaded him not to. I had a good relationship with Steve and felt the same frustrations as he did. I also felt very sorry for Steve because he did not deserve to have to deal with players acting so unprofessionally. They let him down, but he was the one feeling responsible and accountable. It was not his fault.

I suppose it was because Surrey were so used to success, and to winning, but neither I nor Steve could seem to get the message across to the players that relegation was now a distinct possibility, especially after the Kent defeat was followed two weeks later by another loss at Sussex. They just didn't seem to understand that it could happen to us.

But we were relegated, because the team was so unprofessional. Butcher eventually started his captaincy reign in August, but we could not stop the slide towards the bottom three. It was the last season that three sides went down into division two (it has been two since), but that just added to the frustration and the disappointment at how we had performed over the five months of the season.

I have always enjoyed being captain out there on the field, and I also tried my best to communicate with the players during that season, even though I was not the club's official captain and therefore only a stand-in.

What I found especially difficult to understand was why the players, even if they were not enamoured with Rixon's way of doing things, would then go out and let themselves down by giving their wicket away or doing something stupid on the field. That's not being professional and, in my opinion, that is not acceptable.

When I arrived at Surrey, I was told by Keith Medlycott that it was Surrey who were leading the way in the county game; we were the ones being innovative and at the cutting edge of things. We were the most professional. In 2004 and 2005, this was most certainly not the case, and the players' commitment to training and practice was just not good enough. The work you need to do to earn the right to be able to dominate a game of cricket was not put in.

It is shocking how quickly things can fall away, but cricket is a skill game and you have to work at those skills. Also, there are factors like the toss of a coin at the start of a match, or the odd decision that goes against you at a crucial time, that can have a big bearing on the outcome of games. You can build up momentum in cricket, whether it be over the course of a Test series or a county season, but it can also go the other way.

Also, as a team and as individuals, you can be left behind if you are not constantly evolving as cricketers and as a unit, and re-evaluating your game all the time. People can work you out. I stuck an article written by Glenn McGrath on our dressing-room wall at one stage during the 2005 season. In it he said that it was not by chance that he had become a world-class bowler; he had constantly worked at his game and evolved as a player.

He first had to learn how to master reverse swing. Then, to stay in Australia's one-day team, he had to learn to master the slower ball. I hoped those in our dressing-room would read it and get the message – this was the great Glenn McGrath talking! But it didn't look as if they did.

I get told by players, 'Everyone is not like you, Ramps, and a lot of players don't train as hard as you. You have to relax.' When I got frustrated with the players during the 2005 season, I was told that I had to give responsibility to them. But what do you do as captain when it's your opinion that a lot of them are not taking the responsibility for their own performances that you believe they should?

Alan Butcher, who took over as Surrey coach from Steve Rixon, and was subsequently in charge of the team for the 2006, 2007 and 2008 seasons, said to me that he thought my approach to training and practice actually has the effect on some players, who think that they cannot possibly match my intensity of preparation, of making them go the other way and slacken off. So I don't know the answer. I suppose it is up to every player to do what he thinks is right for him and then be judged on the results he gets. But there can be no excuses if he does not perform.

I put my heart and soul into the Surrey captaincy in 2005 and my pride was hurt. We had gone down after a summer during which I was in charge of the team for most of the time, and we had done so with so many good players at the club. When Alan came in to replace Steve, he also took the vice-captaincy away from me and gave it to the most problematic player that Steve and I had dealt with the previous season, all-rounder Rikki Clarke. I could see what Alan was trying to achieve with Rikki by appointing him as number two to Mark Butcher, but that was a lot for me to stomach after the experience of 2005.

During the winter of 2005–06 I hardly hit a ball in practice, which is unheard of for me. But I simply didn't feel like it. I wanted to be in division one of the Championship – that was what I had gone to Surrey for in the first place – and so the prospect of life in division two was very demoralising.

Also, my book *Four More Weeks* had ruffled a few feathers at the club. I certainly don't think I was too harsh on people in that book; I was just being truthful. Maybe I divulged the details of a few dressing-room conversations which some players might have wanted to remain private, but I felt I had written an accurate account of what had been a deflating season for Surrey.

When all the players returned for pre-season, Alan Butcher got everyone together in a meeting room and said that he wanted anyone who had a problem with my book to put their hand up and say it now. He didn't want things left unsaid when the new season started. No one initially said anything. After a bit of prompting, Jimmy Ormond said he had been upset with some of the things I had written about him, but he had thought about it during the winter, had taken on board what I had said and was now prepared to move on. A few others mumbled the same. I felt I had not criticised anyone without good reason; in Ormond's case, not only had he punched that wall at Guildford and stupidly broken his hand but then also just a few weeks later he was two stone overweight when he should have been doing all he could to stay fit for when he could return to the team.

Alan then said he wanted everyone to go on the pre-season trip he had organised to Mumbai, so that we could get together as a squad and prepare for the new campaign. Initially, I thought it was not a good idea – Mumbai in March is incredibly hot and no preparation at all for English conditions in April. I could see no logic to it, but Alan said he wanted me to go so that the group could see that I was also in a positive frame of mind about the summer ahead. He didn't say that I had to go, but he asked me to think about it. So I went, and that is how our 2006 campaign got under way – in the heat of India.

In division two that summer we were able to put the pressure on a succession of opponents, in the Championship, and we dominated enough games to win promotion back into the top tier. Alan Butcher, having been in charge of the club's Second XI, was able to relate to the younger players who had come through the system, and obviously the spirit in and around the club was far better because we were winning games.

As for myself, the 2006 season marked the start of a run of form that was to see me average more than 100 in first-class cricket for two years in succession. As with scoring 2,000 runs back in 1995, it was not as a result of any targets I had set. I don't believe in doing that. What I am, though, is greedy. If I get in, I don't want to throw my wicket away. I enjoy batting too much for that. If I'm in, I want to stay in.

I also began to enjoy my cricket, and my philosophy is that the more runs I make, the better chance my team have of winning that particular match. I remember during that season thinking out there in the middle how lucky I was to be playing cricket for a living, to be batting against good teams and succeeding, and to be enjoying the challenge of seeing how many runs I could score. I also remember chatting to umpires much more than I'd ever done before, and of generally being able to relax a bit more and let things flow.

It was also a case, I think, that I wanted to put the 2005 summer behind me. What do you do? Do you continue to fight with people and disagree with them if there are things going on within the team that you don't think are right, or do you just go out there and do your very best and enjoy your cricket? I decided that my primary objective was to occupy the crease and get runs. Subconsciously, I suppose, getting runs – and a lot of them, if possible – was my answer and my reaction to everything that had gone on the previous summer. I enjoyed being out there in the middle and so I wanted to make the most of every opportunity I got to stay out there!

All the experience that I had accumulated over 20 years in the first-class game came into the equation, too. Whenever people ask me about how I can explain a run of extraordinary form, what I say is always that it is a combination of factors: of fitness and preparation, of motivation in terms of the match situation or the team's needs, of experience, of learning to read the many different types of pitch you come across, of technique against certain types of bowlers, of desire and personal pride, of learning to soak up pressure, and of being patient. It is all these things and more.

In 2006 and 2007, I believe I showed real mental strength in performing to the levels that I did, and to do so after the personal and team disappointments of 2004 and 2005. I was enjoying the game and the art of batting, for the game itself and for what I could achieve if I had the mental resolve not to impose any boundaries upon myself.

When we were back in division one of the Championship for 2007, part of my motivation to do well was also the fact that I had the chance to show what I could do again at first division level. It was a step up from the previous year, in terms of the overall quality of the teams we were now facing, and although I didn't set out to average more than 100 again – that would be ridiculous – I did want to score as many runs as I could once more. No limits, but just bat and see what happens.

But, throughout my career, there has always seemed to be someone wanting to criticise, and at the end of the 2006 season – after I had scored 2,278 first-class runs at an average of 103.54 – it was Steve James, the former Glamorgan opener who is now a full-time cricket writer.

He wrote an article in which he was quite dismissive of my achievement, and the basis of his argument was that it had been done in division two. I felt this was hugely unfair, the main reason being that if scoring 2,000 runs and averaging 100 was that straightforward then why weren't more batsmen doing it? Yet although his article was, in my opinion, ill-judged and quite mean-minded, it also brought it home to me that – whatever else the England selectors might say – there is a general conception now that second division cricket is significantly below first division cricket in terms of both standards and importance.

So, at the start of 2007, I resolved to work harder still and continue to evolve my game on the basis that the first division now represented a new challenge. What could I now achieve in supposedly a higher league?

On a technical level, during the 2006 season I had also slightly changed my trigger movement at the crease, and there is no doubt that this helped me to become more consistent in my performances for the remainder of that summer and throughout 2007 and since. And, although 2007 was a bit of a struggle for Surrey, in that we were in the bottom two for most of the season and only managed to get out of there and avoid relegation right at the end, I found that my own performances carried right on from 2006.

It gave me a great deal of pleasure to get those runs in 2007. Justin Langer was right when he said last year that county cricket has been getting tougher and tougher over the past few years and that, in his opinion, first division cricket in England is now the toughest domestic cricket in the world. Teams have real depth in terms of their squads and, in 2007, batting in particular became much harder work because a new ball was available after 80 overs, and not 100, and the poor weather made pitches and conditions more bowler-friendly than they had been in 2006.

To build up the run of scores I had was very difficult mentally and also extremely tiring physically. By the time we got to our last match, at home to Lancashire at the Oval, I was completely knackered and told Alan Butcher that I wanted to miss the game. We were by then safe in division one, and I initially felt the team would be better off without me.

But after a bit of thought I realised that all of us at Surrey owed it to the rest of the division to put out our strongest side – especially as Lancashire were one of three sides, along with Durham and Sussex, still in with a chance of taking the Championship title.

I was nearly run out for nought, and then got off the mark with a hoick over mid-wicket against Saj Mahmood. Despite trying to tell myself to concentrate, I wasn't at the races and was then dropped in the slips off Glen Chapple. But it was around this time that I also became aware that the Lancashire close fielders were all making a lot of noise and, what is more, were continuing to make that noise even as I was settling over my bat.

This went on for a few more deliveries, so I turned around and said to their keeper, Luke Sutton, 'Have you finished?' Stuart Law tried to step in and apologise to me, but it was a little incident that got me going. Suddenly, I found concentration and extra motivation. I switched on, and now wanted to knuckle down and accept the challenge of taking on their attack. When I got to a hundred, Sutton wandered over to me and said, 'Ramps, I didn't mean it, you know!'

During that game I also became aware of some comments about me made by Mike Atherton on Sky Sports commentary. I have tapes of the game, too, so I have listened to that commentary myself since. I know Mike is being paid to give his opinions, but I have seen a change in him in recent years. At first, when he retired and went into the media, he was always very fair in his comments, but in this instance he was talking about me as if it was the Ramprakash he captained in the West Indies in 1994. That was simply not the case – it was now 2007 and 13 years had gone by.

Of course, even though I made my maiden Test hundred under him in 1998, in his last series as England captain, I am very sad that I didn't make many more runs for him when he gave me chances in 1994 and in subsequent years. But what Athers has got to realise is that I have continued to evolve as a batsman and there is no question that I have become a far better batsman than I was back in 1994.

I have also matured as a person, and as a player. Happily, too, I still have the desire to compete and that has to be the case – otherwise I would give the game up. It was a shame to hear Athers saying things during a game in which I ended up scoring 196 and 130 not out – and batting for more than 12 hours overall – as if it were 13 years earlier in my life. Clearly, he didn't seem to be recognising the fact that, as a player, my results in more recent years have been due to the continual process of trying to improve myself as a batsman.

That Lancashire match, though, was a tremendous contest and a brilliant advert not just for four-day Championship cricket but also for the English domestic game itself. Lancashire, set 489 to win in just over a day and take the Championship, and starting out on the last morning at 27 for no wicket, finally came up just 24 runs short with 4.1 overs remaining. Sussex, as a result, won the title, but we had played the game in exactly the right way and it was a thrilling occasion.

As for myself, my second innings unbeaten hundred had also taken me past 2,000 first-class runs and hoisted my final average above 100 – making me the first batsman to do this for successive seasons. It's another proud achievement, but if I'm honest I didn't have a clue about it when I was out there in the middle.

I just wanted to bat, and for me that has always been more than enough.

CHAPTER 10

AMONG THE BEST

'As soon as he began to play at first-class level, you could see that Mark Ramprakash was going to become a major player in the English game for 15 years or more . . .'

— John Emburey

There were times when I thought it a dubious honour, but during my career I really have been privileged to bat against some of the best bowlers the game of cricket has ever seen. Indeed, the overall standard of international bowling has been lower during the past five or six years, in my opinion, than it was when I was playing for England.

Against the West Indies, I faced up to Malcolm Marshall, Curtly Ambrose, Courtney Walsh and Patrick Patterson; against Pakistan, it was Wasim Akram, Waqar Younis and Mushtaq Ahmed; against South Africa, I batted against Allan Donald and Shaun Pollock; and against India, the spinners Harbhajan Singh and Anil Kumble, while there were also the likes of Muttiah Muralitharan of Sri Lanka and the little matter of Shane Warne, Glenn McGrath, Jason Gillespie and Brett Lee when we played Australia.

In county cricket, meanwhile, I have been tested by other great international bowlers such as Richard Hadlee, Saqlain Mushtaq and Michael Holding, plus of course the best English bowlers of my time — a list which includes Darren Gough, Steve Harmison, Andrew Flintoff, Phillip DeFreitas, Andrew Caddick, Dominic

Cork, Matthew Hoggard and Monty Panesar.

Bowlers such as Warne, Mushtaq, Marshall, Walsh and Donald also played a lot of county cricket during their careers, and I have already mentioned in Chapter 2 the trouble I had with left-arm county swing bowlers like Mark Ilott and Mike Smith before I changed my stance against their type . . . in my 22nd first-class season!

But I have enjoyed the challenge of batting against all types of bowling, in all the many different conditions you experience if you play as long as I have and in every major cricket-playing country in the world.

Perhaps because I averaged more than 40 in Test cricket against Australia in 12 Tests against them between 1993 and 2001, I seemed to cope better with the threat of both Warne and McGrath than some other international batsmen, and certainly some other English batsmen.

McGrath, for example, caused all sorts of trouble for Mike Atherton, who kept on getting out caught at the wicket or in the slips. I'm not saying I found him easy, but the main problems he caused me when I faced him was potential damage to my eardrums.

He was a very strange character, actually. I never understood him or where he was coming from. I remember even in a County Championship match, during the 2000 season, when Middlesex were playing Worcestershire at Southgate, he came rushing over to me from his fielding position at long leg as we left the field to berate me for failing to complete my hundred in the day's final over. I had finished up on 99 not out, despite a couple of late sixes, and duly completed the century the next morning, but for some reason McGrath felt that I deserved an earful of abuse for committing this heinous crime.

Facing him, he was such a metronome, aiming as he did at the line about six inches outside off stump, that I could get across onto off stump and feel fairly comfortable, even though he got steep bounce and was obviously a very fine bowler.

Indeed in the 2001 Ashes series, it was Gillespie who was really the one to watch out of the three main Australian pace bowlers.

Gillespie was then very sharp and could move the ball away towards the slips seemingly at will, while Brett Lee was extremely fast and dangerous simply through that raw speed. At least, with Lee, you did get some four-balls now and again, though.

With Warne, I enjoyed a lot of duels, both in Tests and in county cricket. I first batted against him during the Oval Test in 1993, and in those early years of his own international career – before finger and shoulder injuries began to kick in – he spun the ball prodigiously and, because of the revolutions on it, he managed to get it to dip into your pads quite alarmingly at times. No one else did that as much as him.

He is rightly regarded as one of the great bowlers of all time and he had a great presence at the crease. For myself, however, I found that I virtually always knew which way the ball was turning because I could read him quite well and because he hardly ever bowled a googly. You had to concentrate, and be patient, but as with McGrath I found I could cope most of the time against Shane. Also, the longer I stayed in against them, the more I had to try to match their consistency of line and length with my own concentration levels and control over my shot selection. That was the key to surviving long enough to flourish.

Mushtaq Ahmed, by contrast, was difficult to read. He bowled a lot of straight-on top-spinners and googlies, which were not easy to pick up, but he also bowled a decent leg-break, so I always felt there was more of a danger from Mushy that he could go past you on both sides of the bat.

There were times, too, with Mushtaq when I can freely admit that I did not know which way the ball was going to go. I played an awful lot against him, especially in county cricket when he was at Somerset and then during his phenomenal late career spell at Sussex, and it was always a great challenge to bat against him.

Since he was for a long time a teammate at Surrey, I did not get to play much against Saqlain Mushtaq. On one of the occasions I did, for Middlesex against Surrey in 1997, I was part of a hat-trick by the brilliant Pakistani, who invented his own trademark delivery. Off-spinners since have all tried to develop the so-called 'doosra', the ball that Saqlain first mastered and which flummoxed me in both innings of that match at Lord's.

I had hardly heard of Saqlain at that stage and we were playing on a very flat pitch. We batted first and when I went in during the early afternoon at number five – I had been at my grandad's funeral during the morning – I was surprised by the field that he had for me when he came on to bowl.

He was bowling from the Pavilion end, and the boundary was short on the Tavern side, my legside, as the pitch was nearer to the bottom end of the square. He had a mid-on and a deep square leg, but there was no one fielding at mid-wicket and I couldn't believe it. I thought to myself, after a quick look at him, that I was simply going to put my foot across and hoick him through that gap and into the Tavern stand itself, which was only 50 or 60 yards away. I had been in for a little while and I wanted to get my innings going.

The first ball he sent down I played defensively, and I remember that it went straight on, if anything. Mind made up, I went after the next and, to my amazement, got a top edge and was caught by the fielder stationed behind me at short fine leg. As I walked off, I told myself I was just unlucky. Saqlain then took wickets with his next two balls, too, and completed his hat-trick as our innings subsided miserably.

Surrey made a huge score in reply, underlining what a great pitch it was for batting, but we didn't fare too much better in our second innings either, with Saqlain again ending up with a five-wicket haul, giving him ten in the match, as we lost by an innings and plenty.

When I came in to bat second time around, he was bowling from the Nursery End, but the first thing I noticed was that he had exactly the same field again. I should have smelled a rat, but I merely thought that this was a real bonus and a perfect area for me to get off the mark. I could just flick him away through that mid-wicket gap and it would be an easy two at the least.

Anyway, all that happened was that I somehow got a leading edge and was caught and bowled for nought. It was only after the game that someone said that he was doing something different with the ball and getting it to spin a bit off the pitch away from the right-handers instead of into the pads, but I certainly didn't see anything different in his action, or release of the ball, to suggest this.

Saqlain was a genius, and he could make batsmen look very stupid indeed when he was in his prime. A lot of other off-spinners, with Harbhajan being perhaps the best example, have since followed Saqlain's lead and developed their own versions of the doosra – indeed, it has become almost as necessary a weapon in the armouries of the very best off-spinners as a decent arm ball, or quicker ball.

As for other cricketers I have admired, I would obviously include great modern-day batsmen such as Vivian Richards – my own hero – and Brian Lara and Sachin Tendulkar.

There are others, too, but the cricketers I've most envied and enjoyed watching are the great all-rounders such as Imran Khan, Ian Botham, Kapil Dev and Richard Hadlee.

Then there's Jacques Kallis, Andrew Flintoff, Shaun Pollock and Wasim Akram, who was a fine lower-order batsman as well as being a world-class left-arm quick who could bowl over or around the wicket with equal effectiveness. I would love to have been able to bat and bowl as a genuine all-rounder. Can you imagine how great that must feel?

I often get asked these days about the Indian Premier League and where I stand on Twenty20 cricket in general. For a start, I would love to play IPL cricket, even now, and indeed I wish I had been allowed to go over to India for the inaugural tournament in 2008 when the Rajasthan Royals asked Surrey if I could be released to cover for the injured Graeme Smith for three games. But Surrey chief executive Paul Sheldon would not allow it, as we were well into our own season by then. It was a shame, as the experience I would have returned with would also have been to the benefit of Surrey.

As for Twenty20, my worry about its evolution is that it could eclipse first-class cricket as the main focus of players coming into the game.

I have always regarded the first-class game as the real test of skill and over a period of time the main way that you can be 'graded' as a cricketer, if you like. All the different and varied demands of the longer game – the second new ball, the wear and tear of the pitch, the changing overhead conditions over four or five days, the need to build an innings, or for bowlers to prise out well-set batsmen – challenge you as a player in a way that shortened formats can never do.

Now, however, thinking about how to succeed at Twenty20, in particular, is essential for any young player trying to make his way in the game. Can you play the reverse sweep or reverse paddle? How good is your placement and manoeuvring of the ball, and can you hit the gaps? There is also far more premeditation to batting in Twenty20, and one-day cricket in general, and I am not sure that is good for batsmen.

My father always used to tell me to play each ball on its merits, and I remember Michael Vaughan saying to me once that all he was trying to do at the crease was to make sure he got into a good position to play every ball – with his feet working, and his head still, and his balance good – and then to react to the ball that was bowled at him.

I like that approach to batting. It keeps it simple. To my mind, that is what batting is also about. For instance, if the ball is a full toss, do you have to go down on one knee and sweep it, or reverse sweep it, or paddle it? Can you not just hit it through the offside field for four with a conventional cricket shot?

Twenty20 cricket is about taking risks and a quick 20 or 25 can often be a match-winning innings. The focus now on pre-meditated strokeplay means that there has been a significant shift in many batsmen's approach to the game. Some skills are improving, but there is a danger that young players in particular will lack judgement when it comes to playing in certain different situations and conditions.

I think that the pre-eminence of Twenty20 cricket in the last couple of years has begun to erode some of the skills required in young batsmen if they are also to be successful in the more traditional game. Concentration and the ability to bat time could be two big casualties; in four-day or five-day cricket, you often have to bat through a session, irrespective of how many runs you score, for the benefit of the team.

I also believe that we are now starting to see a split in terms of what young players are coming into professional cricket to achieve:

is it to play Test cricket and/or the first-class game and try to develop themselves as far as they can as cricketers, or is it to make money and therefore to concentrate in the main on becoming good at Twenty20 cricket?

The Kevin Pietersen switch-hit and other innovations such as using the back of the bat to reverse-sweep (so that you don't need to change your grip) are all part of the natural evolution of cricket and there is nothing wrong with that in itself. It is exciting to watch and it builds more interest in the game.

But cricket has to keep everything in proper balance, and I hope that the administrators around the world realise that it is the very richness of the game's variety – in its different formats and challenges to players – that is at the heart of its appeal to the huge overall audience. We cannot afford to alienate any part of that audience by failing to cater for them.

In terms of Twenty20, too, I know that spinners have up to now played far more of a part than was predicted in the outcome of matches at domestic and international level, but would someone like Harbhajan Singh have been so effective if he had grown up in an era in which Twenty20 was as prominent as it is today?

It may be that we have to wait a number of years to see if genuine, world-class spinners are still produced by a system in which the short form of the game is more important than any other. In other words, have genuine spinners been effective in Twenty20 because they already had certain skills before that format came along, and will we now simply have a generation of batsmen who send down 'spinners' like dart-throwers?

A lot of new, highly exciting cricketers have emerged in recent years: players such as Lasith Malinga, the Sri Lankan fast-bowling 'slinger', Ajantha Mendis, the Sri Lankan mystery spinner, England's Ravi Bopara and the Australian opener Phillip Hughes. But they all came through the first-class cricket systems of their respective countries and used them to hone their particular skills. And when so-called Twenty20 specialists have appeared, they also have learned the game in the longer formats.

While on the subject of first-class cricket, it has been a recurring theme of my 20-plus years in the English game that our domestic structure is constantly debated – and in many instances regularly tinkered with.

I began my career in a County Championship (of seventeen, not eighteen counties) that was all-play-all over a fixture list made up entirely of three-day games. We then had two cup competitions, the Benson & Hedges and the NatWest Trophy, both ending in Lord's showpiece finals, and a Sunday League of 40-over matches between, again, all 17 counties.

Over the years, the Championship has gone through stages of being part three-day and part four-day and has evolved into two divisions of nine teams, playing eight four-day games at home and eight away. Limited-overs domestic cricket has also gone through enormous change, with the Twenty20 Cup being introduced in 2003 and that format now dominating to the extent that a second Twenty20 county competition, initially called the P20, is planned for 2010.

This, to me, is total overkill and I hope it never happens. There is just no point at all in having two county Twenty20 competitions. At county level, there simply needs to be one championship of sixteen four-day games, one fifty-over cup and one Twenty20 Cup. That's it.

If we are to have another Twenty20 tournament in the schedule, then it needs to be short and sharp and very different to the existing Twenty20 Cup, which has been hugely successful and does not need tampering with in the way that is being suggested. Also, qualification for the international Champions League Twenty20 event is currently from the Twenty20 Cup and this must also remain – otherwise English cricket's most popular competition of recent times will be instantly devalued.

If the P20 is to come into being in any way and played over a couple of weeks in June, as is being mooted, then it should be as a fully fledged English Premier League with nine regional franchises being formed to give it a parallel profile to the Indian Premier League. This way it would look very different to the Twenty20 Cup and would not threaten either the established strength of that competition or the sovereignty of the 18 counties.

Each franchised team would be based at a Test or ODI ground, or grounds, and would take its base of players from two counties apiece. In other words, Surrey and Kent might be the base for one franchise, and Middlesex and Essex, and Hampshire and Sussex, Lancashire and Derbyshire, and so on. Each franchise could also play up to four overseas players, as in the IPL.

This would make it a big annual event in itself, at a time in our summer when all other overseas cricketers are usually fully available. And if it was kept to a two-week window it would also enable county cricketers not fully involved in it to have a bit of a mid-season break, or to work on their games or play some Second XI or club cricket.

County cricket exists mainly to form the breeding and training ground for players who want to go on to play for England. I realise it is also a competitive environment in its own right and supporters want to see their counties being successful, but it is in everyone's interests to have as tough and as strong a domestic system as possible.

I might be making myself unpopular by saying it, but I also wonder if a nine-team regional 'top division' – possibly even sitting above the current eighteen-county Championship – might not be an even better bet than the present two-division structure with promotion and relegation, and all the self-serving and short-termism that this brings.

Can you imagine a London team, for instance, fielding the combined strength of Surrey and Middlesex – and taking on teams from Manchester, Leeds, Bristol, Birmingham, etc.? A nine-team league on that basis would produce what would be without doubt the strongest domestic league in the world – and therefore the best possible breeding ground for players with England ambitions.

In recent years when I've played in division one of the Championship, I've liked the fact that I was going to play – twice – against the top four teams in the country. Unfortunately, however, when you play in the second division, you get to play eight times against the four worst teams.

In my experience, too, there is now a big difference in the quality of the best four counties in the land and the four worst. David

Graveney, when he was England's chairman of selectors, told me that playing in division two would not harm a player's chances of being chosen for England. But any player, in my opinion, is better prepared for the rigours of international cricket if he has been challenged by playing regularly in the first division of the Championship.

One of the questions I am often asked, now that I've played the game for quite a while, is how cricket in 2009 compares with my professional debut season in 1987.

Well, the first thing I will say is that there seemed to be a lot more genuinely quick bowlers around in county cricket in 1987 and, because Championship cricket was a three-day game, the whole match was played at a quicker tempo. Batsmen went for their shots more, captains kept more slips and other close catchers in for longer, and the overall attitude was that 'a quick game is a good game'.

Now, pitches are a lot flatter and they have been for a while. Yet although there are not the number of really fast bowlers around, teams are much more professional in their preparation and approach. All the so-called 'one-per-centers', such as extra fitness, better nutrition, warm-down and injury preventative activities such as ice-baths, are now the norm in first-class cricket. We travel earlier to away fixtures more often now, so that we can practise at the ground we are due to play at.

But in terms of the quality of the cricket played, and the skills of the cricketers I have played with and against, I wouldn't say there is much difference when you look at the top players of both eras and compare them as individuals.

Take fielding. When I started, guys such as Roland Butcher, Paul Parker and Neil Fairbrother were all top-class outfielders, and players such as John Carr, Chris Tavaré and Brian Hardie were magnificent close-to-the-wicket catchers. In the era immediately before me, too, you had brilliant cover or mid-wicket fielders such as Graham Barlow, Derek Randall and David Gower. The catching at slip was of an equally high standard, with people in England such as Ian Botham and Mike Hendrick and, going back, you heard stories about the prowess of Colin Cowdrey, Bobby Simpson and Walter Hammond.

I think that the basic skills of the top-class cricketers of the day have always been excellent but, across the board, fielding standards in particular have gone up significantly during my two decades in the game.

The tactics of the four-day game now mirror Test cricket in that the main aim of every side is to stay in the game for as long as possible. If the ball is not doing very much, for instance, teams in the field will put sweepers out on the boundary edge and will try to slow the game down. Sides have learned to be defensive better, and they have learned to be negative better.

The authorities in this country were clearly hoping that four-day Championship cricket would encourage leg-spinners to emerge, but I think England remains a very difficult environment for the development of wrist-spin.

In many ways, too, I think that batting techniques against spin (finger spin or wrist spin) have improved, so that it is that bit harder than it was for spinners to flourish in our first-class arena. Again, when I began my career, it seemed as if every county had at least one, and sometimes two, quality specialist spinners: at Middlesex it was Emburey and Edmonds, and then Tufnell, and elsewhere could be found the likes of John Childs, Peter Such, David Graveney, Eddie Hemmings, Vic Marks, Phil Carrick, Jack Simmons and Nick Cook.

Recently, in the Championship, we have been fortunate to have true spin greats like Warne, Mushtaq, Saqlain and Muralitharan playing a lot of matches, but the overall quality of English spinners has declined, in my opinion – despite the proliferation of four-day cricket.

That is not to say there are not very good spinners around. Monty Panesar has an absolutely outstanding record. He has well over 300 first-class wickets at around 30 runs apiece, and his first 125 Test wickets came at 33. He was quicker to the landmarks of 50 and 100 Test wickets than many illustrious names of both the past and recent past, and I think he is an outstanding asset to England and to English cricket.

Yet, in the past year or so, I have heard far more things being

said about Monty in a negative capacity than positive. In the
media, there seems to be far too much attention being paid to
what he can't do. Why don't we ever concentrate, by contrast, on
what he can do? In Monty's case, it is quite a lot more than other
English spinners of his age because, at 27, he is still young for a
class slow bowler.

I felt sorry for him, in particular, during the first part of the 2008–
09 winter when, without any adequate preparation (England didn't
even select him to play in some one-day internationals so as to help
get him match-ready), he found himself being asked to bowl out
Sachin Tendulkar, Rahul Dravid, Virender Sehwag and the rest of
the India batting line-up in the Chennai Test.

The lack of backing and support he has received at certain stages
of his England career has been nothing short of scandalous, and
I only hope the current management regime look after him very
carefully. He loves to bowl and is a proven match-winner at Test
level. He has already won half a dozen Tests in a comparatively
short England career and the way he troubled batsmen of the calibre
of Inzamam-ul-Haq, Mohammad Yousuf and Younis Khan when
England played Pakistan in 2006 showed everyone just what a fine
bowler he is.

Monty is not the finished article yet, by a long way, but he needs
to be encouraged and nurtured – by everyone involved in English
cricket, including our media – as he is someone very capable of ending
up with 350 or 400 Test wickets. I get the feeling that, during the past
year or so, too many people have been trying to get him to be what
he isn't rather than concentrating on helping him to build steadily on
what he has already got, and what he has already achieved.

During my own career a lot was written about both Graeme Hick
and myself, in particular when it came to the question of why we
could not always transfer our prolific county form into the England
arena.

Graeme is a very quiet person, like myself in that sense, and I do
think that England could have got more out of him if he had been
managed better. Although he is four years older than me, and was
25 when we both made our Test debuts together in 1991, against

the West Indies, I feel that England never really had a set plan when it came to helping him to become established and comfortable at Test level.

He was chosen originally at number three, of course, which was always his natural position, and in which he used to stride out for so many years with Worcestershire and put to the sword too many county attacks to mention. But, after four Tests, he was dropped after Curtly Ambrose and Courtney Walsh repeatedly got the better of him.

England were then forced to rehabilitate him in New Zealand the following winter – with myself one of those left out to accommodate him, despite my own creditable showing in my debut series. Graeme only made 134 runs in that three-match series against the far-less-dangerous bowling attack of the Kiwis, at an average of 26, after once more being placed at three in England's order.

He was again started at number three in England's next Test series, against Pakistan in 1992, before being dropped down to number six for the third Test and then one place even lower at seven in the fourth Test – when I was recalled to bat at six – before being omitted altogether for the second summer running.

After that, Hick found himself up and down the order in his own 65-Test career almost as much as I did. Like me, he occupied every batting position from three to seven – although, unlike me, for four Tests in the summer of 2000, at least he was never asked to open the innings as well.

Remarkably, considering his natural reputation as a number three, Graeme only batted there for four of the forty-eight more Tests we played together following the 1991 West Indies series. And it was this lack of a clear policy of where to bat him, and the role he was being groomed (or not, in reality) to play, which I feel contributed to his perceived underachievement.

Like myself, Hick was never allowed to settle into the team for very long and never felt settled. Despite the fact that our careers overlapped and are often compared, I never really talked to him about all this during our times together. Graeme has always been a very reserved and private person and, to be brutally honest, we were both more concerned with our own respective careers than each other!

In my own Test career, actually, I batted in the following different positions: number two (four Tests), number three (six Tests), number four (two Tests), number five (twenty-one Tests), number six (eighteen Tests) and number seven (one Test). And, during those fifty-two Tests, the following different batsmen appeared in the pivotal number three position for England (in addition to my own six appearances there): Hick (eight Tests), Mike Atherton (three Tests), Alec Stewart (four Tests), Robin Smith (one Test), Mike Gatting (one Test), Mark Butcher (eleven Tests), Nasser Hussain (seventeen Tests) and Michael Vaughan (one Test).

So, as these statistics clearly show, there was never in my time any long-term policy of building an England batting line-up around an established number three – apart from when Nasser Hussain, during his own captaincy, took that responsibility upon himself in typical, and sensible, fashion.

You look at other countries, however, and you see the opposite happening in terms of who bats number three – and how that person graduates to that position in the first place.

Take the examples of Viv Richards with the West Indies, Ricky Ponting and Australia, and Ramnaresh Sarwan with the modern-day West Indies. It has happened, too, with other great players from the past few decades, from Greg Chappell to Allan Border to Rahul Dravid. They all began their Test careers deep in the middle order – Dravid was down at number seven when he first played, against England, in 1996 – but graduated to the crucial number three role when they had established themselves and demonstrated that they were equipped both mentally and technically.

To my mind, it is a simple thing. The best established and well-suited player in your side – whether that be a Richards or a Lara or a Bradman or a Gower or a Ponting – takes on the number three position and the rest of the batting order fits in around that person.

Opening the innings, it is a totally different situation. Someone like England's Alastair Cook, for instance, is set up to be an opener and has grown up with the game and the aptitude to do that job. And the middle-order is different again, because everything follows from the number three. If you get that right, you are a long way towards getting the balance of the rest of your batting order right – which is why, so often in recent history, England have had a problem with their number three.

My opinion, despite the emergence of Ravi Bopara early this last summer, is that Kevin Pietersen should be England's number three. He is our best player and he should be challenged to be England's Ponting and bat for the rest of his Test career at three. I think he would rise to that challenge too, and it would elevate his stature even more within the annals of the game.

England's middle-order, going forward in the foreseeable future, should be Pietersen at three, Bopara at four and Ian Bell at five.

I have always been a big fan of Bell. I believe he is an international-class batsman who is as adept against spin as pace and is technically superb. He has no obvious weakness to the technical side of his game and he can score runs all around the wicket.

Where he has struggled, when pushed up into the number-three spot, is in the area of belief. Perhaps he didn't feel comfortable at three. Indeed, he has only ever really looked entirely comfortable when he has batted behind Pietersen in the order. Is this a coincidence? Whatever, he did not seem to be able to put together a big score at number three, whereas he has made a lot of hundreds at five or six in the order.

So why don't England just keep Bell going at five, and push their best and proven world-class batsman up to three? Bopara, too, despite his successes at three, is more of a natural four in my view and this deployment of Pietersen–Bopara–Bell would make the very most of their different skills and aptitudes. It is also, to me, a case of managing your resources to the biggest benefit of the team as a unit.

This, by the way, was exactly the policy that I grew up with at Middlesex, where, at that level, Mike Gatting was our best middle-order player, so he batted for years at three and I gradually worked my way up the order from number six to four, as I became more experienced and comfortable.

Then, eventually, it was time for me to graduate to three, and for Gatting – for his last few seasons before retirement – to drop down the order beneath me. If I had stayed at Middlesex, the proper policy then would have been for someone such as Owais Shah to graduate to the three position, easing me out of it in a similar, planned way.

There was, in short, a plan, whereas with England, especially in the 1990s – and specifically in the case of Graeme Hick – there did not seem to be one. Hick, by the way, saw his own Test career fizzle out at the age of 34 in Sri Lanka in early 2001, twelve months before mine did the same in New Zealand, after spending his last year or so at that level batting down at number six and even, during the 2000 series against the West Indies, at number seven.

I can fully understand the selectors wanting to bat Graeme down the order after his 1991 debut experience, but what would have happened to his Test career if – like so many other super-talented batsmen from other countries – he had been started out at five or six, moved gradually up the order as he became more comfortable in Test cricket, with a view to graduating him in the second half of his career to the number three spot he was destined to fill for England as he did at Worcester?

Sadly, we shall never know how good he could have been as a Test batsman. Instead, he averaged 31 in Tests and only his average of 37 in 120 one-day international appearances really hinted at his true ability.

CHAPTER 11

DANCING KING

'I'm so proud of him – he puts so much effort into everything he does'

– Vandana Ramprakash, after watching
her husband win *Strictly Come Dancing*

Bruce Forsyth was already a show-business legend when I watched him hosting the *Generation Game* on television when I was a kid. Like many families around the country, we would sit round the box and crease up with laughter at some of the antics. It was required viewing in the 1970s (and then again in the early 1990s), when Bruce was the host.

One of the great joys for me of being on *Strictly Come Dancing* was to see Bruce in action up close and to get to know him a little bit. He became one of the patrons of my testimonial year at Surrey in 2008 and played at a Wentworth golf day I had as one of the testimonial functions.

I knew he lived on the Wentworth estate, so it was convenient for him, and he absolutely loves his golf, but it was still a wonderful gesture on his part and he could not have been nicer on the day. He mixed with all the guests effortlessly, moving from one group to the next, realising how important it was for them all to feel that they'd had a chance to speak with him. He is a true professional and a genuinely lovely man.

But it is also an enduring memory of my *Strictly* experience that during one stand-out incident I got to see the real Bruce Forsyth come alive on stage and show just what a brilliant showman and entertainer he is.

I know he gets a lot of stick about the odd mistake he might make, which is actually a bit unfair in that he is now over 80 and amazing for his age. Yet during the incident when my microphone wire got hooked up in my dance partner Karen Hardy's dress and we had to stop our routine, Bruce's mastery of live television took over. His reaction was memorable. I think it is one of the highlights of all the many shows in which he has been involved.

It was during the fourth week of the 2006 competition and Karen and I had to dance a salsa. During the week's practice we had gone along to a salsa club on Fulham Palace Road and we'd had quite a night. There must have been at least a hundred people there, and we had done our routine out on the floor and it had gone down really well.

I really liked that dance and I was really looking forward to the Saturday night live show so that we could perform and hopefully wow the judges and the audience and get big marks. I was confident – perhaps a bit over-confident because the live dance was not going as smoothly as we had expected when, all of a sudden, I became aware that we had a problem.

One part of the dance brought Karen in close to me and somehow the strong black wire cable attached to my neck microphone got caught on her dress. Of course, in the movement of the dance it happened very quickly and before we knew it the wire cable had wrapped around her back as she spun and pulled away from me.

Karen, like all professional dancers, knows only too well that the rules of competition do not permit you to stop a dance. If you do, then that's it. There is no starting again allowed. And so she continued on for a few steps, trying desperately to brush the cable off her.

It was hopeless, of course, because the wire had now got even more entangled with her dress, then I did a step wrong, and then Karen couldn't get into the right position for us to do the next element of the dance. So we had to stop, and we just stood there – not knowing what to do next. Don't forget, it is a live show, and the band were playing on unawares . . . It was all a bit chaotic, as the audience also reacted with some shock to the fact we had stopped. Potentially, it was a very bad situation for us.

What I will say here is that in professional competition the only reason a dancer would stop would be because they had fouled up or had forgotten the routine. They don't wear the microphones we had on, so an incident like this would not happen. Nevertheless, it was our worst nightmare.

Bruce saved us. He rushed onto the stage, quickly assessing the situation and realising why we had stopped. And, for some reason, I suddenly found myself appealing directly to him for us to start the dance again. I wanted another go. Having asked Bruce, I turned to the audience and asked if they thought we should be allowed to untangle ourselves and go again.

Perhaps my competitive spirit was coming out. Perhaps I was revealing my true colours! Karen looked astonished, because it had simply not occurred to her that we should ask for another chance. She thought that was it and that we would simply have to throw ourselves on the mercy of the judges – and the voting public.

But as I was pleading with Bruce, he caught the mood incredibly quickly and – I am sure – instantly recognised the entertainment opportunity this incident had thrown up. So much of what he says on the show is scripted – possibly too much, in a way – but he is so good at ad-libbing and this is one of the best examples of that you will find.

Crucially, too, we were the last couple dancing on that night's show. Bruce immediately began to ask the producers, with whom he was in two-way contact through his earpiece, if we could dance again. I wouldn't say he pushed them into it, but the manner of his management of the situation heavily suggested it, and he was also instantly aware that the audience was very sympathetic towards us.

Then, of course, a lovely lady called Claire, who was one of the floor managers, ran onto the stage to help us to get unentangled and to fix the microphones on again properly. Bruce bumped into

her as she tried to get past him and he immediately jumped back
in mock surprise, pretending not to know who she was, and then
caught hold of her and began to waltz around the room with her. It
was hilarious, and genuinely brilliant by Bruce. It summed up, for
me, why the bloke is such a star.

As a result of all this, we got to dance again – and we danced
extremely well, to loud acclaim. It made the programme even more
entertaining for the millions of people tuning in. A potentially bad
moment was turned into pure TV gold by the skill of Mr Forsyth.

Bruce was always very polite and respectful to all the contestants
and dancers, off stage, and he mixed in well with everyone on the
show. He is old school, I suppose, in that he grew up with live
audiences and performed in his youth on the stage, but his ability
to engage with the viewers is very clever and the huge success of
Strictly is in very large part due to him.

On the evening when Lionel Blair was in the invited audience,
he and Bruce began to do a spontaneous tap-dance routine together.
It was a long day for Bruce as much as anyone – he got in on the
Saturday at around midday and was fully involved in rehearsals all
the way up to the live broadcast – but his energy never flagged, nor
did it flag for the entire series.

Tess Daly, meanwhile, is not only stunning but also great fun
and a brilliant co-presenter alongside Bruce. She complements him
superbly, and when she is interviewing the contestants, she judges
perfectly the need sometimes just to let the contestants talk.

My own favourite moment involving Tess came after one of the
Saturday night shows when a big group of us, including quite a few
of the dancers and a number of other contestants, went out to a
club in London. During the evening I found myself in the middle
of a heaving dance floor, sandwiched between Tess and Karen, as
the three of us gyrated to the dance music. It was so funny, as Tess's
husband Vernon Kay and Karen's husband Conrad were standing
chatting together and having a beer while we danced.

As for the judges, I found I got along with all of them very well
– Arlene in particular, of course! Over the weeks of the show, you
got to chat to them a bit behind the scenes. They did tend to keep

themselves away from the contestants for much of the time, but whenever you met in the bar after a show, or when they were in and out of make-up or involved in the rehearsals, they were all very friendly and pleasant.

Len Goodman, the head judge, is a real gentleman and he loves his cricket too, which meant that we chatted about that a bit. He supports Kent, and last year when they reached the Friends Provident Trophy cup final at Lord's I got him some tickets to go along to watch them. He has this 'Cockney cab driver' charm about him, and he is very fair in his comments. Then again, if he criticises you, you really know you are in trouble.

Arlene Phillips very quickly let it be known that she liked my style, and it was very much one of the running jokes that she would get a bit flustered and hot and bothered when talking about my dancing. A lot of that, of course, is for the cameras – and all the judges play up to that very well. It's all great fun.

When, during the show, the stuff came out in the papers about my personal life and some problems Van and I were having at the time, Arlene was very supportive and she made a point of speaking with both Van and me about it. She had gone through a similar experience in her life and she just wanted to be supportive to us.

It is a shame, as far as I am concerned, that Arlene will no longer be a member of the judging panel – although she will still appear on the *Take Two* programme during *Strictly*. I can understand why the BBC have decided to replace Arlene on the panel with Alesha Dixon, and Alesha will clearly bring her insight of having won the competition into that job. They wanted to change things around a bit and I can't criticise because they want to evolve what is primarily an entertainment show, but Arlene is synonymous with *Strictly Come Dancing*. Obviously I have a great memory of her as a judge. I am available, by the way, if the BBC ever want to give Len a bit of a rest and want to appoint another former winner to the judging panel!

Craig Revel Horwood is known for his acid tongue, and he doesn't care about ripping a contestant to pieces, but I get on very well with him. During my Surrey testimonial year in 2008 he came to a couple of my functions. At one of them, a salsa ball at the Grosvenor Hotel, I actually awarded him the best dancer prize – which I think went down well. And although on the show he can come across as quite nasty, he doesn't discriminate and I've no problem with that.

My one after-dinner joke, meanwhile, features Bruno Tonioli. It is about what happened after one of the shows midway through the competition. Quite a number of my Surrey cricket teammates had come along to watch that show as my guests and we were all standing at the BBC bar afterwards when Bruno bounced over to say hello.

He came straight up to me and began to rub his hands all over my chest and shoulders while saying, 'Mark, Mark, didn't you dance well tonight!' The other cricketers loved all this, of course, and one of them piped up, 'But why then, Bruno, didn't you give him a ten?' Bruno, with a cheeky look in his eye, said, 'Well, I think Mark knows what he has to do to get a ten!'

I don't need to spell it out here that both Bruno and Craig bowl around the wicket as well as over and, to start with, all that luvvie stuff can be a bit off-putting – especially when, like me, you've been used to the rather more macho, testosterone-filled world of professional sport, and 20 years and more of cricket changing-rooms! But after a short while, you do get used to it and you take it as the norm. It's just the banter that happens in that world.

Claudia Winkleman, meanwhile, who hosts the *Take Two* midweek show during *Strictly*, is another real character. The first time that Karen and I appeared on her show, I was a bit shy in answering some of her questions. And so, on air, she threatened to jump into my lap if I didn't liven up!

Like a lot of contestants, I went into the show ready for anything but not really knowing what to expect. And, like a lot of those lucky enough to be chosen to participate, I found that the whole experience creeps up on you until you feel that it is the most important thing in your whole life.

At first, of course, all you want to do is make sure you are not the first to be voted off – that is the biggest fear of every single competitor – but by the time you get to week five or six (if you have survived, of course!) you are totally wrapped up in the *Strictly* bubble. The weekly schedule, as I have described earlier, takes over and provides a forward momentum and a structure in itself.

And, above all, the adrenalin every Saturday night is like a drug. Although it is terrifying, especially in the early weeks when the experience is all so new, the feelings of satisfaction and elation if you nail a performance are so good. Playing in a Test match for England pales into insignificance, in terms of your nerves, compared with what you feel waiting to perform on live television in front of the cameras, the audience and 12 million or so viewers. But, in the same way, the buzz of it is heightened, too.

Very soon, as a contestant having the time of your life, you simply don't want to go. You are learning so much – and the adrenalin rush more than makes up for the terror. You are desperate not be voted off and are desperate to do your best.

Karen and I never set out to win the competition; it did not even enter our minds that we could be winners until we got to the final weeks of the show. At the start, it was all about learning the process, and enjoying the process, and week-to-week that was everything for me and for Karen. In that respect, there are similarities between how we approached *Strictly* and how I approach my cricket. You don't focus on the possible prizes, you focus on the process and the method. Then, if you apply your skills accurately and well, there is a better chance of being successful anyway.

Before the first show I remember I was given quite high odds – at 16–1 to win, I seem to remember. I wasn't one of the favourites, like Emma Bunton, who we all knew would be good because of her dancing experience, but after the first live show I was joint leader in terms of the points awarded that night, so my odds then came down. I know a fellow who won more than £1,000 by putting a bet on me right at the start: full marks to him, but I would have laughed out loud if you had said then that I would get into the final, let alone win it.

Louisa Lytton, the young *EastEnders* actress, was another contestant who picked things up so quickly. At one stage I thought she might be a big rival to Emma for the title. As it was, I was soon having to deal with the added pressure of being called one of the favourites myself and there were a few comments about this from the other contestants in rehearsals.

Karen and I just concentrated on performing as well as we could and on keeping the process fun. There were plenty of times, however, when I had self-doubts and when I couldn't seem to get a routine right, but, by the Thursday or the Friday, everything always seemed to come together.

In the week building up to the final, Karen had booked a three-hour session for the Sunday with a couple who were world show-dance champions, on the basis that it was the show dance in the final itself which could make all the difference. Also, we learned to do three lifts which, again, Karen wanted us to include in our routine for the all-important 'wow' factor.

By this stage, the final was being billed as rugby v. cricket, as Matt Dawson had come through so strongly from the early rounds that he had seen off both Louisa and Emma. There was a lot of banter, too, between us – we had by then struck up an excellent relationship and become good friends.

I didn't know Matt at all before the show began, and he took it well when in the first week he was duped into wearing a hideous pink shirt after all the blokes said that we would dress up colourfully and then turned up for the Saturday show in more sober blacks and whites. He was stitched up good and proper, but he didn't seem to mind.

At first, too, Matt didn't look as if he cared too much about whether he stayed in or went out, but in the fourth week he went to see an acting coach and suddenly he became a seriously good dancer. It was like a switch being flicked. After that he also really got into it and, of course, as a top-class rugby player and a World Cup winner with England he was a serious competitor.

Peter Schmeichel, the former Manchester United and Denmark goalkeeper, was a fellow contestant I got on very well with, and he was an absolute gent. As a big Arsenal supporter – and especially as Ian Wright (someone Peter clashed with a few times during their football careers) is my Arsenal hero – I wondered how I would take to him, but he couldn't have been nicer.

In fact, during the first live show, when I didn't really know what to do with myself, Peter saw that I was a bit nervous about being there and came over and we had a good chat. I really appreciated that – some people talk a lot when they are nervous, but I'm the sort who does the exact opposite. It was great of Peter to recognise that and try to help me out.

Schmeichel was not only a great keeper, but he has also done everything in football and won so much as a player. But he was also quick to say that football was serious and *Strictly* was really just a bit of fun. He had everything in perspective and he impressed me a lot.

Jimmy Tarbuck was another contestant who I got along very well with. He is, literally, cracking jokes all the time and is obviously an old and close friend of Bruce. They still play a lot of golf together. I went to one of his golf days as a result of getting to know him on *Strictly*, which was also a lot of fun.

He was partnered with Flavia and he kept on joking that dancing so close to such a lovely lady was going to give him heart trouble. It wasn't a joke. Two weeks later, he did suffer heart problems and had to withdraw from the show on health grounds.

Emma Bunton was obviously the most high profile of all the celebrity contestants. As a former Spice Girl, and now a solo singer, she has been, and is, a huge star. But she is a really down-to-earth and very nice person, and was liked by everyone. Forget the pop star thing, I think she's just naturally a lovely girl with absolutely no side to her.

There was a very funny episode when Emma invited everyone involved in the show to come along to a big house near Baker Street, in central London, to take part in a promotional video she was making for a single she was releasing at the time, a version of 'Downtown'. It was a bizarre experience.

The place itself was huge, on several storeys, and it was like a madhouse. Everyone had to dress up in various uniforms, or flouncy Victorian dresses and things like that, and we were all asked to perform certain little skits for the cameras.

I was put in a huge pair of Wellington boots, plus army fatigue trousers and an army jacket, unbuttoned, with nothing on underneath it. Karen, meanwhile, emerged from the dressing-room area wearing thigh-high boots, fishnet tights and a marionette outfit, with huge hair and lots of make-up. Very fetching.

I had to carry her into a room, drop her onto a bed and then do a little dance routine. In the final video, our act lasted about a split second. Karen absolutely loved it. I wondered what the hell it was all about, but I admit it was an enjoyable afternoon!

Anyway, back to the week of the final and those lifts that Karen and I were practising. They were challenging, to say the least, and it wasn't as if Karen had done them before either. As a Latin and ballroom expert, she had never had to do lifts in her professional career, but she was confident that we could both pull them off in the competition finale.

All through the week, however, we were struggling to get them just right, and of course it is physically demanding – and tiring – to keep doing them so much. When it came to the Saturday, and the Band Call rehearsal, and then the full dress rehearsal, we also had a decision to make.

What we decided was that we could not physically do the lifts in the rehearsals as it would mean doing them ten times each – in other words, thirty lifts – because there were five run-throughs at the Band Call and five more in the dress rehearsal, so we left them out.

There was also more than a bit of tactical canniness in this decision. All the rehearsals are watched keenly by your opponents and by everyone else in the studio and there was definitely an element of us wanting to keep the lifts under wraps until the main live performance itself. I noticed, in rehearsals, that Matt was going flat out all the time – but he's a bit younger than me, and rugby players have far more muscles.

On the Saturday of the final, part of me was feeling that I would be happy to get through it, whatever happened, just get it over and done with! But mainly both Karen and I wanted to perform to the best of our ability – and to hit the show dance as hard as we could, hoping the adrenalin of the occasion would make those lifts far easier than they had seemed in practice.

It had been such a long journey, from that first meeting through all the practice sessions either in Hackney or in Chiswick, which was a little bit closer to Karen's home in south London (I say Croydon, she says Purley!) and therefore a better option when we tried to cut down her travelling.

But we felt prepared. I had eaten my usual jacket potato and tuna for lunch and had had my usual 4 p.m. Mars bar, so I was as ready as I could be! Of course, getting four marks of the maximum ten from all the judges for our salsa was a huge moment and set up the victory, yet I felt there was still everything to play for when we came to our show dance.

I felt confident in the routine that Karen had put together for us and, as we prepared to go out there on the floor for the last dance of the competition, I drew on all my experience in cricket – and especially of waiting to go out to bat – and made sure I had the right balance between really attacking the performance and enjoying it.

All my family had come to watch the final – Van and the children, and my mum and dad – and they had suffered a bit early on when I was slightly down on Matt in the judges' scores. He was strongest in ballroom, and I was stronger in Latin, but when we nailed the salsa I knew we would have a great chance.

Karen and I really performed that dance as smoothly as we could ever do it and I was very happy at the way we had risen to the occasion. Those four tens also put us on the top of the leaderboard after the second round of dances.

Then there was a break before the results show, in which we would perform our show dance. Karen had also chosen some great music for it, and the three lifts all worked out well. The adrenalin did make a massive difference! At the end of our dance, the immediate reaction from the audience was amazing and the feedback we got afterwards was excellent.

I can promise you that those few minutes were as important to me as anything I had ever done in my life, on the cricket field or off it. And I got so much pleasure out of performing as we did, and I put so much into it.

Karen also had the same emotions, which just shows how much the professional dancers also get into the competition. We both wanted to win the final so much. Karen took a lot of pride out of the way we had performed throughout our 14 weeks together, and I knew just how much pressure she had been under during the show's entire run to get everything right each week.

I was never in the bottom two, but we did have some poor weeks, so it was certainly not all plain sailing. But we did always enjoy a strong public vote, and I know that in the final we had a huge vote from the public, which meant an enormous amount to me.

When you consider everything that I have had to put up with during my cricket career – with all the ceaseless comment about my supposed mental frailty in particular – it was so nice for me to get that sort of public recognition and support.

For someone like myself, on that sort of reality television show, with a lot of people far more famous than me, it was quite humbling to see the level of public support that was coming in every week for Karen and me.

However I think a lot of that was also down to Karen's personality and the way our relationship, friendship and partnership developed. The public clearly enjoyed the way we went about things, and Karen is someone who really wants to entertain and to come up with routines that are interesting.

As for my emotions when it was announced that we had won, all I can say is that I was overwhelmed. The adrenalin, the euphoria of it all was just incredible. It was the same for my family, too. I think we all found it an overwhelming experience.

It was certainly a bit of a comedown, I can tell you, when in January I found myself coaching some of the Surrey U13 cricketers in a quiet indoor school at Wellington College! Nothing against the Surrey U13s, but being back in the real world, and outside of the show-business bubble in which I had been submerged throughout the autumn months, felt very strange and staid.

I have a DVD of the performances that Karen and I put together during *Strictly* and I watch them now and again. It is good to remind myself of it all every so often!

But it has also been noticeable, during these past two and a half years or so, how many people have wanted to talk to me about the dancing. Even when I am at cricket functions, more people seem to want to chat to me about *Strictly* than about my 23-year professional cricket career!

My daughters, Cara and Anya, both enjoyed seeing their dad on the show, of course, and they loved coming along with Van to join the live Saturday evening audience. Sometimes, at school, the attention they got because of it became a little bit too much and on a few occasions some of the older girls at their school got a bit overexcited. Cara in particular, being that much older, had more instances of that to deal with than Anya.

Meanwhile, when I used to drop them off at school, a lot of the mums would come up to us to chat about the previous Saturday night show, and thankfully most of the time it was also to congratulate Karen and me on our performances. It was funny to get all that attention, but it just shows what a high-profile and hugely popular show *Strictly Come Dancing* is. And, above all, it is just great fun.

Since my win, I've been involved in a *Strictly* Christmas special and have been invited back to watch several shows in recent series. I really do enjoy that, watching the dances while in the live audience, being able to sit back and totally relax. That is very pleasurable.

I have even ended up judging a couple of amateur dance competitions in the London area in the past couple of years. You see, those 14 weeks that I was on *Strictly* changed my life in so many ways, and they live on still.

CHAPTER 12

MENTALLY TOUGH

'Mark Ramprakash should be playing for England now, and should have been for most of the last seven years'

– Tom Graveney, the former England batsman, who is 15th in the Hundred Hundreds Club, with 122 first-class centuries

I have played 23 seasons as a professional cricketer and during that time I have scored more than a hundred first-class centuries and more than 30,000 first-class runs. I have represented my country 52 times at Test match level. I have won a lot of trophies during my county cricket career and also countless other individual awards.

But one irritating, and in my opinion unfair, tag has wrapped itself around me throughout the past two decades or so, which is that I have never possessed the mental toughness to play my cricket in a manner that – it is claimed – would have seen me achieve even more success in my years in the game.

I was so taken aback by something Nasser Hussain, a friend of mine, said during a television-commentary stint back in May that it moved me to write a column that I felt was my only proper right of reply on my own dedicated page on the English cricket website, testmatchextra.com.

I was watching England's second Test against the West Indies on television when Nasser, on commentary, brought my name from out of the blue into his assessment of Alastair Cook's batting.

Cook, he said, had battled hard to get to his century on the
first day of the Test at Riverside and had shown enormous mental
strength, as he was struggling with aspects of his game, but had just
concentrated on getting the runs in the book.

He added that Cook was not afraid to get ugly runs and that this
was where he differed from players like me, who – he said – were
too intent on the way we made runs, especially in terms of wanting
to play the 'perfect stroke' to every ball.

'Mark Ramprakash,' he said, 'always wanted to make pretty runs.'
Now I know Nasser was not being malicious, and he has often
commented very favourably about me as a cricketer and batsman, as
I also know Mike Atherton has not meant to be when he has also
said similar things about me on Sky Sports commentary. Indeed,
both Nasser and I have attracted a lot of comment during our
respective careers about our cricket and our personalities. There are
some writers and commentators who I won't take much notice of,
but those I respect I do read or listen to, and I have always valued
Nasser's opinion, and any feedback from him I would always take
constructively. But the continual inferences, in the media generally,
that I in some way lacked mental strength is now playing like a
broken record, especially when examples can be obtained of
contemporary Test batsmen who have been dropped or are having
a lean spell. I had thought that my dancing triumph live in front of
12 million viewers would have nailed that myth; or my resilience
in scoring more than a hundred centuries during a career that has
spanned many setbacks. The trouble is that if you repeat a myth
often enough it becomes a 'fact' that feeds on itself.

As for the subject of 'ugly' or 'pretty' runs, that's a bizarre concept.
Your fluency varies between matches and even in the same innings.
It depends on the state of the pitch, the overhead conditions and
the quality of the bowlers. I have seen Cook bat beautifully in fine
weather, especially against short bowling. So apart from not making
sense, Nasser has done his fellow Essex player no favours by saying
he is an ugly batsman.

Commentators have every right to give their opinions, of course,
but unfortunately I far more often than not don't have the facility to

join the debate because I am not there when these things are being said. That is why I used my website column early last summer to enter the debate and put forward my side. Moreover, I have been doing more and more coaching in recent years and one of the big things I teach young batsmen is the need to look at batting as being all about the end result – the runs in the book.

Before I leave this subject, let me give you two more examples of why I feel – during my England career especially – I was always swimming against the tide in terms of the opinions formed inside the game (as well as outside) about my perceived character and temperament.

Both examples come from my most successful time (and tour) as an England batsman, the 1998–99 Ashes tour to Australia. This was the trip on which I scored 845 runs from 19 first-class innings at an average of almost 53 and topped the Test series averages for England with 379 runs at 47.37. This success also came towards the back end of a run of 18 successive Tests that was, by some distance, the longest spell I ever enjoyed in the England side. A coincidence, I wonder?

The first example from this trip concerns an incident just before the second warm-up match of the tour, a four-day game against South Australia at Adelaide. Now, bearing in mind that I had played in the previous nine England Tests, starting the previous winter in the West Indies, where I had made my maiden Test century, and then continuing through five summer Tests against South Africa and one against Sri Lanka, you would have thought that my place in the opening Ashes Test that winter might have been assured. Not a bit of it.

I had been suffering quite badly with flu and when we all turned up for nets at the Adelaide Oval on the day before this game I was asked by the England management (Alec Stewart was captain, David Lloyd was coach and Graham Gooch was tour manager) if I wanted to have a bat in the nets. I said that I didn't feel 100 per cent and that it might be better if I didn't net.

Towards the end of the session, I was asked again. I repeated that I didn't feel quite right. Then came the reply, totally out of the blue, that it was a new rule that if a player didn't net the day before a game then he would automatically not play in the game. I protested, saying that I very much wanted to play in the match, but that it was just a case of trying to make sure I had shaken off the flu in time.

However, the management were adamant, and so I got up and literally ran to the dressing-rooms to get my pads, bat and other batting gear so that I could fulfil their decree of needing to net if you wanted to play in the actual game.

It was a charade, but I am sure that what lay behind all this, in my case, was that the selection committee were very keen to get John Crawley into the Ashes Test line-up because, at the Oval in the one-off Test against the Sri Lankans that ended our summer, he had scored a very fine 156 not out in our first innings. Who was being lined up to be eased out to make way for Crawley? I'll leave you to guess . . .

As it was, I had the net and fulfilled their criteria and, in the game against South Australia, ended up helping Graham Thorpe to add an unbroken 377 for our fifth wicket in the second innings. Thorpey scored 223 not out and I ended the game unbeaten on 140. It was the highest England partnership since Peter May and Colin Cowdrey had added 411 in the Edgbaston Test of 1957 against the West Indies and also a record stand for any touring team to Australia.

After that, of course, I played in the opening Test and went on to have my most successful series with the bat. This is why I think there were plenty of occasions in my England career when I was required to show real mental toughness – with this almost farcical incident being one of them.

I was always playing for my place and I never felt established. Just look at what happened in my final year of Test cricket. In August 2001, I scored 133 against McGrath, Warne, Gillespie, Lee and a rampant Australia at the Oval and yet, by April 2002, just eight months later, I was being consigned to the Test match scrapheap at the age of 32.

The second example I want to give from that 1998–99 Australia tour shows how differently I was treated in contrast to other England players of recent times whose public images are different from mine.

It happened during an on-field incident at Melbourne, in a game against Victoria, in between the second and third Tests.

During our second innings I was dismissed for 33 by a fast bowler playing for Victoria who was making his first-class debut. His name was Ashley Gilbert and perhaps the most remarkable thing about him was that he was (and still is, I imagine!) 6 ft 10 in. tall. Now, if bowlers are good enough to get me out – well done. I can take that, even though I might be extremely disappointed to get out. But what I cannot take is someone seriously abusing me, as this fellow did, and in particular abusing me racially. He basically marked my dismissal by running up to me and telling me to go back to where I had come from.

It is such a cowardly thing for a bowler to do and is inexcusable. Good bowlers do not need to do anything like that and some of the greatest, such as Curtly Ambrose, for instance, hardly ever said a single word to the countless batsmen they saw off.

What this bloke did was totally out of order and I felt, as I walked off, that I simply should not have to put up with it. Later in the day, when we were pressing for victory and he came out to bat in the final few overs, Dean Headley immediately bounced him and I ran in from cover and gave him a few choice words, saying exactly what I thought about him and his behaviour.

Because I am a full foot shorter than him, the resulting pictures of me 'getting in his face' were, more accurately, me looking up to him from his chest level, as I gave him my opinion. It must have looked quite amusing from the boundary edge and certainly afterwards the management passed off the incident as 'funny', even though I had been deadly serious and what I said to him was certainly not in jest.

The incident was reported in the London *Evening Standard* back home in a distinctly unflattering light, as far as I was concerned. Once again, the perception of me to the public was being portrayed in an all-too-familiar way, even though the writer of the article did not have a clue about the reason why I had taken it upon myself to follow up Headley's very intentional bouncer with the only challenge I could offer myself.

Indeed, compare that negative portrayal of my aggression with the way the verbal assault on Matthew Hayden, the Australian opener, by England fielders, including Paul Collingwood and Andrew Strauss – two players who have since captained England and have excellent images – was reported during and after the NatWest Series one-day international at Edgbaston in the run-up to the 2005 Ashes.

Hayden had reacted angrily to Simon Jones, the England bowler, hitting him with the ball when fielding Hayden's straight drive and flinging it right back at him in what technically was an effort to run him out but which, in reality, was a deliberate attempt to rough up the Australian.

Jones, to his credit, immediately realised he was in the wrong and held up his hand in acknowledgement to Hayden, but that did not stop Collingwood and Strauss – and a few others, I think – running up to Hayden, much in the manner I had done to Gilbert six and a half years earlier, and giving him the benefit of their views.

The only difference in the way this incident was portrayed, of course, was that this time the England players in question were widely praised for their outward show of aggression against the 'old enemy'. Double standards?

So many cricketers, and sportsmen, have a natural competitiveness in their make-up; they sometimes need the blood to stir to get themselves going, in the way Steve Waugh used to deliberately pick fights with close fielders when he was batting if he felt he wasn't concentrating properly or didn't feel quite on top of his game. That was his way of getting himself going sometimes, but it is amazing how some players get their shows of aggression portrayed in a positive way and others consistently do not.

My passion for the game even got me into a bit of trouble in the 2008 summer, first in a spat with a Sky Sports cameraman during a Twenty20 Cup match between Surrey and Hampshire at the Rose Bowl, and then in an incident involving Murray Goodwin in a Championship fixture against Sussex at the Oval, which ended up costing me a two-match suspension at the start of this last season, plus a total of £2,500 in fines.

I have since apologised to Sky for the Rose Bowl show of temper, which had occurred when one of their cameramen shoved his camera right into my face at the side of the Surrey boundary-edge dugout just after I had been dismissed and was feeling very upset.

But it was the Oval incident which ended up with me being put on trial in the media and again, because of the image of me that has been cultivated in the press over the years, culminating in an unprecedented two-match ban.

Let me give you the facts. The Championship game against Sussex began on 20 August and, at that time, we had five games to play and were very aware that Sussex were also one of the other teams in the bottom part of the table. They were also missing Chris Adams, Mushtaq Ahmed (who was going to retire because of injury) and Matt Prior, so we fancied our chances of beating them.

I was still acting captain, as I had been since the beginning of June, when Mark Butcher injured his knee, and after I had won the toss we batted and both Jon Batty and myself got hundreds while putting on 232 for the third wicket. We were heading for a big first innings total and that would enable us to put Sussex under a lot of pressure.

All through my innings of 178, however, the Sussex players had been niggling away and things were happening out there on the field that do not normally happen. It was obvious that Sussex felt they were under huge pressure. I had scored a double-hundred against Somerset at Taunton in our previous Championship match and my hundredth hundred up at Yorkshire ten days before that, and I was clearly a man they were desperate to get out.

Indeed, when I had scored about 20, I glanced a ball wide of Corey Collymore at long leg off the bowling of Robin Martin-Jenkins and turned to look for two. But Robin had moved into my path, so I ran into him and came to a halt. Meanwhile, Collymore's throw had come in but had gone over their keeper's head, so I was able to sprint back after all to get a second run on the overthrow. Then, about 15 runs or so later, the same thing happened again when I turned to look for a second run.

Moreover, after reaching 45 a ball from Martin-Jenkins cut back and went through my defensive push at about waist height. It clipped something, but not my bat, and Sussex went up for a catch at the wicket. Murray Goodwin, who was fielding at cover, was appealing particularly aggressively. From cover, what sort of view would he have had?

When I got to 96, I went down the pitch to have a chat with my partner, Batty, and when I then walked back to my crease Goodwin came over to me and accused me of cheating. What he was accusing me of was deliberately walking on the pitch to scuff it up.

I immediately responded to this, telling him that he should know all about cheating, as he was the one who was appealing for an edge to the keeper from cover when he simply would not have known if the ball had hit the edge of the bat or not. He replied that he had lost all respect for me. I said that respect was a two-way thing.

John Steele, one of the umpires, came over and said to cut it out, and I thought he had dealt with it. I walked back into my crease and began to prepare to face the next ball. But Goodwin continued to have a go at me. I thought he was totally out of order, so, once again, I walked back towards him and continued to remonstrate with him. Angry words were spoken and at this stage we both became quite animated.

Both umpires, Steele and Rob Bailey, approached and told me to be quiet. No doubt they were sincerely doing their job as they saw fit, but I felt their intervention was so one-sided. They should have known that any batsman who is on 96, as I was, does not want to get involved with a fielder. It is a time when we want to be concentrating fully on getting to the century; it does not make any cricketing sense to pick a fight in that situation.

But now the crowd could see that something was happening out in the middle and it was rapidly becoming a bit of an incident that was going to get reported and grab people's attention. Umpires do try very hard, but I felt that on this occasion they had not policed the whole day as well as they might have done. In my opinion, they should have reprimanded Goodwin also, not just me, and they had not said anything to Martin-Jenkins either, when I could have been run out as a result of his block on me.

I had sworn quite loudly during the exchanges and the umpires were not happy with that. Both of them had told me to stop. I actually get on very well with both John and Rob; both are excellent umpires and very nice men.

The incident made me even more determined, by the way, not just to complete my hundred but also to go on and make it a very big one for my team – which I did. I often get targeted by the opposition, verbals-wise, as they want to upset me, but I always just use it as extra motivation to bat well.

At the end of that day's play, though, I was summoned into the umpires' room. Still disappointed at what had happened, I gave them my views about the fact that they had not umpired the game very well and, although Alan Butcher (the Surrey coach) tried to dissuade me, I felt I was in the right to put my views across. But being Surrey captain went against me and I was told I would be the subject of a disciplinary hearing after the season in October.

We would have gone above Sussex, swapping places with them, if we had won the game, but despite our best efforts we could not stop them forcing the draw. In the media, it was soon reported that I could be facing a lengthy ban because of the incident between Goodwin, the umpires and myself.

I felt at the time that someone at the England and Wales Cricket Board had spoken to the media and told them that I could be facing a ban. If so, this would surely have been prejudicial to my case.

However, ahead of the disciplinary hearing I prepared my case thoroughly. I didn't like getting into trouble, but I was determined to put my side of the affair to the disciplinary committee in a clear fashion. I told them exactly what had happened, and the context of it, and they accepted my argument that there had been provocation. They accepted my good character over more than 20 years in the professional game, and in essence they accepted my case.

Nevertheless, because of the media spotlight surrounding the initial incident and its aftermath, I was banned from playing in the first two Championship matches of the 2009 season on the grounds that (a) I had sworn at John Steele, the umpire, and (b) I had acted inappropriately for a captain. Although my arguments were accepted, it was the severest punishment the ECB had dished out.

The whole affair left a very bad taste in my mouth, but I had to accept it and move on. What was most upsetting of all, though, by the time the season ended, was that Surrey finished bottom of the table and we were relegated into division two of the Championship.

In so many ways, the 2008 season felt like 2005 all over again, especially in that I had been the one who had tried to take on the captaincy – and all the leadership responsibilities, both on and off the field, that this entails – following Mark Butcher's unfortunate injury in the first week of June.

However, the difference between 2008 and 2005 was that the team spirit was very good last year. It was simply that we could not get going, we suffered too many injuries at the wrong times and too many players did not perform.

Only six players appeared in more than nine Championship matches, and although Usman Afzaal proved to be a decent signing, almost joining Scott Newman and me with more than 1,000 Championship runs, we did not have any stand-out bowlers and our main overseas player, the wholehearted Australian fast bowler Matt Nicholson, took only eleven wickets in his nine matches at more than fifty-six runs apiece.

We actually began the season well, scoring a lot of runs and drawing our first five matches, but then Butcher was injured and it was also decided to make changes that altered the dynamic of the team. Form and forward momentum are precarious things; in sport, situations can change so quickly, but we also didn't help ourselves.

A failure to show consistency in our bowling was a familiar problem of recent seasons, and particularly of 2005, but we also dropped around fifty catches in Championship cricket in 2008. If there is one damning statistic that condemned us to relegation, then that was it.

I remember having dinner with Justin Langer, during our match down at Somerset in mid-August, and he stressed just how tough a division he thought it was. Justin has played in some hard cricket in his long career and he is not a person given to hyperbole, so his words underlined to me just how difficult it is now to win games of cricket in the top division of our Championship. It is a tough school and there are no easy pickings.

That is how it should be, of course, and although we were one of the teams relegated I can only applaud the fact that the strength of English domestic first-class cricket is making an impression on the likes of Langer. And look at Kent's fate at the end of the 2008 season, if you need any more evidence of just how competitive things are in county cricket's top division. With two games to go, they were in with a chance of making up for being beaten finalists in both the Friends Provident Trophy and the Twenty20 Cup by winning the Championship title. What happened? They lost both those last two matches and went down with us.

Our main problem at Surrey, however, was the loss of Butcher as both a captain and a batsman, who, before his injury, had scored more than 500 runs from ten Championship innings. As in 2005, he was always going to come back before the season was out, but never did, and as the accepted captain of the club he is a crucial figure in the dressing-room and out there on the field.

I was happy, and honoured, to captain the side on the field, and I had a good relationship with Alan Butcher, the coach, but the second half of the season in particular was very difficult for me. I tried my best to give a lead, both in the field and with the bat, but our bowling attack never measured up and Nicholson struggled with illness as well as with his form. It was also my testimonial season in 2008, and of course that brought with it a lot of off-field work and responsibilities. Overall, it was very difficult.

The club were strongly criticised towards the end of the season for signing the Pakistan Test fast bowler Shoaib Akhtar for the last two Championship games in a last-ditch bid to avoid relegation. By then, Nicholson had returned to Australia, and Shoaib was available and keen to come.

I feel that his signing was a legitimate one because we were in a situation in which we had to take a risk. We had to add something different to our bowling attack. And Shoaib, in fact, should have played in our last three games but, on the practice day before the vital fixture against Kent, at Canterbury, we were told that he had encountered problems getting his visa and could not get to England in time to play.

We desperately needed a boost at that stage and this news was like a hammer blow to the team. As it was, it rained for two days at Canterbury, but it still felt like the last straw when Shoaib's arrival was delayed.

Shoaib did get things sorted out in time to play in our penultimate match, at home to Hampshire at the Oval. He did bowl pretty quickly for someone who had not played a first-class game for seven months, and he was fit. He was also a player whose extrovert nature meant he fitted in straightaway in our dressing-room. He was very polite and nice, and he tried very hard.

But, after just an hour's play, and despite the fact that he had taken the wicket of Michael Carberry, we were seven overs behind where we should have been in terms of the over-rate, and Shoaib's overs were taking an age to complete because of his long run and his slow walk back to his mark.

As captain, I felt things could not get any worse. On top of everything else, we were now facing the prospect of being docked points for a slow over-rate. But as it happened, our relegation was all but assured when Hampshire ran up a big first innings total and then dismissed us cheaply twice. We should have batted it out in our second innings for the draw, but by now all the fight had gone out of the team.

The criticism of Shoaib was unfair, too, in that his attitude and approach to those two games were excellent; against Nottinghamshire, in our last match, he was also hit on the head when he batted but still came out and bowled. It was a courageous thing to do. After bowling for a while he had to go back into the dressing-room because he felt unwell and ended up vomiting as a result of his distress.

I have to confess that, from a personal point of view, I felt somewhat downhearted at the end of the 2008 season. I didn't want to play second division Championship cricket again, and I did a lot of thinking about my future and my motivation for playing on.

With only one year left on my Surrey contract, I also had to consider whether my last years as a professional would be spent at the club. Were Surrey about to enter the situation that Middlesex had been in when I decided to leave them following the 2000 summer? Did I feel that Surrey, as a club, were going to get their house back in order?

Alan Butcher was relieved of his job as coach at the end of the season and I feel it was the players who let him down rather than the other way around. But Chris Adams, who had retired as a player after so many years of leading Sussex to great success, including the first three Championships in their history, was appointed as the new cricket manager under the managing director of cricket, a newly created role, taken by Gus Mackay.

Moreover, a clutch of former players – Graham Thorpe, Ian Salisbury, Martin Bicknell and Alec Stewart – joined the club in varying coaching roles, and it was obvious that Surrey were serious about turning around their fortunes.

From my personal angle, and after some extended negotiations, I asked for and was kindly granted a new three-year deal – in effect a two-year extension of my previous contract – because I felt I too wanted to make a commitment to Surrey for what would surely be the final seasons of my career.

I decided to commit myself to just beyond my 42nd birthday, in September 2011, for a couple of prime reasons: one, that I will always be hugely grateful to Surrey for offering me the chance to come to the club in 2001, and therefore want to repay them to the very best of my ability for the faith they then showed in me; and, two, because I want to play a part in the development of some young and talented players currently in the Surrey squad.

The Oval is also a fantastic ground to play at, and to practise at, and in my view there is nowhere better in England to be a professional cricketer.

With two more first-class centuries in my first three Championship innings of the 2009 season, I was happy to begin the last phase of my career still on top of my game, still highly motivated and still making runs for Surrey's cause. I have no specific individual targets now, other than to make the very most of the time I have left in the first-class game, as well as picking up the gauntlet of the Twenty20 challenge.

First and foremost, I am still enjoying playing cricket so much. People might think I would be considering retirement, but why should I retire when I am still fit and when I feel so lucky to have a great life playing professional cricket? As you get older, you do appreciate things even more.

Many of my contemporaries have retired because they lost that enjoyment factor. I haven't at all. I enjoy so much about the game: the buzz, the banter in the Surrey dressing-room, batting, and little things like going down to my bat manufacturers, Gray-Nicolls in East Sussex, during the winter and getting my new bats made.

When we got our first win of last season, by beating Yorkshire in the Friends Provident Trophy the day after the huge frustration of losing to Durham by just one run, it was a great feeling and it is important to me that I still get that thrill.

There was a great mix of experience in the Surrey dressing-room in 2009, with home-grown talent playing alongside the likes of Andre Nel from South Africa, Grant Elliott from New Zealand, Ryan Harris from Australia, Pedro Collins from Barbados and Gary Wilson from Ireland. The atmosphere was excellent and everyone has been working so hard.

I would be the first to admit that there have been times when I have found myself wondering if I am running out of steam. Early on last summer, for instance, I suffered at times from a sore neck and a sore lower back. They were not bad injuries, just a sign of advancing old age, but as someone who has always felt fit and kept myself on top of my fitness, they were hard to accept.

The development aspect of a few Surrey team selections was another thing I found a little strange at times, though this gradually took shape. I am someone who has always needed to go out on the field looking to win every game and needing my own mindset to be full-on. Not being passionate about winning has not been my style during my professional playing career. But blooding new players while also wanting to win is never easy.

I need to feel a hunger and a desire, and a belief that I can still improve myself and my team, if I am to keep getting up at seven o'clock in the morning to come into the ground to prepare myself properly for the game ahead, or to practise or train.

For me, though, enjoyment of batting and of cricket itself is the most important thing – because what else would I do that is so fulfilling as playing the game? I am still not sure what I will do when my career finally comes to an end. When I chatted with Mike Atherton down at Bristol early last summer, he agreed that it will be highly unlikely that I find anything so fulfilling as doing what I do now.

Perhaps mentoring younger players is something that will grab me. As I've said, I thoroughly enjoyed the work I put in over several years while qualifying to be a Level Four cricket coach and found it very interesting, but it may be that working one-on-one with selected players might appeal to me more than a general coaching or management role.

Let's see what happens, and how I feel when I do finally get to the end of my career. Cricket has been a way of life for me for a long time – from the age of 17, when I first played for Middlesex in 1987 – and I don't want to give it up yet.

These days, too, I have other interests away from the game to help me to put things into perspective, and I am not just talking about dancing! As an Arsenal season-ticket holder and a keen fan, plus someone who now enjoys the odd round of golf, as well as playing some amateur football to keep fit in the winter, I feel I have enough outside interests to balance my continued passion for cricket.

Indeed, I wish I had given more time to these sorts of other interests during the early part of my career. I was incredibly focused on my cricket in those years and I did not have enough other interests to even things up.

But one thing I need never do is look back and say that I didn't try hard enough to achieve success or was not dedicated enough in my chosen profession. Looking back now with all that hindsight, from the age of 40, I can say with absolute certainty that I did all that I could to be as successful as possible in my chosen profession.

While I am very grateful for the opportunity to play for my country, I do think in retrospect that I was picked a little too early for England, especially when you consider that my debut came at the start of a five-match Test series against a great team such as the West Indies were in 1991.

I was 21, and I believe the England selectors could have managed my entry into Test cricket a little better than they did. Indeed, if they had rated me as a young cricketer with a long future at international level, then I should have been managed better in an overall sense, too.

Then again, I was not the only cricketer of my generation – or of any generation, for that matter – to suffer from insufficient management in terms of how my career at international level progressed. I think that the English management set-up is better now in this regard. And at least the selectors gave me my chance.

Nevertheless, I also believe England's selectors could have handled me more sensitively at this end of my career. In late 2007, for example, I was not chosen for the tour to Sri Lanka despite a concerted media call for my inclusion. Of course, one has to accept team selection and I would have left it there. However, I was then asked if I would go on standby in case a senior batsman was injured.

My reply to Geoff Miller, the chairman of selectors, was to ask why I would be on standby just for a senior batsman? To my mind, you pick your best group of batsmen in your squad and then you put your next best on standby in case of any injury. It was kind to make the offer, but my feeling that this was a PR palliative was inescapable.

Even since then England keep saying that the door is not shut for me, but I feel the reality is that it is not open – and probably never has been since 2002.

I am very grateful for all the opportunities given to me. A large number of people have been very nice to me. I am proud of all that I have achieved in cricket, both during my Test career and in the years since. And, of course, in the autumn of 2006, I achieved something else in my life that resonates still. Indeed, in terms of nerves and pressure, playing in a Test match pales into insignificance when compared with what I came through triumphantly in *Strictly Come Dancing*.

ACKNOWLEDGEMENTS

I have been so lucky to have such fantastic parents, who worked incredibly hard to provide for me. I know their circumstances were a real struggle at times and when cricket arrived in my life they were so supportive, juggling commitments and giving up their time to taxi me around all over the country. I continue to benefit from their wisdom. They are inspirational.

My sister is often introduced by friends to other people as 'Mark Ramprakash's sister'. This must be really annoying for her, especially as I have always taken seriously my job of being an irritating little brother! Just to let you know, Zara, that whenever I speak of you to others – you with a degree from Oxford and made partner of a prestigious London law firm by the age of 33 – I am the one glowing with pride.

To my wife Van, my soulmate, who has always been there for me through thick and thin: this book and the achievements chronicled in it are very much ours. You have given so much love since we have been together, and it has been a roller-coaster ride. Thank you for giving so much. I hope we will continue to give to each other. I am very proud to call you my wife.

To Karen Hardy and her husband Conrad, for showing me a whole new world. It was a truly amazing life experience that will always stay with me, make me proud and make me smile.

To Sam Donnelly and Charlotte Oates, for somehow having the courage to cast me on *Strictly Come Dancing* series four.

I was lucky enough to have a number of outstanding coaches in my cricket career who were not only technically good but also displayed so much patience. They gave up their time selflessly with no personal reward bar the fact that they were giving young boys an opportunity to enjoy the game. To them, I am so very thankful. They are Graham Sainsbury, Jack Robertson, Viv Feltham, Alan Dutch, Gordon Jenkins, Chris Winn, David Green, Dave Josephs, Ted Jackson and Don Bennett.

There have also, of course, been many managers and players who have helped me throughout my cricket career. This list would be too long to mention here. However, first in this list is Mike Gatting, who always believed in me and backed me 100 per cent through thick and thin. When I was starting out, he was a tremendous role model. I learnt so much from him about how to play the game, especially when he was batting at the other end. He was always a great pleasure and an inspiration to bat with.

The same must also be said about that great West Indian batsman Desmond Haynes, who embodied everything good about what overseas players can bring to the English game. He took a keen interest in my development at Middlesex, and was always on hand to talk about the game and lend advice.

Another great role model has been and continues to be Alec Stewart. I always admired the way Alec would go out and play his game at international level with a 'live by the sword or die' attitude. That way you will never look back with any regrets. He always conducts himself incredibly well whatever the situation or company. This only slips slightly when Chelsea lose at home!

I would like to say a special thank you to Adam Hollioake and Keith Medlycott for giving me the opportunity to sign and play for Surrey. To come and experience the environment that they had created rejuvenated me as a player and a person. They managed me superbly well, which enabled me to kick my career onto a new level. For that I shall always be grateful.

In terms of the production of this book, I first have to thank Mark Baldwin of *The Times*, who also covered most of my England and England A tours and many county games in which I have played, plus all at Mainstream Publishing, especially Bill Campbell and associate publisher Iain MacGregor; Deborah Warner, who worked on the original manuscript; Emily Bland, who designed the jacket, and Adrian Pope, who took the cover photograph. In addition, I must thank Nick Canham, my agent, and MC Entertainment for all their help.

Finally, I want to extend a huge thank you to Darren Gough for writing his foreword to this book, alongside Karen's. Thanks for being a true mate in the cricket world but most importantly giving me the push I needed to take the plunge and enter *Strictly Come Dancing*.

STATISTICS

MARK RAVIN RAMPRAKASH

Born 5 September 1969 in Bushey, Hertfordshire
Middlesex 1987–2000, Surrey 2001–present
Tests: 52 (1991 to 2001–02)
One-day internationals: 18 (1991 to 2001–02)
Cricket Writers' Club Young Cricketer of the Year 1991
PCA Cricketer of the Year 2006
Wisden Cricketer of the Year 2007

In 2006, Mark Ramprakash became the first cricketer to score 2,000 runs in twenty first-class innings (beating the previous record of twenty-one innings, set by Don Bradman in 1938 and Graham Gooch in 1990), the first to make scores of 150 in each of five successive first-class matches (eclipsing the previous record of four set by Vijay Merchant in India in 1941–42), and the first to reach double figures in each of his twenty-four first-class innings in an English season. His first-class average of 103.54 was also the highest by an English player in a home season, beating Geoff Boycott's 102.53 in 1979.

In 2007, Ramprakash topped 2,000 first-class runs and averaged more than 100 for the second successive season, the first player to do so in consecutive English summers. His 2,026 runs (at 101.30) was also a remarkable 30.02 per cent of all Surrey's runs from the bat (out of 6,747), a record for all counties, beating Graeme Hick's 28.96 per cent for Worcestershire in 1988. The previous Surrey record was Tom Hayward's 23.98 per cent in 1906.

THE HUNDRED HUNDREDS' CLUB

Mark Ramprakash was at equal 16th place on the list of those in the Hundred Hundreds' Club when this book went to press, with 108 first-class hundreds.

'I am very proud of the fact that my name is now in such an exclusive list of some of the true greats of the game,' he said. 'In fact, all the names on this list are legends of cricket and are synonymous with great cricketing achievement. I cannot claim to have been as successful at international level as a lot of the other 24 players who have scored a hundred hundreds, or more, but I am honoured to be classified among them. As for Jack Hobbs scoring 98 of his hundreds after the age of 40 . . . well, that is something which I imagine will be a bit beyond me!'

	Year reached	Age	Total 100s
W.G. Grace	1895	46	126
Tom Hayward	1913	42	104
Jack Hobbs	1923	40	197
Phil Mead	1927	40	153
Patsy Hendren	1928	39	170
Frank Woolley	1929	42	145
Herbert Sutcliffe	1932	37	149
Ernest Tydesley	1934	45	102
Wally Hammond	1935	31	167
Andy Sandham	1935	31	107
Don Bradman	1947	39	117
Les Ames	1950	44	102
Les Hutton	1951	35	129
Denis Compton	1952	34	123
Tom Graveney	1964	37	122
Colin Cowdrey	1973	40	107
John Edrich	1977	40	103

Geoff Boycott	1977	37	151
Glenn Turner	1982	35	103
Zaheer Abbas	1982	35	108
Dennis Amiss	1986	43	102
Vivian Richards	1988	36	114
Graham Gooch	1993	39	128
Graeme Hick	1998	32	136
Mark Ramprakash	2008	38	108*

as at 14 August 2009

Ramprakash is the fifth Surrey batsman to score 100 first-class hundreds, following Tom Hayward, Jack Hobbs, Andy Sandham and John Edrich.

THE HUNDRED HUNDREDS

After completing his hundredth first-class hundred, at 4.12 p.m. on Saturday, 2 August 2008, with a four cut away off David Wainwright, the slow left-arm spinner, Ramprakash put the fact that ten innings had passed since his 99th century down to the loss of his favourite bat. 'After scoring the 99th at Hove, I broke the bat I'd been using for the past two years,' he said. 'I've used five bats since and I've not played that well.'

1	128	Middx v. Yorks	Headingley	20 July 1989
2	118*	Middx v. Camb Univ	Fenner's	3 May 1990
3	146*	Middx v. Somerset	Uxbridge	24 July 1990
4	100*	Middx v. Kent	Canterbury	26 July 1990
5	125	Middx v. Kent	Canterbury	27 July 1990
6	132	Middx v. Notts	Lord's	7 Sept. 1990
7	158	Eng A v. Sri Lanka A	Kandy	10 Feb. 1991
8	119	Middx v. Sussex	Lord's	11 May 1991

9	110	Middx v. Notts	Trent Bridge	3 Sept. 1991
10	108	Middx v. Lancs	Lord's	9 May 1992
11	233	Middx v. Surrey	Lord's	23 May 1992
12	117	Middx v. Surrey	The Oval	14 Sept. 1992
13	140	Middx v. Yorks	Scarborough	14 August 1993
14	117*	Middx v. Lancs	Lord's	11 Sept. 1993
15	154*	Eng v. WIBP XI	Guyana	10 March 1994
16	135	Middx v. Durham	Lord's	23 June 1994
17	131	Middx v. Derbys	Derby	1 July 1994
18	123*	Middx v. Essex	Uxbridge	29 July 1994
19	124	Middx v. Surrey	The Oval	27 August 1994
20	163*	Middx v. Hants	Lord's	5 May 1995
21	214	Middx v. Surrey	Lord's	29 June 1995
22	133	Middx v. Glos	Bristol	7 July 1995
23	205	Middx v. Sussex	Lord's	27 July 1995
24	155	Middx v. Durham	Chester-le-Street	11 August 1995
25	235	Middx v. Yorks	Headingley	24 August 1995
26	111	Middx v. Northants	Uxbridge	31 August 1995
27	158	Middx v. Leics	Uxbridge	8 Sept. 1995
28	111*	Middx v. Leics	Uxbridge	11 Sept. 1995
29	115	Middx v. Som	Taunton	16 Sept. 1995
30	134	Middx v. Yorks	Lord's	30 May 1996
31	169	Middx v. Warwicks	Lord's	27 June 1996
32	108	Middx v. Hants	Portsmouth	30 August 1996
33	110	Middx v. Som	Uxbridge	16 Sept. 1996
34	108*	Rest of Eng v. Eng A	Edgbaston	20 April 1997
35	145	Middx v. Sussex	Lord's	7 May 1997
36	111	Middx v. Northants	Lord's	29 May 1997
37	113*	Middx v. Kent	Lord's	25 July 1997
38	190	Middx v. Hants	Lord's	7 August 1997

39	123*	Middx v. Worcs	Kidderminster	30 August 1997
40	154	Eng v. West Indies	Barbados	13 March 1998
41	122	Middx v. Worcs	Uxbridge	23 May 1998
42	108	Middx v. Worcs	Uxbridge	24 May 1998
43	128*	Middx v. Glam	Lord's	1 June 1998
44	110	Middx v. Leics	Leicester	19 August 1998
45	140*	Eng v. South Australia	Adelaide	10 Nov. 1998
46	101	Middx v. Glos	Bristol	30 April 1999
47	209*	Middx v. Surrey	Lord's	12 Sept. 1999
48	101	Middx v. Worcs	Southgate	8 July 2000
49	110*	Middx v. Sussex	Southgate	28 July 2000
50	112	Middx v. Sussex	Southgate	30 July 2000
51	120*	Middx v. Warwicks	Edgbaston	19 August 2000
52	146	Surrey v. Kent	The Oval	22 April 2001
53	143	Surrey v. Som	The Oval	7 June 2001
54	133	Eng v. Australia	The Oval	25 August 2001
55	131	Surrey v. Yorks	The Oval	7 Sept. 2001
56	105	Eng v. IBP XI	Hyderabad	22 Nov. 2001
57	119*	Surrey v. Lancs	The Oval	11 May 2002
58	121	Surrey v. Camb Univ	Fenner's	15 May 2002
59	218	Surrey v. Som	Taunton	3 July 2002
60	210*	Surrey v. Warwicks	The Oval	11 July 2002
61	205	Surrey v. Lough Univ	The Oval	24 April 2003
62	152	Surrey v. Leics	The Oval	15 May 2003
63	110	Surrey v. Middx	Lord's	29 June 2003
64	182*	Surrey v. Warwicks	Edgbaston	10 July 2003
65	104	Surrey v. Sussex	Hove	1 August 2003
66	279*	Surrey v. Notts	Whitgift Sch.	13 August 2003
67	113*	Surrey v. Oxford Univ	The Parks	10 April 2004
68	157	Surrey v. Kent	The Oval	25 May 2004

69	145*	Surrey v. Warwicks	Guildford	22 July 2004
70	161	Surrey v. Northants	Northampton	29 July 2004
71	130	Surrey v. Worcs	The Oval	4 August 2004
72	100*	Surrey v. Worcs	The Oval	5 August 2004
73	134	Surrey v. Lancs	Whitgift Sch.	12 August 2004
74	152	Surrey v. Sussex	The Oval	16 April 2005
75	107	Surrey v. Glamorgan	Cardiff	29 April 2005
76	107	Surrey v. Notts	The Oval	9 May 2005
77	192	Surrey v. Glos	The Oval	17 August 2005
78	126	Surrey v. Warwicks	Edgbaston	13 Sept. 2005
79	252	Surrey v. Middx	The Oval	22 Sept. 2005
80	113	Surrey v. Leics	Leicester	26 April 2006
81	292	Surrey v. Glos	The Oval	4 May 2006
82	118	Surrey v. Worcs	The Oval	18 May 2006
83	156	Surrey v. Glam	Swansea	22 June 2006
84	155	Surrey v. Northants	Northampton	16 July 2006
85	167	Surrey v. Som	Guildford	21 July 2006
86	301*	Surrey v. Northants	The Oval	3 August 2006
87	196	Surrey v. Worcs	Worcester	9 August 2006
88	115	Surrey v. Yorks	The Oval	20 April 2007
89	107*	Surrey v. Hants	The Oval	27 April 2007
90	120*	Surrey v. Warwicks	The Oval	12 May 2007
91	266*	Surrey v. Sussex	Hove	16 May 2007
92	108	Surrey v. Kent	Whitgift Sch.	2 June 2007
93	142	Surrey v. Worcs	Guildford	26 July 2007
94	188	Surrey v. Hants	Rose Bowl	30 August 2007
95	175	Surrey v. Warwicks	Edgbaston	7 Sept. 2007
96	196	Surrey v. Lancs	The Oval	19 Sept. 2007
97	130*	Surrey v. Lancs	The Oval	21 Sept. 2007
98	118	Surrey v. Lancs	The Oval	16 April 2008

| 99 | 123 | Surrey v. Sussex | Hove | 3 May 2008 |
| 100 | 112* | Surrey v. Yorks | Headingley | 2 August 2008 |

BREAKDOWN OF GROUNDS ON WHICH RAMPRAKASH MADE HIS 100 HUNDREDS:

26 – The Oval; 18 – Lord's; 8 – Uxbridge; 5 – Edgbaston; 3 – Guildford, Hove, Headingley, Southgate, Whitgift School (Croydon); 2 – Bristol, Canterbury, Fenner's (Cambridge), Leicester, Northampton, Taunton; 1 – Adelaide (Australia), Cardiff, Chester-le-Street, Derby, Georgetown (Guyana), Hyderabad (India), Kandy (Sri Lanka), Kensington Oval (Barbados), Kidderminster, Portsmouth, Rose Bowl (Southampton), Scarborough, Swansea, The Parks (Oxford), Trent Bridge, Worcester

CAREER RECORD

TESTS

M	Inns	NO	HS	Runs	Ave	100	50
52	92	6	154	2350	27.32	2	12

TESTS V. AUSTRALIA

M	Inns	NO	HS	Runs	Ave	100	50
12	24	2	133	933	42.40	1	6

ONE-DAY INTERNATIONALS

M	Inns	NO	HS	Runs	Ave	100	50
18	18	4	51	376	26.85	0	1

FIRST-CLASS

M	Inns	NO	HS	Runs	Ave	100	50
424	698	89	301*	33103	54.35	108	138

as at 14 August 2009

COUNTY CHAMPIONSHIP

M	Inns	NO	HS	Runs	Ave	100+	150+	200+
317	521	70	301*	27188	60.28	97	33	14

as at 14 August 2009

LIST A ONE-DAY

M	Inns	NO	HS	Runs	Ave	100	50
396	384	62	147*	12923	40.13	17	83

as at 11 August 2009

TWENTY20

M	Inns	NO	HS	Runs	Ave	100	50
52	52	8	85*	1388	31.54	0	10

as at 14 August 2009

FOR MIDDLESEX (FIRST-CLASS)

M	Inns	NO	HS	Runs	Ave	100	50
211	345	47	235	15046	50.48	46	73

FOR SURREY (FIRST-CLASS)

M	Inns	NO	HS	Runs	Ave	100	50
123	200	27	301*	13294	76.84	55	40

as at 14 August 2009

FOR SURREY AT THE OVAL (FIRST-CLASS)

M	Inns	NO	HS	Runs	Ave	100	50
52	84	9	301*	6124	81.65	26	14

as at 14 August 2009

ALL FIRST-CLASS AT THE OVAL (FOR MIDDLESEX, SURREY AND ENGLAND):

M	Inns	NO	HS	Runs	Ave	100	50
64	107	10	301*	7167	73.88	29	19

as at 14 August 2009

FOR ENGLAND YOUNG CRICKETERS (1986–89)

M	Inns	NO	HS	Runs	Ave	100	50
7	12	2	120*	519	51.90	2	0

FOR ENGLAND YOUNG CRICKETERS (ONE-DAY MATCHES, 1986–87 TO 1989)

M	Inns	NO	HS	Runs	Ave	100	50
14	14	0	61	332	23.00	0	3

Note: To 14 August 2009, Ramprakash had taken 34 first-class wickets at an average of 64.58, including 4 in Tests, and 46 wickets in List A one-day cricket at 29.43, including 4 in ODIs.

CAREER BREAKDOWN

FIRST-CLASS CRICKET

1987 – Middlesex

M	Inns	NO	HS	Runs	Ave	100	50
8	14	3	71	321	29.18	0	2

1988 – Middlesex

M	Inns	NO	HS	Runs	Ave	100	50
9	13	4	68*	421	46.77	0	3

1989 – Middlesex

M	Inns	NO	HS	Runs	Ave	100	50
21	34	5	128	1052	36.27	1	7

1990 – Middlesex

M	Inns	NO	HS	Runs	Ave	100	50
24	42	10	146*	1541	48.15	5	6

1990–91 – England A in Pakistan and Sri Lanka

M	Inns	NO	HS	Runs	Ave	100	50
5	7	0	158	250	35.71	1	0

1991 – Middlesex

M	Inns	NO	HS	Runs	Ave	100	50
15	26	4	119	964	43.81	2	7

1991 – England v. West Indies

M	Inns	NO	HS	Runs	Ave	100	50
5	9	0	29	210	23.33	0	0

1991 – England v. Sri Lanka

M	Inns	NO	HS	Runs	Ave	100	50
1	1	0	0	0	0.00	0	0

1991–92 – England in New Zealand (first-class matches)

M	Inns	NO	HS	Runs	Ave	100	50
4	5	2	19*	47	15.66	0	0

1991–92 – England A in West Indies

M	Inns	NO	HS	Runs	Ave	100	50
5	9	1	86	322	40.25	0	3

1992 – Middlesex

M	Inns	NO	HS	Runs	Ave	100	50
16	27	1	233	1156	46.24	3	5

1992 – England v. Pakistan

M	Inns	NO	HS	Runs	Ave	100	50
3	5	1	17	31	7.75	0	0

1992 – England A v. Essex

M	Inns	NO	HS	Runs	Ave	100	50
1	1	0	12	12	12.00	0	0

1993 – Middlesex

M	Inns	NO	HS	Runs	Ave	100	50
16	22	1	140	813	38.71	2	4

1993 – England v. Australia

M	Inns	NO	HS	Runs	Ave	100	50
1	2	0	64	70	35.00	0	1

1993–94 – England in West Indies (Tests)

M	Inns	NO	HS	Runs	Ave	100	50
4	7	0	23	73	10.42	0	0

1993–94 – England in West Indies (other first-class matches)

M	Inns	NO	HS	Runs	Ave	100	50
4	7	2	154*	384	76.80	1	2

1994 – Middlesex

M	Inns	NO	HS	Runs	Ave	100	50
18	26	2	135	1270	52.91	4	6

1994–95 – England A in India

M	Inns	NO	HS	Runs	Ave	100	50
2	4	1	99	210	70.00	0	2

1994–95 – England in Australia (Test)

M	Inns	NO	HS	Runs	Ave	100	50
1	2	0	72	114	57.00	0	1

1995 – Middlesex

M	Inns	NO	HS	Runs	Ave	100	50
17	27	3	235	2157	89.87	10	6

1995 – England v. West Indies

M	Inns	NO	HS	Runs	Ave	100	50
2	4	0	18	22	5.50	0	0

1995 – England A v. Warwickshire

M	Inns	NO	HS	Runs	Ave	100	50
1	1	0	79	79	79.00	0	1

1995–96 – England in South Africa (Tests)

M	Inns	NO	HS	Runs	Ave	100	50
2	3	0	9	13	4.33	0	0

1995–96 – England in South Africa (other first-class matches)

M	Inns	NO	HS	Runs	Ave	100	50
3	5	0	70	170	41.32	0	1

1996 – Middlesex

M	Inns	NO	HS	Runs	Ave	100	50
16	29	2	169	1406	52.06	4	8

1996 – The Rest v. England A

M	Inns	NO	HS	Runs	Ave	100	50
1	2	0	18	35	17.50	0	0

1997 – Middlesex

M	Inns	NO	HS	Runs	Ave	100	50
17	27	3	190	1293	53.87	5	7

1997 – England v. Australia

M	Inns	NO	HS	Runs	Ave	100	50
1	2	0	48	52	26.00	0	0

1997 – The Rest v. England A

M	Inns	NO	HS	Runs	Ave	100	50
1	1	1	108*	108	-	1	0

1997–98 – England in West Indies (Tests)

M	Inns	NO	HS	Runs	Ave	100	50
3	5	1	154	266	66.50	1	1

1997–98 – England in West Indies (other first-class matches)

M	Inns	NO	HS	Runs	Ave	100	50
2	3	1	77	123	61.50	0	1

1998 – Middlesex

M	Inns	NO	HS	Runs	Ave	100	50
9	15	2	128*	635	48.84	4	0

1998 – England v. South Africa

M	Inns	NO	HS	Runs	Ave	100	50
5	9	1	67*	249	31.12	0	1

1998 – England v. Sri Lanka

M	Inns	NO	HS	Runs	Ave	100	50
1	2	0	53	95	47.50	0	1

1998–99 – England in Australia (Tests)

M	Inns	NO	HS	Runs	Ave	100	50
5	10	2	69*	379	47.37	0	4

1998-99 – England in Australia (other first-class matches)

M	Inns	NO	HS	Runs	Ave	100	50
5	9	1	140*	466	58.25	1	3

1999 – Middlesex

M	Inns	NO	HS	Runs	Ave	100	50
12	22	2	209*	929	46.45	2	6

1999 – England v. New Zealand

M	Inns	NO	HS	Runs	Ave	100	50
4	6	1	69*	127	25.40	0	1

2000 – Middlesex

M	Inns	NO	HS	Runs	Ave	100	50
13	21	4	120*	1088	64.00	4	6

2000 – England v. Zimbabwe

M	Inns	NO	HS	Runs	Ave	100	50
2	3	0	56	75	25.00	0	1

2000 – England v. West Indies

M	Inns	NO	HS	Runs	Ave	100	50
2	4	0	18	20	5.00	0	0

2001 – Surrey

M	Inns	NO	HS	Runs	Ave	100	50
9	14	0	146	776	55.42	3	4

2001 – England v. Australia

M	Inns	NO	HS	Runs	Ave	100	50
4	8	0	133	318	39.75	1	0

2001–02 – England in India (Tests)

M	Inns	NO	HS	Runs	Ave	100	50
3	5	0	58	159	31.80	0	1

2001–02 – England in India (other first-class matches)

M	Inns	NO	HS	Runs	Ave	100	50
2	4	0	105	159	39.75	1	0

2001–02 – England in New Zealand (Tests)

M	Inns	NO	HS	Runs	Ave	100	50
3	5	0	31	77	15.40	0	0

2001–02 – England in New Zealand (other first-class matches)

M	Inns	NO	HS	Runs	Ave	100	50
2	3	0	42	48	16.00	0	0

2002 – Surrey

M	Inns	NO	HS	Runs	Ave	100	50
15	25	4	218	1194	56.85	4	6

2003 – Surrey

M	Inns	NO	HS	Runs	Ave	100	50
15	23	4	279*	1444	76.00	6	2

2004 – Surrey

M	Inns	NO	HS	Runs	Ave	100	50
17	29	5	161	1564	65.16	7	6

2005 – Surrey

M	Inns	NO	HS	Runs	Ave	100	50
14	23	2	252	1568	74.66	6	5

2006 – Surrey

M	Inns	NO	HS	Runs	Ave	100	50
15	24	2	301*	2278	103.54	8	9

2007 – Surrey

M	Inns	NO	HS	Runs	Ave	100	50
15	25	5	266*	2026	101.30	10	4

2008 – Surrey

M	Inns	NO	HS	Runs	Ave	100	50
14	23	3	200*	1235	61.75	6	1

2009 – Surrey

M	Inns	NO	HS	Runs	Ave	100	50
9	14	2	274	1209	100.75	5	3

as at 14 August 2009

* denotes not out

INDEX

Abbreviations used: d. – daughters, f. – father, m. – mother, MR – Mark Ramprakash, s. – sister, w. – wife